· America's Aging ·

The Social and Built Environment in an Older Society

Committee on an Aging Society
Institute of Medicine and National Research Council

NATIONAL ACADEMY PRESS
Washington, D.C. 1988

National Academy Press • 2101 Constitution Avenue, NW • Washington, DC 20418

NOTICE: The project that is the subject of this report was approved by the Governing Board of the National Research Council, whose members are drawn from the councils of the National Academy of Sciences, the National Academy of Engineering, and the Institute of Medicine. The members of the committee responsible for the report were chosen for their special competences and with regard for appropriate balance.

This report has been reviewed by a group other than the authors according to procedures approved by a Report Review Committee consisting of members of the National Academy of Sciences, the National Academy of Engineering, and the Institute of Medicine.

The Institute of Medicine was chartered in 1970 by the National Academy of Sciences to enlist distinguished members of the appropriate professions in the examination of policy matters pertaining to the health of the public. In this, the Institute acts under both the Academy's 1863 congressional charter responsibility to be an adviser to the federal government and its own initiative in identifying issues of medical care, research, and education.

This study has been supported by funds from the National Research Council Fund, a pool of private, discretionary, nonfederal funds that is used to support a program of Academy-initiated studies of national issues in which science and technology figure significantly. The NRC Fund consists of contributions from a consortium of private foundations including the Carnegie Corporation of New York, the Charles E. Culpeper Foundation, the William and Flora Hewlett Foundation, the John D. and Catherine T. MacArthur Foundation, the Andrew W. Mellon Foundation, the Rockefeller Foundation, and the Alfred P. Sloan Foundation; the Academy Industry Program, which seeks annual contributions from companies that are concerned with the health of U.S. science and technology and with public policy issues with technological content; and the National Academy of Sciences and the National Academy of Engineering endowments. The study was also supported by the Charles A. Dana Foundation and the Retirement Research Foundation.

Library of Congress Cataloging in Publication Data

Committee on an Aging Society (U.S.)

The social and built environment in an older society / Committee on an Aging Society, Institute of Medicine and National Research Council.

p. cm. — (America's aging)

Bibliography: p.

Includes index.

1. Aging—United States—Social conditions—Congresses. 2. Aged—Services for—United States—Congresses. 3. Quality of life—United States—Congresses. I. Title. II. Series.

HQ1064.U5C535 1988

305.2'6'0973—dc19 88-17837

CIP

ISBN 0-309-03780-8

Cover photograph: © by Ron Blakeley/UNIPHOTO.

Printed in the United States of America.

COMMITTEE ON AN AGING SOCIETY

FREDERICK C. ROBBINS (*Chairman*), Professor Emeritus, Case Western Reserve University School of Medicine, Cleveland, Ohio

LAWRENCE K. ALTMAN, Medical Correspondent and "The Doctors' World" columnist, The New York Times, New York, New York

WILLIAM G. BELL, Professor Emeritus, Institute on Social Research, Florida State University, Tallahassee, Florida

ROBERT H. BINSTOCK, Henry R. Luce Professor of Aging, Health, and Society, Case Western Reserve University School of Medicine, Cleveland, Ohio

ALEXANDER M. CAPRON, Norman Lopping Professor of Law, Medicine and Public Policy, University of Southern California, Los Angeles

CARROLL L. ESTES, Chairman, Department of Social and Behavioral Sciences, School of Nursing, University of California, San Francisco

JACOB J. FELDMAN, Associate Director for Analysis and Epidemiology, National Center for Health Statistics, Hyattsville, Maryland

JOSEPH HENRY, Associate Dean, Professor, and Chairman, Department of Oral Diagnosis and Radiobiology, Harvard School of Dental Medicine, Boston, Massachusetts

M. POWELL LAWTON, Philadelphia Geriatrics Center, Philadelphia, Pennsylvania

F. PETER LIBASSI, Senior Vice-President, Travelers Insurance Company, Hartford, Connecticut

ROSLYN LINDHEIM,* Professor of Architecture, College of Environmental Design, University of California, Berkeley

THOMAS W. MOLONEY, Senior Vice-President, The Commonwealth Fund, New York, New York

JAMES N. MORGAN, Program Director and Professor of Economics, Survey Research Center, University of Michigan, Ann Arbor

GEORGE C. MYERS, Professor of Sociology and Director, Center for Demographic Study, Duke University, Durham, North Carolina

---

*Deceased.

BERNICE L. NEUGARTEN, Professor of Education and Sociology, School of Education and Social Policy, Northwestern University, Evanston, Illinois
ALAN PIFER, President, The Carnegie Corporation of New York, New York, New York
ELIZABETH RUSSELL, Senior Staff Scientist, Jackson Laboratories, Bar Harbor, Maine
BERT SEIDMAN, Director, Department of Occupational Safety, Health, and Social Security, AFL-CIO, Washington, D.C.
T. FRANKLIN WILLIAMS, Medical Director, Monroe Community Hospital, Rochester, New York
MICHAEL ZUBKOFF, Professor and Chairman, Department of Community and Family Medicine, Dartmouth Medical School, Hanover, New Hampshire

Study Staff

ENRIQUETA C. BOND, *Study Director* and Director, Division of Health Promotion and Disease Prevention
LINDA DEPUGH, *Administrative Assistant*

Consultant

ROGER EGEBERG

Preface

Substantial increases in the number and proportion of older persons in the decades ahead portend significant changes in American society. Indeed, demographic projections of a population rapidly growing older have led some observers to characterize the United States as an "aging society."

The ways in which an aging society might be a different society, in other than demographic characteristics, are not entirely clear. But it is evident that the changing age distribution of the population will have major implications, at the very least for the following:

- financing, development, organization, and use of health care systems;
- patterns of family life, social relations, cultural institutions, living arrangements, and physical environments;
- distribution of jobs among older and younger workers, as well as the earnings, status, and satisfaction that these jobs may provide, within the context of age discrimination laws, seniority practices, and technological innovation;
- economic aspects of providing retirement income through various public and private mechanisms;
- quality of life of the population throughout the life course including functional status, well-being, legal status, and personal autonomy; and
- an ever-shifting agenda of related public policy issues.

If we are to deal effectively with these issues, our current understanding of the specific implications—for older and younger persons, for age relations, and for the institutions of our society—must be expanded.

The Committee on an Aging Society was organized to identify selected issues that need to be confronted, both soon and over the longer term. Recognizing that many organizations and ad hoc groups have been addressing a range of issues associated with aging and with older persons as an age group, the committee has attempted to emphasize broader societal issues as well. From among those issues the Committee on an Aging Society suggests topics that warrant systematic investigations fostered by the National Research Council, the Institute of Medicine, and other organizations. It is the committee's belief that such investigations of these topics will provide a basis for action by policymakers in both the private and public sectors.

This volume is the third report in a series, called America's Aging, in which the committee calls attention to issues that emerged from symposia convened to explore selected topics. Other reports or proposed symposia focus on health in an aging society, productive roles, and legal and ethical issues.

This report summarizes the conferees' recommendations and the discussions on which they were based and presents the papers commissioned for the December 1985 Symposium on the Social and Built Environment in an Aging Society.

FREDERICK C. ROBBINS
Chairman
Committee on an Aging Society

Acknowledgments

As with many reports issued by the Institute of Medicine, this report represents the collaborative efforts of the committee, the project staff and individuals who contributed specific papers in this report. Several participants at the meeting also contributed to the report. We wish especially to thank Michael Rodgers, then Staff Director of the Subcommittee on Housing and Consumer Interests, Select Committee on Aging, U.S. House of Representatives, for his contribution on federal legislation on housing for older persons now part of the first summary chapter. Two committee members, William G. Bell and M. Powell Lawton, made major contributions to the planning, convening, and summarization of the symposium. Without their continuing contributions, this volume would not have been possible.

Contents

▪ AMERICA'S AGING ▪

The Social and Built Environment in an Older Society

Summary

INTRODUCTION

Among the challenges posed by our aging or "graying" society is the relationship of the elderly to the social and "built" or physical environment. The changes that have already affected the growing elderly population in the United States point to a number of continuing trends: a majority of the aged increasingly will be female, older, better educated, and probably better off financially, although there will continue to be a "hard-core" group of poor older persons. Demographic projections also estimate that, as longevity continues to increase, there may be more very disabled people, as a function both of the changed age distribution in the population and of lifesaving medical technology. What changes must be made in our social and physical methods of organizing the environment to accommodate the needs of these citizens? What policies should be formulated to effect these changes, and what more do we need to know to carry out our plans effectively?

To address these issues, the Committee on an Aging Society convened a symposium in Washington, D.C., in December 1985.

The Summary and the Proposals for Policy and Further Research are based on contributions from a number of committee members and symposium participants. We wish to acknowledge particularly William Bell, M. Powell Lawton, George Myers, and Michael Rodgers.

The symposium focused on selected aspects of the social and built environment and on new ways in which the environment might be restructured to achieve two essential goals: (1) enhance the social productivity of aging persons and (2) prolong the residence of older persons in the community in a manner that enhances the quality of their lives and fosters ties with formal and informal support systems.

In selecting the symposium topic, the committee recognized that policies influencing the social and built environment have been largely value driven, often reflecting goals and standards of decision makers, in both the public and private sectors, that have remained undefined.

PREVIOUS STUDIES

Although domiciliary and institutional living for the elderly have been favorite topics from the beginnings of gerontology as a field of study, their first consolidation in a more scientific form came in the chapters of the handbooks of gerontology published almost 30 years ago (Birren, 1959; Tibbitts, 1960). Vivrett (1960) provided a chapter summarizing much of the service-, policy-, and design-relevant information of the day; similarly, Kleemeier's (1959) chapter was the first attempt to formulate an environmental psychology of later life. Subsequent writings by Carp (1966), Rosow (1967), Pastalan and Carson (1970), and Lawton and Nahemow (1973) developed the issues further in a period that saw the emergence of a national housing program, the redefinition of the home for the aged, and the stimulation and facilitation of nursing home development by the federal government.

The first and perhaps most influential project of research, policy, programming, and education in the aging-related environmental area was that of the Gerontological Society (later to become the Gerontological Society of America or GSA) from 1971 to 1978, which was supported by the U.S. Administration on Aging and directed by the late Thomas O. Byerts. This multifaceted project treated many of the topics presented in this volume and resulted in a series of conferences, books, policy statements, and teaching materials on aging persons and the built environment. The project succeeded in engaging the attention of many scientists and professionals who had not previously been involved in the field of aging, and it also contributed to an enrichment of the general methodology of studying person–environment relations specifically focused on older people. (For example, throughout its history, meetings and publications of the Environment Design Research Association have featured gerontological material in substantial quantity, much of it attributable to the Gerontological Society's project.)

In 1981, GSA provided the U.S. Department of Housing and Urban Development with a research agenda and annotated bibliography (Taylor, 1981; Taylor et al., 1981, 1982). Other relevant projects funded by the Administration on Aging dealt with transportation (Cantilli and Schmelzer, 1971; Institute of Public Administration, 1975) and gave financial support to help establish the National Center on Housing and Living Arrangements for Older Americans at the University of Michigan, a project that is now continuing with university support.

Other organizations have also begun to address the issue of the elderly and their environment. In revising its standards for facilities for the physically handicapped, the American National Standards Institute (ANSI, 1980) engaged a gerontologist–architect, Edward Steinfeld, who succeeded in stimulating the thinking of design practitioners and administrators. Most recently, the American Institute of Architects mobilized some of its resources to encourage architects to be increasingly sensitive to the housing needs of older persons. Unfortunately, the AIA project appears to have been terminated after the publication of a single book (American Institute of Architects, 1985).

THE CURRENT FRAMEWORK

The current framework of research on the social and built environment of an aging society acknowledges a basic tenet that has been suggested by Howell (among others): to understand and address the interaction between the environment and an aging population, one must take into account concepts from and the knowledge bases of diverse fields (Howell, 1980). The design of the symposium reported in this volume reflects that stance in that the eight papers commissioned for it were prepared by authors from such fields as sociology, economics, psychology, medicine, planning, and architecture.

The Demography of Current and Future Aging Cohorts

The demographic changes in the elderly population of the United States are central to addressing the social and built environment of an aging society. In a review of current demographic trends and projections, William J. Serow and David F. Sly (in this volume) suggest the need for a basic understanding of the characteristics of the various subpopulations of older persons and how the elderly population as a whole evolves within the larger aggregate of the general population. The authors emphasize that neither of the two aggregates can be viewed in isolation:

> . . . the needs of this subpopulation (of the aging) and its resulting demands are going to be strongly influenced by its size. In this sense, it is important for us to know much more about patterns of mortality and longevity and how these are changing. This may sound simple, but the complexity of such knowledge is evident when we consider that the size of this population is influenced by historical patterns of fertility and mortality to the point at which persons enter old age, as well as by patterns of mortality throughout the older years of life—to say nothing about the patterns of immigration and emigration over the whole course of life. Similarly, the structure of the processes that are responsible for growth in the elderly population (fertility, mortality, and migration) and the changes that are likely to occur in that structure will influence the demand for "needs" and even influence what these needs are and will be. For example, temporal patterns of child-bearing (when combined with increased longevity) across generations influence how old children are when their parents reach old age and may have profound influences on the physical, economic, and social ability of children to care for their aging parents. Similarly, changing patterns of mortality may not only influence the number of people who reach old age but may also affect how many people survive for longer periods after reaching old age. In addition, changes in mortality may have an impact on the physical, economic, and social abilities of this subpopulation's members to care for themselves (in old age).

The period examined by these two researchers comprised 1940–1980, and it is apparent from their findings that the composition of the population of those aged 65 years or older has changed sharply. Two features stand out, both of which are associated with a distinct increase in the educational level of older persons. First, in general, the economic status of the elderly has improved, although, according to Serow and Sly (in this volume), "different cohorts have quite different savings and labor force opportunity patterns, which can have quite different consequences for the financial abilities of the population during the *early* years of old age" (emphasis added). The second feature is increased longevity: older people are living longer after reaching age 65. Regarding the interaction of these trends, Serow and Sly (in this volume) commented: "increased longevity among the aged will have important consequences for how long savings and retirement income will have to last, which in turn may have important consequences for how the elderly dispose of income and savings through old age." The level of disposable income and the extent of savings on the part of elderly persons will also dictate the size of the dependent population to be supported publicly, the period and scope of support to be provided, and the nature of the private sector's response to the changed economic position of the elderly.

Yet none of the recent indications of improved economic position of the elderly should obscure the continued presence of a "hard core" of poor older persons, which was estimated in 1980 to be about 12.5 percent of all those aged 65 and older in the United States. In general, poor older persons are women drawn from many different minority groups, but most of them are black, without spouses, and with limited educational achievement. Higher Social Security benefit levels have helped to lift a proportion of the elderly out of poverty but not by much. It is estimated that approximately 40 percent of older persons on Social Security must survive financially on their monthly payment, a function that Social Security was not designed to perform when it was begun in 1935.

A substantial group of poor elderly persons, combined with the increased longevity of the subpopulations of all older people is a factor that must be reckoned with in planning social services and housing for the elderly. Other recent demographic trends that are also likely to affect the social and built environment of older persons include changes in labor force participation (in particular, the increased numbers of women working) and decisions about when to retire; divorce among couples with substantial years of marriage, often on the threshold of old age; the diminishing number of family members available to provide social support of a family's elders as more married women enter the labor force; and changes in mortality differentials by sex. Collectively, these changes suggest an expanded role for formal services to the aging and their families.

One segment of the aging population in particular—those 85 years and older, the oldest of the old, frequently characterized as the frail or vulnerable elderly—has grown at a dramatic rate over the past four decades and is likely to exercise a strong influence on the social and built environment of the future. Between the census periods of 1940 and 1980, the population aged 85 and older expanded by more than 500 percent from 364,752 to 2,240,067. The growth of 85-and-older persons in this period was almost two to one in favor of women. There is little known about this age group, largely because of the paucity of tabulations from published U.S. census data, and the marked growth in their numbers appears to have surprised some U.S. policy analysts, despite signs of this potential growth as early as 1950. (Serow and Sly point out that in the census periods 1940 through 1970, the population aged 90 and older increased by 68, 90, and 75 percent, respectively, before tapering off to an increase of 45 percent in the census period 1970–1980.)

The future "old old" may differ in important ways from the current elderly cohort. For example, Serow and Sly (in this volume) argue that the 1980 group aged 55–64 represents the cutting edge of critical differences between the elderly of yesterday and the elderly of tomorrow in the composition of the population and their life-course experiences. The new old are better educated and have higher incomes, although such economic betterment may be offset by other trends. Men may retire earlier, and women will probably have considerably more labor force experience. Smaller families portend fewer familial resources to care for the future old old. Furthermore, despite a better economic outlook for many of the future oldest old, a substantial group will still fall under the poverty line.

To summarize briefly, three new factors of importance in the design of social and physical environments for community-based elderly persons have become apparent. First, the survivorship of elderly persons in the upper ranges of the age scale appears to be increasing. Second is a major demographic trend that will greatly influence the social and built environment: the emerging cohort differences by composition and life-course experiences that suggest the future old old may differ in important ways from the current elderly cohort. Finally, we may note the substantial growth of an elderly subpopulation whose members are potentially susceptible to decrements in health and related conditions that may accompany advanced age, suggesting an increasing vulnerability among elderly persons who choose to maintain their independent residences.

The Concept of Vulnerability Among the Oldest Old

With increased longevity, vulnerability among the elderly has assumed growing importance. As a result, the changes associated with the normal process of aging are being subject to increasing scrutiny. Beth J. Soldo and Charles F. Longino, Jr. (in this volume), for example, have proposed the following:

- Changes among elderly persons are not correlated with chronological age but exhibit variance.
- Changes among older people are not manifest as a simple linear decline but show a variety of rates; change may even be arrested.
- Changes in function may produce different effects in the same person, and the variance among older persons tends to increase with age.
- The rate of change can proceed along some dimensions relatively independently of change in others, but the serious loss or compromise of functional capacity in one area can accelerate the rate of decline in others.
- A supportive social or physical environment or positive change can retard the rate of functional loss to some degree.

These findings, which were derived from research by Soldo and Longino and others, suggest not only that changes associated with the aging process are multidimensional but that vulnerability among aging persons should be conceptualized similarly because it includes physical, environmental, economic, social, and mental health factors. Indeed, Soldo and Longino suggest that the assessment of vulnerability among older persons calls for an integration of qualitative information (derived from biomedical research and service delivery experiences) and quantitative data gleaned from demographic analyses.

Soldo and Longino (in this volume) measured vulnerability

according to five specific areas: (1) income, (2) the existence of care services, (3) social contact, (4) an unmet but perceived need for special housing, and (5) satisfaction with one's neighborhood. Using such a quality-of-life deficiency index to discover vulnerability in disabled elderly persons living with or without a spouse and living with or without relatives, the authors found that "nearly 90 percent of the frail are not simply disabled but also socially, economically, or environmentally impoverished as well. Nearly two-thirds are deficient in at least two areas, and slightly more than one-fifth have problems in three or more areas." The authors concluded that the gradient of need on the part of the vulnerable elderly is matched imperfectly with the gradient of available community-based services offered to them. Citing the work of Glick (1979), the authors suggest that the demand for community long-term care may far outpace the growth in members of the disabled portion of the elderly. Barring changes in service delivery approaches, Glick's projections also suggest that the proportion of the elderly with an unmet need for long-term care and the proportion with multiple social and environmental deficiencies may increase over time. To understand better why this mismatch of need and service exists, it is necessary to examine recent federal housing policies and what current policies portend.

Federal Housing Policies

Over the years, federal policy on housing for the elderly has been directed toward two elderly groups. The first, and by far the largest in monetary terms, comprises moderate and upper income groups. Tax expenditures, in the form of mortgage interest and property tax deductions, have been extremely successful in promoting and subsidizing home ownership for elderly persons. By 1986, over 75 percent of the elderly owned their own homes, and 80 percent of those owned their homes outright.

The second track of federal policy has been directed toward providing housing and adequate shelter for low-income individuals. Initiated during the Great Depression as part of the Roosevelt New Deal, federal involvement in housing for the poor of all ages has a 50-year history. In 1949, Congress adopted a national policy aimed at ensuring a decent home and suitable living environment for every American family. Over the years, the federal government has developed a number of mechanisms to achieve this goal including the direct provision of housing through new construction, rental assistance, mortgage interest subsidies, and other financing arrangements with local governments and housing development agencies. Currently, these programs account for well over 3.5 million units, some 1.5 million of which are occupied by older persons.

Although the low-income housing created under the Housing Act of 1937 was not initially intended to provide special assistance to the elderly, it has evolved into one of the principal forms of housing assistance for this age group. As a result of legislative changes enacted in the late 1950s, the proportion of housing units occupied by people over age 65 jumped from 10 percent in 1956 to 46 percent in 1984 (U.S. Senate, Special Committee on Aging, 1986).

The first program specifically designed for the elderly—Section 202 of the Federal Housing Act of 1964—was initiated in 1959. It has become the centerpiece of federal housing policy for the elderly, providing low-interest loans to private, nonprofit sponsors for the construction of subsidized rental units. As of 1985, it had provided an estimated 188,000 units of assisted housing for this age group.

Yet despite this construction, one estimate is that approximately 2 million of the 3.2 million low-income elderly who are eligible for federal housing assistance currently are not served by federal programs (U.S. Senate, Special Committee on Aging, 1984). Recent congressional studies show that, today, over a quarter million older persons are waiting to gain entrance to Section 202 projects nationwide. With the continued "graying" of the population, this demand is expected to grow.

Although the federal response to assisted housing has been the major source of low-income housing in this country, critics maintain that the current approach has been deficient in several areas. First, unlike health and income security programs, housing has never been seen as an entitlement. Some housing specialists feel that this narrow vision has exacerbated the problems of existing substandard housing and resulted in long waiting lists for housing assistance.

Second, the government's response to assisted housing has been predominantly production oriented. This "bricks and mortar" approach has failed to address the support service needs of those requiring help. As indicated by several of the authors whose papers are presented later in this volume, programs of nutrition, health, day care, and other social services have not been fully integrated into assisted housing, which results in a fragmented and confusing array of service initiatives and considerable unmet needs.

Third, economic concerns in the 1980s, fueled by inflation and changes in federal spending priorities, forced shifts in public policy on many domestic programs. Although much of the consequent budget-cutting attention was directed toward health and income transfer programs, federally assisted housing also came under scrutiny. Administrative and legislative initiatives in the early 1980s substantially reduced assisted housing programs, resulting in a 70 percent loss of budget authority since 1981.

In light of these economic and political changes, many observers believe that federal housing programs are undergoing a gradual evolution that may alter the future of housing policy for the aging. Three major trends are likely to have an impact on these developments.

First, a renewed emphasis on federalism in the early 1980s produced a shift to state and local governments of the responsibility to provide for the shelter needs of low-income persons. State governments have experimented with a variety of creative financing arrangements. Tax-exempt bonds, the integration of state funds with existing federal dollars from such sources as community development block grants or urban development action grants, and the allocation of a portion of state revenues for low-income housing have all produced promising results. Seven states now have substantial congregate housing programs for the elderly, and at least one local community has promulgated zoning laws requiring developers to earmark a portion of new developments to low- and moderate-income housing.

Second, the federal government has moved away from its historic role in the direct provision of housing and now promotes private sector and philanthropic initiatives. Rather than building new public housing units, the Reagan administration has emphasized stabilizing existing housing programs for the elderly. Additionally, the private sector, which has traditionally been motivated by economic returns, has been encouraged to adopt new marketing strategies in conjunction with the human service agencies to ensure older citizens continued opportunities for independent living. In recent years, a number of national and regional organizations have been formed to foster such new partnerships.

Finally, the economic pressures of rapidly escalating health care costs, especially among the elderly, are driving the move toward the development of a comprehensive approach to community-based long-term care services. (Only recently, however, have the shelter needs of the elderly been recognized as a vital component in such a system.) Research on congregate housing demonstration programs at both the federal and state levels has shown that a mix of support services tailored to individual needs in an assisted housing environment can reduce more costly institutional alternatives (U.S. House of Representatives, Select Committee on Aging, Subcommittee on Housing and Consumer Interests, 1987). The hope of the advocates of comprehensive services is that substantial savings in both Medicare and Medicaid may be possible through programs designed to provide in-home support services; yet even if savings are not realized, the programs may succeed in enhancing the quality of life and prolonging community residence for older people.

In short, the federal government's 50-year commitment to housing for the elderly is likely to continue, although probably in a changed form to meet new needs. Public sentiment and the congressional priorities that have been established during the last several decades will ensure that these needs receive the attention of policymakers. As our society becomes progressively older and changes occur in the social and economic environment, housing policy must keep pace to address these new and varied challenges.

Public Intervention in Housing Programs for the Aging

Raymond J. Struyk's review (in this volume) affirms the relationship between housing and long-term care and endorses the role of community-based housing as a major environmental element in a multidimensional response to vulnerability among the aging. Viewing housing programs provided by the public sector as a form of public intervention, Struyk asserts:

The dominant issue in the debate surrounding the housing environment of the elderly is how to construct public assistance to support those housing transitions that are necessary to allow community-housing to become an active and integral element in the overall long-term care system.

His view of the needs of older persons for a social and built environment include the following propositions:

- changes in health, in the availability of social supports, and in income level accompany persons moving into old age;
- the intact elderly differ among themselves in basic health condition, level of household income, and preferences for renting or owning a home; and
- the elderly are prime candidates for long-term care, a system that ought to transcend the traditional institutional solution and include the provision of supportive services to help the vulnerable elderly with the normal tasks of daily living while they retain residence in community-based housing.

What is required but is currently absent as part of an effective social and built environment is a set of national policies and practical, flexible options to respond to the elderly, whose housing demands may change as subjective conditions change in the course of the process of aging.

In analyzing the extent to which older persons in need of supportive services should remain at home, Struyk (in this volume) distinguished between two types of housing problems: the difficulties associated with the more traditional issue of housing condition and the deficiencies of the dwelling itself are referred to as dwelling specific, whereas problems associated with activity limitations of the housing occupant in the use of the dwelling are termed dwelling-use problems. The former category of issues tends to be related to income level rather than age and can be addressed by paying to have repairs made or having repairs provided by volunteers. The latter set of problems may be attributed to advanced age exacerbated by physical impairment and may be offset by assistance from family or others or by modifications in the design features of the dwelling.

Struyk found that about 12 percent of persons aged 65 and older need some form of supportive service in the home—7 percent of those aged 65–74 and 21 percent of those aged 75 and older, totaling an estimated 28 percent of all elderly households.

A more conservative approach to estimating the elderly in households with functional limitations receiving formal supportive services calculates that 25 percent of the elderly are in receipt of such services, paid for either by themselves or by an agency. The estimates of the number of elderly with housing-specific problems tend to be more accurate and exceed the number of elderly with housing-use problems. Approximately 10 percent to 17 percent of the elderly are said to have both types of problems.

Two strategies are available for tailoring housing to a person's needs as health conditions change: one is the modification of the dwelling, and the other is the person's relocation to alternative housing more suited to his or her physical status.

The intent of housing modification is to enable the older person to continue to live as independently as possible while remaining in the same dwelling, thereby diminishing actual or potential dependence on others. The cost of modification is a major consideration, however, although some of the costs are one-time expenditures and some changes may not require the outlay of funds. For example, one possible solution for a person with heart disease residing in a home in which the bedroom is on the second floor is to convert one of the downstairs rooms to a bedroom. Yet despite the rationality of a strategy of housing modification, Struyk (in this volume) reports that a 1982 study showed that only 10 percent of the elderly who resided in households with at least one member with health and mobility problems carried out any modification of the dwelling.

The second strategy, relocation to alternative housing, may include moving to a smaller home, entering a shared housing arrangement, or moving into one of several forms of residential congregate housing. According to Struyk, Heumann (1985) calculated that congregate facilities were about one-third less expensive overall than institutional long-term facilities for the same care services. But most older people, whether impaired or not, tend to resist relocation. In many instances the older person is intuitively correct for it may not be possible to replicate his or her current housing, despite its limitations, with an equivalent dwelling. Some older people may not be aware of available alternatives. Relocation need not be threatening if the decision is made voluntarily, but the social costs of relocation should be considered.

The security of familiar surroundings is valued by most older persons. Sweden, among other countries, exercises what it calls a "first line of defense" against moving older pensioners from familiar environments. This policy includes making improvements in the housing unit and providing a program of home help (SPRI, 1979). The Swedish system of home help is worth examining as one way of addressing services to the vulnerable elderly. The service is national in scope; in 1979 it employed some 70,000 paid workers throughout the country. The provision of home help, as of other social services, is the financial responsibility of municipal authorities and is usually paid for out of tax funds. It is offered without cost to the recipient. Home help services are provided by a combination of paid staff and volunteers, preferably neighbors and friends. The tasks are divided: those tasks requiring specialized knowledge and skill are performed by the paid staff, and those tasks that are routine and easily manageable are performed by the volunteers. It is not unusual for the home helper to undertake minor health care such as help with medications, but full nursing service is not provided by this individual. It is not unusual, therefore, to have a consortium of helpers working collaboratively under a case manager, drawing on the varied contributions of a family member, a neighbor in the area, a nurse, and a home helper to provide the range of support services necessary to get the older person through the day's routine.

Struyk (in this volume) concludes that making the current housing program in the United States more responsive to the frail or vulnerable elderly will require enlarging housing alternatives for older people. Also needed is an evaluation of the effects of the housing options now being tested. He argues that the federal government should expand the array of residential solutions to meet various levels of vulnerability among the elderly.

The prospects of any change in national policy to incorporate the provision of supportive services in community-based housing as part of a modernized long-term care system appear to be slim. Resistance on the part of the current and previous national administrations to any expansion of long-term care programming beyond the present institutional solution is deeply rooted. Nor are the prospects made better by current shifts in budgetary priorities for social programs.

Mobility and Social Integration of the Aging

As the number of elderly persons surviving into their eighties and nineties increases, the issue of mobility takes on an added priority. Mobility, which can be defined as the capacity to travel from home to essential destinations at reasonable cost, is interdependent with housing location. The opportunity for older persons to maintain a reasonable level of mobility, regardless of the choice of residential location, contributes to the continued independence of the aging. Yet the role of transportation in connecting people to places seems to have received insufficient attention by policy planners. Wachs (in this volume) has noted that, for the elderly, housing choice often involves a trade-off in mobility:

> If one chooses a low-density suburban living environment, far from friends, relatives, and services, it may entail high mobility costs for the individual and society, especially in old age. High-density inner-city environments may impose high housing costs and less aesthetically pleasing environments on their residents, but it may cost individuals and society much less to provide access to services at such locations. Although we recognize these principles, we know less than we would like to know about the economic, social, and cultural trade-offs between housing and mobility. Therefore, any investigation of the relationships between housing and mobility in old age must include attitudinal and social dimensions as well as physical and economic ones.

Planning for the mobility of older people should be incorporated into environmental planning for the intact as well as for the vulnerable elderly. As Wachs suggests, the absence of transportation may be the means by which our environment conspires to isolate the elderly; the presence of transportation may be one of the keys to an active and healthy old age.

Access to transportation services, whether self-provided or provided by public resources, is particularly important for vulnerable persons, regardless of age. Such persons should be assisted by all reasonable means to maintain a pattern of living that approximates the norm in a given society if they are to perform appropriately and effectively in that society.

The mobility problems of inner-city elderly illustrate the complexity and importance of understanding the transportation needs of older persons. Many urban elderly have never driven and, being economically limited to infrequent taxi use, must rely on public transit or relatives and friends who drive. Depending on friends and relatives fosters a sense of dependency and obligation in a group already prone to such feelings. And unfortunately, public transit is not always a good alternative because its use may involve substantial physical barriers such as long walks, high steps, narrow doorways, and exposure to the elements. Although attention has been directed toward the removal of such physical barriers, Wachs found a distressing lack of security for persons using public transit (incidence rates of crime perpetrated on older people are 30 times the crime victimization cases reported by local transit police). Greater attention to security—for example, such inexpensive changes as relocating bus stops and better street lighting—might be one of the most important initiatives by which public policymakers may better tailor transportation to the needs of the elderly.

Older Americans in this decade are different in demographic terms compared with their counterparts in the 1970s. It may be helpful to review some of these major changes and to extract their transportation implications:

- Older people are living longer, thereby swelling the ranks of the elderly in the upper ranges of the age span.
- The women-to-men ratio has become even more pronounced than in prior decades, with the disparity between the two sexes widening with increasing age.
- As measured by the proportion of elderly persons with a high school diploma, educational achievement has risen steadily, thus improving the income, health status, and well-being of older people.
- The percentage of older persons voluntarily leaving the labor force has increased for both sexes.
- Although a smaller proportion of older persons are now below the poverty line, at least one older person in eight can still be classified as poor.
- Minorities have increased as a proportion of the aging population, and all projections indicate they will continue to gain on the white majority.

According to Bell and Revis (1983), the transportation implications of these changes appear to be the following:

- Car ownership will be maintained by many older persons, and the private automobile will continue to be the preferred and main source of transportation both for disabled and for intact older persons.

- Specialized transportation, estimated by one study to be used by less than 10 percent of all elderly persons, will have to serve an older group of riders who are mostly female, less physically able, and drawn heavily from minorities.
- Work-oriented trips will decrease as a trend toward early retirement continues and as elderly riders seek trips to other destinations.

In keeping with the phenomenon of a more heterogeneous older population, Wachs (in this volume) states that the travel patterns and mobility requirements of the elderly are a function of life-style. He argues that it is not possible to predict the travel patterns of older people without a grasp of the variations in activity that reflect differences in life-style.

The concept of life-style is a useful analytic tool in dealing with the residential location and mobility patterns among the elderly living in a diversified urban setting (Wachs, 1979). Life-style takes into account socioeconomic and demographic variables that singly or collectively affect the elderly differentially. For example, in a study carried out in the Los Angeles area, Wachs identified and subdivided the elderly in the region according to six life-style groups: the central-city dwellers, the financially secure, the new suburbanites, the early suburbanites, the blacks, and the Spanish-Americans. A different set of life-style groupings could be devised for geographic regions other than Los Angeles.

The utility of the life-style concept, in terms of mobility among elderly persons, is that it raises the possibility of differentiating among their travel patterns according to variations in housing location, car ownership, reliance on public transportation, and degree of vulnerability.

The Swedish Perspective on Housing and Social Environments for the Elderly

The pattern of growth of the elderly population in industrial countries tends to be similar, but the cultural interpretation of independence in old age differs among countries. All industrialized nations have exhibited a change in the age pyramid as a result of a falling birth rate and the increased longevity of the population. In the short run, urbanization and industrialization minimize cultural and social differences and may appear to form a tendency toward increasingly uniform life patterns for older people. In the long run, the demands of industrialization are likely to become dominant in shaping residential arrangements among older parents and their adult children, even in cases in which such arrangements conflict with existing cultural patterns. Sven Thiberg, a research architect from Sweden (in this volume), cites the cases of Japan and Sweden, two countries that are similar in living standards, education, and methods of production but quite dissimilar in their cultural norms regarding the care of parents in old age:

> It is not merely that 7 percent of the elderly in Sweden and 60 percent in Japan live with relatives. The declared social goals of the two nations differ just as much. In Sweden, the national policy is that an independent life is desirable and that it can only be attained if older people live in their own homes; in Japan, the state advocates that the elderly shall live with their relatives. Great efforts are made in Sweden to support old people living on their own; in Japan, no reason is seen to develop such support because it is considered to conflict with the desirable social pattern.

Thiberg concludes, however, that "everything indicates that a growing degree of industrialization leads to increased mobility, the splitting up of households, and less stable families. In the long run, these trends have the effect of separating the young and the old even more than they are at present, and in general, cultural ties do not appear to be strong enough to prevent this development." Cultural influences may become subordinate to the forces of industrialization, and older people increasingly may tend to live near but not with adult children, in most instances by mutual agreement. Rosenmayr and Kockeis (1962) have termed this expression of independence in living arrangements on the part of older people in most modernized countries "intimacy at a distance."

To keep older people out of institutions or delay their entry into that form of living arrangement, Sweden has experimented with several types of specialized housing for the elderly. These include pensioners' flats in normal housing, which are usually one- or two-room apartments dispersed within a residential area; temporary pensioner flats, which are located mostly in sparsely populated areas; old-age homes for the elderly who could not look after themselves because of deficiencies in their prior housing or who require considerable social assistance from paid staff; and flats in service blocks. Originating in the early 1970s, service blocks are apartment buildings that are designed to complement housing in the normal market for older people and in old-age homes. About 40 apartments per service block is common, but some local councils (which sponsor service blocks) prefer a smaller number—10 to 15 flats—to avoid segregating large numbers of the elderly in service-oriented buildings.

The primary purpose of the service block is to provide housing and support services for its elderly residents. The internal services offered in the blocks vary but are likely to include a central dining room, hobby shops, social services, podiatry services on a scheduled basis, and limited medical supervision. Some blocks incorporate a child care center on the premises or build a children's playground on open space owned by the service block thus allowing elderly residents to serve as volunteers in the children's programs. Frequently, the physical location of the service block advances its integration with other resources and other generations. For example, a block is often located so as to take advantage either of adjacent health resources or to encourage the interaction of the service block with neighborhood social life. Some local councils have built service blocks that are linked by covered passageways to a contiguous nursing home or health clinic. In such instances, the service block is located in close proximity to a local shopping center. To encourage the use of the service block by area residents and shoppers, it may include services for the public such as a cafeteria, a post office, a library, and a social insurance office. The policy thus encourages elderly residents to remain in their own dwellings, aided when necessary by publicly provided forms of social support and informal care by relatives offered voluntarily, in that order of priority. Thiberg (in this volume) indicates that housing programs for older people are sustained both by the general aims of housing policy and housing provision, which are listed below.

The aims of Swedish housing policy are as follows:

- to guarantee an abundant supply of forms of housing for all ages and types of household;
- to make forms of housing economically and technically

available through government financing and distribution policies; and

- to give the elderly their choice of dwelling according to need and desire and not move them to special forms of residence as long as adequate care can be provided in their own home.

The aims of housing provision are as follows:

- to convert the existing housing stock by such methods and such financing as to make it easier for the elderly to remain in their homes, modernization comprising the external environment, service establishments, and communications;
- to ensure that new housing is directed toward strategic additions to the existing housing stock (especially important is the provision of new forms of living environments that are difficult to realize in existing housing); and
- to plan reconstruction and new construction so that medical care for the elderly occurs to an increasing extent in their own homes, ensuring that administration, maintenance, and care of the residential environment shall be of good quality and take place in consultation with the residents in order to increase well-being and security and reduce the risks of accidents.

What lessons can be learned from Swedish policy on designing appropriate environments for the aging? First, elders are encouraged to "age in place" as long as it is feasible to remain in one's home. Second, housing is viewed as an integral part of a holistic approach to publicly provided social services for all of the elderly, thus reducing the need for recurring problems of shelter. For aging persons to pursue an independent life in old age requires economic, social, and cultural measures in support of the goal of normalization.

New Technology and the Productivity and Independence of the Elderly

With increased longevity and, in general, a more affluent old age for the elderly in the United States, the possibilities for enhancing the productivity and independence of older persons have attracted considerable interest. A number of authors have examined new technologies relevant to the social and built environment that might allow the elderly to lead lives of greater productivity and independence.

Robert L. Kane (in this volume) has focused on the role of technology and its effect on individual well-being. He views the growth of new technology as a given that we must assess mainly in terms of how to establish priorities and how to finance what is chosen. He holds that there are collective (societal) benefits as well as individual benefits from the new technology that must be evaluated and reminds us that the people who will be affected by the technology of the future will differ from the aged of today.

Kane offers some insight into the assessment of various types of technological achievements in medicine, preventive health, and communications. For example, in communications, he foresees the use of personal computers in ways that will not only increase the pleasure of learning and entertainment but that will also reshape traditional patterns of social contact. Kane (in this volume) notes: "The ability to interact with machines as well as with other people may provide the elderly with a much more patient, reinforcing set of social patterns than they have experienced before."

Victor Regnier's contribution (in this volume) focuses on the more traditional aspects of how housing for the elderly, particularly for the frail elderly, can emphasize "user-friendly" housing designs. Regnier maintains that to achieve a complete, behaviorally based design, all of the desirable goals must be specified beforehand (e.g., social mix, identity, unobtrusive care, etc.) and specifically addressed by certain physical design features. Regnier also emphasizes that housing designs must be evaluated empirically in a formal postoccupancy study. Thus, the design model that he proposes for the built physical environment must be carefully integrated with considerations about the intended social environment. Moreover, the physiological and sensory aspects of design must be evaluated within a behavioral context.

Regnier also discusses a number of other considerations in designing housing for the elderly including the neighborhood setting, together with appropriate accessibility to varied services, and more knowledgeable management of facilities. In the case studies of congregate residence that Regnier presents, an assessment is offered of how these two factors are taken into account in housing design.

Both the Kane and Regnier papers call attention to the circumstance that regulatory design requirements often militate against desirable outcomes. Yet often, these regulations are intended to ensure the implementation of new technologies and products to replace old materials and practices (e.g., using polyplastics instead of wood) and are further examples of innovations in the built and social environment that may produce unintended consequences.

Working within a somewhat visionary framework, James N. Morgan's thesis (in this volume) calls for a radical reshaping of the physical and social environments of elderly persons. His concern is to seek suitable accommodations for older persons in their passage from wellness to infirmity. He believes this may best be achieved by exploring the potential for productivity in older persons. Already in American society, most elderly persons live long enough to experience an extended period of postretirement; increasing longevity also carries the increased likelihood that many older persons will spend a large part of those remaining years with functional disabilities that require assistance from others. Considering the growing costs of long-term care, Morgan proposes harnessing the productive capacity of older persons to handle some of the burdens of such care. To do so, however, requires the removal of barriers—economic, legal, social–organizational, and environmental. He proposes mega-experiments: large-scale demonstrations or trials that involve creating new, flexible, self-regulated communities of older persons operating with a system of nonmonetary currency to facilitate the exchange of services among people who help one another. Such communities presumably would be self-supporting (i.e., unsubsidized), more efficient, and equitable as well as encouraging an increase in productive activity.

What would be the essential features of such new communities? Morgan believes they would have to be newly constructed, with homelike living quarters and shared facilities. The communities would be compact with a maximum of several hundred units so as to encourage close contact and interaction among the residents. The age composition would be adjusted to maintain a spread of persons 55 years of age and older, but the residence would be viewed as permanent for the remaining years of one's life.

For Morgan, the "glue" that could hold such a community together would be the mode of exchange: a resident would be able to help others in the community who are disabled and thus earn exchange credits that would be claimed when he or she needed help. Unlike currently planned old-age communities and most congregate housing arrangements, the case services in such a community would be provided mainly by neighbors rather than by professionals.

The design of the symposium and of similar efforts to address systematically a major social issue relevant to the aging illustrate a basic principle that is recognized especially, but not exclusively, by researchers and planners in social gerontology. One way of conceptualizing this principle is to characterize it as the vertical–horizontal dilemma in the social problem-solving process. That is, given the scope and breadth of knowledge in many areas of social life, it is deemed more efficient and appropriate to slice that knowledge into vertical segments, thus creating areas of specialization or disciplines. Yet the problems of the elderly, among others, frequently fail to confine themselves to these arbitrarily created divisions of knowledge but rather transcend and cut across separate disciplines, requiring the collaboration of specialists from several disciplines for problem-solving purposes.

To that end, the eight commissioned papers presented in the volume are largely specialized analyses of aspects of the general subject of this symposium. The remainder of this first part includes a brief discussion of previous studies and a summary of the current framework of thought in a number of areas covered by the symposium. The next section represents the committee's views on a feasible policy and research agenda for the future. Ideas in the agenda for the future were drawn from the positions articulated in the commissioned papers, modified by the discussion held at the symposium as well as the perspective of some committee members.

REFERENCES

American Institute of Architects. 1985. *Design for Aging: An Architect's Guide.* Washington, D.C.: American Institute of Architects Press.

ANSI (American National Standards Institute). 1980. "Specifications for Making Buildings and Facilities Accessible To and Usable By Physically Handicapped People." ANSI 117.1. New York: ANSI.

Bell, W. G., and J. S. Revis. 1983. *Transportation for Older Americans: Issues and*

Options for the Decade of the 1980s. Office of Technology and Planning Assistance, Office of the Secretary of Transportation. DOT 1-83-42. Washington, D.C.

Birren, J. E. 1959. *Handbook of Aging and the Individual.* Chicago: University of Chicago Press.

Cantilli, E. J., and J. L. Shmelzer, eds. 1971. *Transportation and Aging.* Washington, D.C.: U.S. Administration on Aging.

Carp, F. M. 1966. *A Future for the Aged.* Austin: University of Texas Press.

Glick, P. C. 1979. "The Future Marital Status and Living Arrangements of the Elderly." *The Gerontologist* 19:301–309.

Heumann, L. 1985. *A Cost Comparison of Congregate Housing and Long-Term Care Facilities in the Mid-West.* Urbana: University of Illinois, Housing Research and Development Program.

Howell, S. S. 1980. "Environments and the Aging." Pp. 237–260 in *Annual Review of Gerontology and Geriatrics,* vol. 1, C. Eisdorfer, ed. New York: Springer.

Institute of Public Administration. 1975. *Planning Handbook: Transportation Services for the Elderly.* Washington, D.C.: Government Printing Office.

Kleemeier, R. W. 1959. "Behavior and the Organization of the Bodily and the External Environment." Pp. 400–451 in *Handbook of Aging and the Individual,* J. E. Birren, ed. Chicago: University of Chicago Press.

Lawton, M. P., and L. Nahemow. 1973. "Ecology and the Aging Process." Pp. 619–674 in *Psychology of Adult Development and Aging,* C. Eisdorfer and M. P. Lawton, eds. Washington, D.C.: American Psychological Association.

Pastalan, L. A., and D. H. Carson, eds. 1970. *The Spatial Behavior of Older People.* Ann Arbor: Institute of Gerontology, University of Michigan.

Rosenmayr, L., and E. Kockeis. 1962. "Family Relations and Social Contacts of the Aged in Vienna." In *Social and Psychological Aspects of Aging,* C. Tibbitts and W. Donahue, eds. New York: Columbia University Press.

Rosow, I. 1967. *Social Integration of the Aged.* New York: Free Press.

SPRI. 1979. *Primary Care and Care of the Elderly.* Special Publication S100-107. Stockholm: SPRI, Fack, 102 50.

Taylor, P. S. 1981. "Long Range Research Agenda for Elderly Housing and Related Services." Report prepared for the U.S. Department of Housing and Urban Development. Gerontological Society of America, Washington, D.C.

Taylor, P. S., E. D. Sclar, and B. Soldo. 1981. "Research on Housing and Related Services for the Elderly. An Annotated Bibliography." Report prepared for the U.S. Department of Housing and Urban Development. Gerontological Society of America, Washington, D.C.

Taylor, P. S., E. D. Sclar, and B. Soldo. 1982. "Research on Housing and Related Services for the Elderly. An Annotated Bibliography." Report no. 2 prepared for the U.S. Department of Housing and Urban Development. Gerontological Society of America, Washington, D.C.

Tibbitts, C., ed. 1960. *Handbook of Social Gerontology.* Chicago: University of Chicago Press.

U.S. House of Representatives, Select Committee on Aging, Subcommittee on Housing and Consumer Interests. 1987. *Evaluating the Congregate Housing Services Program.* Staff report. Washington, D.C.: Government Printing Office.

U.S. Senate, Special Committee on Aging. 1984. *Section 202 Housing for the Elderly and Handicapped: A National Survey.* Staff Report 98-257. Washington, D.C.: Government Printing Office.

U.S. Senate, Special Committee on Aging. 1986. *Developments in Aging: 1985,* vol. 1. Staff Report 99-242. Washington, D.C.: Government Printing Office.

Vivrett, W. K. 1960. "Housing and Community Settings for Older People." Pp. 549–623 in *Handbook of Social Gerontology,* C. Tibbitts, ed. Chicago: University of Chicago Press.

Wachs, M. 1979. *Transportation for the Aging: Changing Lifestyles, Changing Needs.* Berkeley and Los Angeles: University of California Press.

Proposals for Policy and Further Research

When the housing problems of older people first arose as a matter of public concern during the late 1950s, the direction of policy and the programs to implement it were relatively clear: to build good-quality shelter for the large number of older people who were relatively self-supporting but who were limited by income in their ability to find decent housing on the open market. New housing production was one way to provide economic relief for the poorer elderly. At about the same time, methods were also under consideration for providing economic relief in long-term health care for the elderly. Two strategies that were implemented were the redefinition of the home for the aged and federal facilitation of nursing home development.

Simply stated, then, the federal government wanted to elevate the quality of life for the low-income independent older person through improved housing; it wanted to do the same for the low-income disabled older person through nursing home care. Yet these intended policies did not readily accommodate subsequent changes in American society in general and in the elderly population in particular.

First, the income of older people improved measurably, shrinking the size of the financially indigent population. Second, the distinction between independent and dependent elderly persons became blurred: an elderly person's health status could vary, and there were often unequal rates of change among older residents clustered in the new housing of the 1960s. Third, the OlderAmericans Act, the Social Security Act, and Medicare established the concept of chronological age as a basis for entitlement to national programs.

In housing and health programs, it became recognized that prospective clients were not dichotomously healthy or unhealthy but could exhibit health conditions of any stage in between. Thus, the nation saw the development of intermediate residential models—housing for the elderly that fell somewhere between their own residences and the total care provided by nursing homes—as well as the emergence of local, home-delivered services that came to be known as community-based long-term care. All of these developments seemed to be going in the "right" direction—that is, working toward a greater ability to match the characteristics of environments and services to the varied needs of elderly people. But expectations about the country's ability to produce enough housing units, enough varieties of residences, and the right mix of services were diminished by the economic downturn of the late 1970s.

At this writing (1987), all federally assisted new housing construction programs have been terminated except for the Section 202 program, which survives on a year-by-year basis over the recurring objections of the national administration. Nursing home construction with the aid of public funds has been greatly reduced. Experimentation with locally provided community-based long-term care continues in spite of reduced public funding fueled by private sector innovations and a demand by elderly clients.

Although the present may be a time for the consolidation of these efforts, it may also be an appropriate time to identify objectives in environmental policy for the future. This chapter discusses four policy areas: age and disability, environmental services and the well-being of older people, person and environment in life-span perspective, and self-determination in environmental decision making.

AGE AND DISABILITY

Neugarten (1982) and Binstock (1983) have suggested that there should be no ambiguity in an elderly person's eligibility for services and programs. One form of eligibility may be chronological age; another is need as defined by levels of disability or poverty. As some gerontologists have warned might happen, the United States is currently in the midst of a disruptive quarrel over "age equity" (Kingston et al., 1986; Preston, 1984), a quarrel fed by the resentments of people who believe that benefits are going disproportionately to older people who are not necessarily in economic need. Thus, a first question is whether national housing policies have emphasized chronological age in their definition of entitlement in a way that undermines the credibility of the policies. In general, they have not. There was a time when substantial federal support went into mortgage insurance and low-interest loans to housing or nursing homes that served older people who had incomes well above the poverty level, but those subsidies have for the most part ended. The attention of national housing policy is now focused on low-income persons.

Another complaint that is sometimes made is that the new construction of public programs became concentrated on older income-eligible clients, some believe to the neglect of younger families. This trend can be seen in the high proportion of public housing and Section 8 units that were provided for elderly persons in the 1970s. Thus, age can be said to have been an advantage in the distribution of scarce national housing resources.

Currently, there is concern that almost no new housing for low-income people is being built to replace units being lost through the normal processes of housing turnover. However one may applaud programs to conserve and rehabilitate older housing, it ought not to occur at the expense of the program that has produced 800,000 or so new units over the years. Moreover, in the process of modifying the original objectives of federal housing policy and defining its target group more carefully, in addition to income the age criterion must be redefined to recognize the housing needs of people of all ages.

It is possible that limiting high-expense programs to the most financially needy may require the introduction of an added criterion in addition to age and income. Some discussion is needed to develop a consensus about whether less expensive forms of assistance should be substituted for new dwelling units for poor older people, reserving the more expensive programs for poor older Americans who are also disabled. A question that is often raised is the issue of what minimal level of quality is everyone's right. Having been guided so strongly and for so long by the simple view that our national programs could provide quality housing for all, insufficient attention has been paid to specifying the minimum right versus the purchasable options. Whether health should be an additional eligibility criterion introduces a second major policy issue: that of the relationship between the environment of the elderly and their health and social services.

ENVIRONMENTAL SERVICES AND THE WELL-BEING OF OLDER PEOPLE

The demographic and health data presented in this volume (see the eight commissioned papers) quite effectively portray the size of the "vulnerable" population as a minority of all aged persons. Yet what must also be considered is that elderly persons who are vulnerable by reason of health deficits are likely to be vulnerable in other ways.

Historically, federal housing programs housed older tenants who grew less independent with the years, creating a growing group of disabled people who required something more than mere shelter. The congregate housing model—that is, a facility with supportive services that is clearly a housing unit and not an institution—became firmly established during the one phase of housing development for the elderly (although never as ubiquitously as is sometimes presumed). For a time, it seemed as if three models of residence would serve most elderly people's housing needs: independent housing, congregate housing, and nursing homes.

The reluctance of society to support these three housing models financially forced us to search for alternatives to these relatively expensive physical facilities. Social gerontologists were probably late in recognizing the strength of older people's wishes to remain in their own homes in the community. Indeed, there may be a ceiling in terms of the proportion of older people who may be candidates for planned housing, given improvements in the access of older people to good supportive services that would enable them to remain in their own homes.

An apparent failure to pool housing-related resources at the federal level may be traced to an attempt to maintain separate programs by the U.S. Department of Housing and Urban Development (HUD) and the U.S. Department of Health and Human Services (HHS). This lack of integration of related services was extended to the local level, and as a result, opportunities to develop integrated services were missed. Such opportunities included planned small-scale equivalents of congregate housing, (Lawton et al., 1985), supportive small-scale housing alternatives for the marginally independent, and the incorporation of a strong housing-quality component in local community-based long-term care programs.

The papers by Soldo and Longino and by Struyk in this volume discuss the importance of a health component in housing programs and the connections between housing, health, and social service programs. As these authors point out, major policy issues remain. For instance, where does the responsibility lie for facilitating, by a policy of housing maintenance, the continued residence of older people in homes of their own choice? On balance, it is clearly more cost effective to subsidize the maintenance of the usual older existing home rather than pay the costs of replacing it with a new home. Yet the problem confronting policymakers is the large backlog of potential clients and the high administrative costs of a centralized small-repair and maintenance program for older homes (Struyk, 1985).

In attempting to delimit the scope of public responsibility and establish priorities for housing assistance, it may be necessary to exclude health and disability criteria to qualify for federal assistance in home adaptation. Soldo and Longino (in this volume), Newman (1985), and others have demonstrated that multiple deprivations tend to occur in the same people, who then exhibit a combination of unmet needs: insufficient income, poor housing, ill health, and apparent social needs. More specifically, the impaired elderly who are now being served by subsidized in-home service programs may well constitute a pool of possible candidates for home repair and home adaptation services. Such services might make the critical difference that would enable these people to remain at home instead of moving to a more expensive residence.

One value issue, then, is whether the nation (like some other countries that assist the elderly in maintaining their independent living) is prepared to pay for additional services that may reduce the necessity for the institutionalization of older persons. A policy dilemma that must also be faced is the failure to address quality-of-life issues for healthy but low-income elderly who live in deficient housing. Does one approach take precedence over the other?

The first two policy areas reviewed in this section have involved vulnerable older people who constitute a high-priority group even though they may be a minority of older people. Needy as this group may be in terms of policy attention, the field of person–environment relationships has much to offer in improving the quality of life for all older people. Two further policy-relevant areas suggested by the papers presented in this volume are the life-span view of person–environment transactions and the issue of self-determination in environmental decision making.

PERSON AND ENVIRONMENT IN LIFE-SPAN PERSPECTIVE

Although the authors of papers in this report were not asked specifically to address life-span issues, any broad approach to housing policy must place some of the major policy issues within the context of the life-span perspective. One proposal made earlier suggests that the needs of the larger society require that some measure of equity be established regarding the housing needs of people of different ages. An important moderator of concern about age equity, however, is the realization that the beneficiaries are seldom restricted to one specific age group: benefits for one generation often produce benefits for other generations. For example, housing subsidies for older people in the form of planned housing developments are likely to remove financial burdens from younger wage earners, allow more dwelling-unit space for growing children, and diminish the intrafamily conflict that is often associated with involuntary home sharing by adult children and their elders.

Yet what is equally important is to conceptualize a person's life as an "environmental career," a notion that introduces basic theories of persons in environments with each person shouldering the task of maximizing the gains and minimizing the stresses of the various environments inhabited over the course of one's lifetime. If we agree with Campbell et al. (1976) that people make a continuing series of choices and engage in active behaviors that lead to their successful approximation of an ideal environment, it is not surprising to find that older people are more satisfied with their ultimate housing, their neighborhoods, and other facets of their environments than are people of younger ages.

One line of reasoning suggests that planning for one's housing environment in old age should be a lifelong process. This approach may be intuitive for many older people for despite the problems of nonliquidity, some 75 percent of all elderly in the United States own their own homes. Buying a home is only one of a variety of "housing adjustments" (in Struyk's terms) that a person is required to make. If we enlarge the foregoing concept to "environmental adjustments," it is possible to identify a large category of tasks and decisions that extend across the life span and for which there is need for intervention. The promotion of national policy to direct such interventions is urgently needed. The concept of environmental adjustments clearly includes the transportation concerns expressed in this volume by Wachs, the specific housing interventions discussed by Regnier, and the radical readjustment proposed by Morgan, together with the outcome of "quality-years" cited by Kane.

Perhaps the most useful general policy directive emerging from a proposed life-span view is that priority should be given to interventions whose benefits are germane to multiple age groups. Indeed, any proposed program should be analyzed for its contemporary effects on multiple generations in addition to its probable effects on recipients at later stages of their lives.

To reiterate, one principle that ought to guide policy development in the environmental area is that what is found to be useful for older people is likely to be useful for people of any age as well as for disabled persons. Contributions to the improvement of housing, neighborhoods, and consumer products for most people may begin in a search for user-friendly designs specific to the elderly; yet many of the design adaptations discussed by Regnier have the capacity to enhance the quality of residential life for people at any stage of life.

There are many implied policy proposals contained in the papers included in this volume. For example, Struyk's plea for enlarging the opportunities for timely modification of older persons' housing might well influence the building of age-irrevelant housing with features that increase the adaptiveness of the residence to the changing needs of its occupants over time. Wachs has noted that security is a major need for older people as they traverse their neighborhoods or use local transportation. Improving security for them will improve the quality of life for all transit users. And as Kane suggests, the processes of teaching and establishing an older person's familiarity with new housing-relevant technologies will reveal useful methods that may apply to younger users as well. (This principle applies despite a mistaken assumption that user-friendly technology is not relevant to the young.)

In summary, the life-span conception of an environmental career leads the process of policy formulation toward a broader conception of the common good in the realization that there are few environmental benefits for one group that cannot be made to work to the advantage of people of any age. This broad conception argues against the idea of age-targeted environmental designs. In contrast to this point of view, however, is the notion of disability-oriented or deprivation-targeted housing design.

SELF-DETERMINATION IN ENVIRONMENTAL DECISION MAKING

There are a number of particular ways in which the varying needs, preferences, personalities, competencies, and disabilities of a person influence his or her use of the environment. The personal factor in environmental interactions should be addressed to give adequate recognition to individual needs and the ability of older people to shape their own living environments, both as individuals and as a group.

The environmental career of a person is determined in part by the nature of the environment into which the person is thrust and partly by the active choices the person makes in the selection of environments and in the shaping of either the given or the chosen environment. It may be useful to think of the way people interact with allotted or chosen environments as a tension between reactivity and inactivity. In addition to this behavioral dialectic, there is a conflict-laden need between the wish to be challenged and the wish to be secure. National housing policies for the elderly tend to assume that old age is only a time of reactivity and a striving for security.

The wish to remain in one's own home is but one instance of the preference in the elderly for autonomy within the limits of a person's physical, mental, and economic capabilities. Yet how can housing policies be modified to facilitate such active choices as proposed by several authors in this volume? Community-based services for elderly persons in congregate housing and in other housing alternatives can extend the period of community residence. Although neighborhood dynamics were not originally to be part of this volume's scope, Wachs' underlining of how a lack of physical security may limit personal autonomy commands attention. Other forms of neighborhood-wide interventions that help people form at least preliminary relationships with one another need to be supported by policies affirming the worth of neighborhood preservation.

An important feature of Sweden's in-home services for the elderly, as described by Sven Thiberg (in this volume), is the assistance given by close neighbors, stimulated by small organizational and financial incentives provided by the federal government. Such an approach has the advantage of enabling active roles for neighbors who are prepared to help the less independent in their vicinity.

There are few older people who are so impaired that some degree of choice or autonomy is not within personal range. Our policies regarding institutional care, as Regnier noted, however, have supported many regulations that work against preserving even limited independence for people who must live in a particular setting. Institutional regulations that import rules from acute care hospitals or that place an undue premium on the maintenance of rigidities and internal order defeat the provision of a flexible living environment for residents. In practice, in such a situation, few independent behaviors are rewarded. The performance of instrumental roles such as the making of one's bed or the assumption of responsibility for one's small living area is discouraged in the name of conforming to internal regulations.

In practice, there are few incentives for designers, sponsors, or administrators to attempt innovative efforts in providing environments that maximize choice. For example, consider the small manufactured home and its relative, the "granny flat." Current technology can produce such units at reasonable cost to accommodate a person's changing needs, but local zoning, land use restrictions, and building codes have hindered the implementation of this approach.

Some of the authors of the papers in this volume emphasize

the importance of consumer preferences in giving direction to technological developments in housing. Certainly, demographic projections support the idea that an unprecedented number of older individuals will be financially and intellectually capable of expressing and acting on personal preferences in the open economic market. At the same time, consideration must also be given to raising the quality of housing for the segment of the older population that is not financially solvent or knowledgeable enough to participate fully in the market economy. One way to achieve this goal is to target life-enriching programs more toward the poor older person. Such publicly subsidized programs as senior activity centers, transportation, and educational activities are likely to elevate the quality of life, but a substantial proportion of these resources tend to be consumed by people who may not require subsidizing. On the other hand, targeting such programs only to the poor may mean they are politically less viable and poor in quality. In any case, a policy that leads to creative efforts to design aspects of the physical and social environment that challenge and engage healthy but economically deprived older persons should be a priority.

To sum up, the prevalence of a proportion of elderly persons with poor health and economic deprivation identifies one target group of older people on whom it is appropriate to focus as subjects for environmentally significant subsidy programs. Yet the majority of older people are healthy when they enter old age, and they may remain in good health for most of their lives; in such cases, their relationship to the environment is a continuous process of active choices and self-determinative behavior. Therefore, each proposed housing policy must consider carefully its effect on the use of the environment in bolstering the quality of a person's life. From this perspective, policies are not age specific but contribute to the autonomy and well-being of people of all ages.

RESEARCH AND POLICY NEEDS

An important function of the papers prepared for this volume was to point to research needs whose implementation might lead to better theory, policy, services, and design of the social and built environment of an aging society. Yet the concept of person-in-environment is by its nature quite broad because it must integrate discrete elements that are usually treated separately for convenience: that is, the person, the small group, larger aggregates of people, social institutions, culture, values, and the physical environment. To achieve an integrated policy and research product requires a multidisciplinary array of participants that includes but is not limited to physicians, psychologists, sociologists, anthropologists, policymakers, architects, and planners.

Precisely because the field of person–environment relationships is so wide-ranging, it requires a special category of research to address the knowledge-implementation process. It is not accidental that specific attention to these special research needs was cited in the papers in this volume by the two architects in the group, Regnier and Thiberg. The "doers"—those who actually design our physical and to some extent our social environments—and the risks of such housing are at the far end of the chain of knowledge generation that begins with theoretical biology, psychology, and other academic disciplines. Although some designers active in the investigation or exploration of person–environment relationships are themselves researchers or are research oriented, the majority of their peers are not. The latter group depends on socially determined channels of communication for their knowledge, a process strewn with many barriers, as documented by Regnier and Thiberg.

Thus, one major research need is for a focused inquiry into the life course of design-relevant ideas: the multiplicity of sources of the idea such as the potential user, the scientist, and the professional; the way the idea is subjected to verification; the multiple modes of transmission of the information; and the determinants of the extent and manner of its adoption, both informally in common practice and formally in regulations, housing codes, law, and broad special policy.

The knowledge-implementation process is a special research need and is therefore given special priority in this section. Yet there are also other research needs that have been suggested in the papers included in this volume and in discussion on the topics that follow.

Population Issues

The many compositional changes that have already occurred within the aging population and future projections of coming change (see Serow and Sly, in this volume) constitute an essential aspect of the social environment of older Americans. Research is needed to study the effects of such changes on the aging individual at the micro end of the scale and on the total society at the macro end. One poorly understood determinant of the behavior of the elderly is the effect on an older person of having aggregates of people in close physical proximity or within the person's subjective awareness—what may be called the suprapersonal environment. Thus, as older people migrate from one location to another, differing mixes of individuals—in terms of age, health, condition, ethnicity, and other characteristics—are available with which the older person may interact.

The effects of comparative changes in the educational and income levels of aging cohorts on their social attitudes is another phenomenon requiring study. For example, will the greater numbers of the old old reinforce the social stereotype of age as a period of disability? How much will the growing affluence of new young old cohorts counteract any negative social valuation of the broad category of older persons? In fact, what will the economic status of future cohorts of older persons be, given the shifts now occurring in the economy (from industrial to service jobs, earlier retirement, etc.)? How will all of these trends affect housing policy?

Researchable questions also arise regarding the effects of the migration of older people into an existing community, including the net effect on demands for local services and amenities, as well as their integration with the nonmigrant population.

Housing Programs

Housing adjustments within a life-span perspective are a primary focus for research because they allow the study of the process by which changing needs, social conditions, and family status interact with housing and other environmental attributes. The manner in which residential decisions are made and the nature of the barriers and facilitators—what Struyk calls timely adjustments—are areas about which too little is known. Research is also needed on the multigenerational effects of housing services directed toward older people. There is a need to document more thoroughly the indirect benefits to adult children and to grandchildren of the economics of housing assistance and the social consequences of separate living arrangements.

The conditions under which alternative housing is acceptable to older individuals is an area that requires further research, including community-level studies of how such enterprises as shared housing, match-up services, and other housing forms get started and under which conditions they succeed or fail. In addition, the last word on congregate housing for older people has not been written. One of the messages from HUD is that better targeting of services for older persons and the adjustment of services to local needs would work in the interest of improved efficiency and cost-effectiveness. A series of variations on the basic model of housing for older persons should be implemented and evaluated. For example, the service block concept used in Sweden is one of many forms evolving outside the United States that could be tested experimentally in this country. Congregate housing service programs could be effectively concentrated in housing sites that will give preference to elderly persons.

Finally, research and demonstration efforts could be directed toward identifying a feasible way to introduce a modest home repair/maintenance/home adaptation program into local communities. The administrative overhead costs seem to preclude the establishment of such a program in a centralized form, but there are excellent models currently working at local levels in cities such as Everett, Washington. Another promising demonstration project idea would be to train social- or health-oriented in-home workers in basic skills that could then be transmitted to newly impaired older residents to make their current home functionally usable.

Technology

The interaction between the elderly and technology is just beginning to receive research attention. A somewhat abstract question raised by Kane deserves attention: how to introduce and measure the benefits or other effects of technology on the quality of an older person's life. A general recommendation might be that every attempt to assess the economic effect of a new technology be expanded to include its psychological and social impact on the user.

Finally, on the macrosocial level, research is needed on the way political decisions that control the accessibility of various innovations are conditioned by community attitudes and value judgments regarding the aging.

Productivity and New Environmental Forms

The massive field trial proposed by Morgan on the pooling of resources is an appropriately researchable idea on the productivity of older people. What is needed is to determine the limits of older people's abilities to "bank" the services they give and to accept an economy based on the exchange of services rather than on money or the use of volunteers. In addition, another issue is raised by a proposal of this kind. Morgan, as does Regnier, poses a clear trade-off between the need for privacy and individuality on the one hand and for sociability and integration on the other. Research on this issue, both at the level of the individual home and at the level of group housing environments, is recommended.

The Vulnerable Aged

In portraying some of the current approaches to the problems of the vulnerable aged, Soldo and Longino raise many as yet unanswered questions about the alternative pathways to care by household members versus nonhousehold members and to care by family versus formal organizations. For example, would it be helpful to know what personal characteristics of an impaired person generate the desire to continue to live alone and retain autonomy? What is the best route toward achieving changes in the physical configuration of the home to support independence? What kinds of compromises are involved for various family and household members when an impaired older person is maintained at home?

Related to the concept of the environmental career that subsumes a lifetime of housing adjustments, a more limited "caregiving/care-receiving career" is also deserving of study. In addition, the course of beginning impairments and the overlay of multiple impairments, other issues raised by Soldo and Longino, require study in relation to residential decision making.

Finally, a careful analysis needs to be made of the environmental behavior of cohorts of affluent older persons as they move into old age. Their choices and preferences will provide preliminary information on the consumer preferences of larger numbers of older people in the future. It is also possible to use and adapt such knowledge in planning for the needs of the poor and the near-poor elderly, the groups identified by Soldo and Longino as the most likely to be deprived of adequate housing.

Transportation

The specific ideas on research in Wachs' paper in this volume recognize the importance of differences in types of neighborhoods in planning services for the older person. It seems clear that the effects of differing physical and social forces at the neighborhood and community levels are poorly understood in addressing the environment of aging persons.

Although Wachs points out that transportation is primarily an instrumental activity rather than a goal in and of itself, this very observation raises the question of identifying the conditions under which transportation per se may be a primary goal. Is it possible to walk, drive, or ride public transportation for sheer enjoyment? Is such transportation behavior likely to be attractive to older people? Can research on this topic lead us to a broader repertoire of life-enriching experiences in an aging society?

Concern about the possible restrictions of experience engendered by the inaccessibility of transportation has engendered questions about the processes by which a person's "social space" becomes restricted. Growing disability may lead to a diminishment in the geographic extensiveness of activity patterns; another possibility is that an involuntarily imposed restricted range of transportation alternatives may blunt the desire for new experiences. These several aspects of the mobility of older persons deserve study.

A host of cost and cost–benefit issues are raised by Wachs including the dichotomy of mainstreaming versus tailored specialized transportation services. Wachs' identification of such factors as institutional resistance to resource pooling and the incentives to potential fraud in the voucher approach illustrate the multiplicity of unanswered questions still remaining after years of demonstration transportation projects. There is a clear need for more disciplined research in evaluating contrasting approaches to satisfying the mobility needs of an aging population.

CONCLUSION

Although the researchable issues articulated in the preceding pages were implicitly or explicitly suggested by the authors of the papers in this volume, the issues proposed for study tend to exhibit a bias toward the individual in relation to the larger environment. Yet there is also great richness in terms of policy implications and research needs in the macrosocial and economic areas that were not covered in this review. Similarly, there are many important environmental topics that simply could not be addressed within the limits of the resources available for this project. Some of the missing topics include such areas as rural aging; neighborhood and community planning; the performance of nursing homes, acute hospitals, mental hospitals, and nonresidential facilities; the role of the family; the ethical underpinnings and values to be achieved; and the cultural aspects of person–environment interactions. Additionally, resources limited a consideration of how data and policies in other countries (beyond Sweden) can enrich and inform our policies. A complete agenda for future policy consideration should include these areas.

REFERENCES

Binstock, R. H. 1983. "The Aged as Scapegoat." *The Gerontologist* 23:136–143.

Campbell, A., P. G. Converse, and W. Rodgers. 1976. *The Quality of American Life.* New York: Russell Sage Foundation.

Kingston, E. R., B. A. Hirshorn, and J. M. Cornman. 1986. *Ties That Bind: Interdependence of Generations.* Washington, D.C.: Seven Locks Press.

Lawton, M. P., M. Moss, and M. Grimes. 1985. "The Changing Service Needs of Older Tenants in Planned Housing." *The Gerontologist* 25:258–264.

Neugarten, B. L., ed. 1982. *Age or Need?* Beverly Hills, Calif.: Sage.

Newman, S. J. 1985. "Housing and Long-Term Care: The Suitability of the Elderly's Housing to the Provision of In-Home Services." *The Gerontologist* 25:35–40.

Preston, S. H. 1984. "Children and the Elderly in the U.S." *Scientific American* 25:44–49.

Struyk, R. J. 1985. "Future Housing Assistance Policy for the Elderly." *The Gerontologist* 25:41–46.

The Demography of Current and Future Aging Cohorts

William J. Serow and David F. Sly

For a number of years, demographers have been making periodic forays into the realm of aging issues (Hermalin, 1966; Keyfitz, 1968; Lopez and Hanada, 1982; Manton, 1982; Pearl, 1940) and in fact much of their general subject matter deals either directly or indirectly with population aging (Coale, 1964; Cowgill, 1974; Myers, 1985a). Yet systematic efforts to define and give legitimacy to "population aging" as a subfield of demography are of relatively recent vintage (Myers, 1985b; Siegel, 1980). These excellent essays nonetheless accomplish their objective of providing clear, concise statements about the substantive domain of the field and the approaches that demographers can use to analyze and explain the causes and consequences of population aging. Moreover, some legitimacy has been given to the field by the extent of agreement these researchers show concerning the basic parameters that define it.

For example, demographers generally agree that they should be primarily concerned with aging as an aggregate phenomenon and that there are two aggregates of primary concern: (1) the total population and (2) the population older than some specified

---

William Serow is professor of economics and associate director at the Center for the Study of Population at Florida State University, Tallahassee. David Sly is professor of sociology and director of the Center for the Study of Population. Their research for this paper was supported by National Institute of Aging research grant AG05395.

age. With respect to the former, demographers concern themselves with how general population processes influence the age composition of populations and the causes and consequences of changes in that composition. In terms of the latter, demographers consider the older population as a subpopulation and study the causes and consequences of changes in its size, composition, and distribution. Although there is agreement that these two aggregates are clearly distinguishable as different points of analytical departure, there is also consensus that neither can be viewed in total isolation from the other. That is, an understanding of how aging evolves in a population is crucial to understanding changes in the older population and the causes and consequences of such changes.

Just as these essays reflect a high level of agreement about the general domain of the demography of aging, so too do they reflect accord when it comes to general analytical strategies and techniques of analysis. Clearly, then, the demography of aging has gained legitimacy as a specialized subfield in an academic sense, but a question essential to our undertaking here is whether it can also be given legitimacy in a more practical sense. More specifically, we need to ask how an awareness of the knowledge provided by the demography of aging can help policymakers and others charged with the responsibility of planning for the needs of this group as well as for the consequences of changes in it.

It is not possible here to present a fully developed response to this question, but it is possible to provide a broad overview of some of the general ways in which knowledge of the demographic structure of the population as a whole and of the changing demographic structure of the elderly will assist policymakers and planners. For example, the needs of this subpopulation and its resulting demands are going to be strongly influenced by its size. In this sense, it is important for us to know much more about patterns of mortality and longevity and how these are changing. This may sound simple, but the complexity of such knowledge is evident when we consider that the size of this population is influenced by historical patterns of fertility and morality to the point at which persons enter old age, as well as by patterns of mortality throughout the older years of life—to say nothing about the patterns of immigration and emigration over the whole course of life. Similarly, the structure of the processes that are responsible for growth in the elderly population (fertility, mortality, and migration) and the changes that are likely to occur in that structure will influence the demand for "needs" and even influence what these needs are and will be. For example, temporal patterns of childbearing (when combined with increased longevity) across generations influence how old children are when their parents reach old age and may have profound influences on the physical, economic, and social ability of children to care for their aging parents. Similarly, changing patterns of mortality may not only influence the number of people who reach old age but may also affect how many people survive for longer periods after reaching old age. In addition, changes in mortality may have an impact on the physical, economic, and social abilities of this sub-population's members to care for themselves.

In short, we must understand how trends in basic demographic processes have operated (and will operate) over time so we can better estimate the size of this subpopulation and the level of demand it will create for various needs. Similarly, variations over time in the levels and structures of basic demographic processes have important implications for both the types of specific needs likely to arise and the types of options available for meeting them.

Population composition and distribution will also affect demand. The socioeconomic status of the elderly subpopulation will influence both the level of demand for needs and the types of needs that will emerge. In this sense, it is important for us to understand more clearly how the economic composition of the elderly population is changing and the factors that are responsible for this change. Different cohorts have quite different savings and labor force opportunity patterns, which can have quite different consequences for the financial abilities of the population during the early years of old age. In a similar fashion, increased longevity among the aged will have important consequences for how long savings and retirement income will have to last, which in turn may have important consequences for how the elderly dispose of income and savings throughout old age. Levels of income and savings are also likely to have important consequences for how much support will have to be provided through the public sector; longevity will influence not only how many persons will have to be supported, but also when in old age such support will begin and for how long it will be needed.

We can also expect the economic composition of the elderly population to have important consequences for the private sector. Although we cannot explore the full range of such possibilities here, it should be obvious from what has already been said that everything from product development and retailing to financial markets and the structure and availability of credit could be significantly affected by changes in the economic composition of the elderly population.

The economic structure and circumstances of the elderly are not the only compositional factors that will influence the social and built environment. Other important elements include the level of labor force participation and the structure of the elderly labor force including the age of exit. In addition, we must take into account changes in the marital status composition of the elderly, which are affected by cohort patterns of divorce and singleness as well as by changes in mortality differentials by sex. All of these factors are likely to influence the demand for and types of needs in such areas as housing, health care, recreation and leisure, and living arrangements.

Population distribution will also be an important consideration in determining the level and types of needs prevalent in the elderly population. Redistribution of this population occurs essentially as a result of areal differentials in mortality and migration. Where the elderly reside will obviously play a key role in determining where services will have to be delivered and what needs must be satisfied, but equally important is that, to the extent these processes operate in a selective manner, we can expect that areas with different redistribution experiences are likely to have elderly populations with different needs. Unfortunately, little is known about areal differentials in mortality and migration and the factors that affect them, especially for some very important types of areas such as metropolitan areas. For our purposes here, however, and probably of greater importance is the fact that even less is known about the population compositional differentials among areas that are being created by redistribution.

To this point, we have focused almost exclusively on how a knowledge of demographic trends can further our understand-

TABLE 1 Size of the Older Population by Age and Sex, 1940–1980

	1980			1970			1960
Age Group	Male	Female	Totals by Age	Male	Female	Totals by Age	Male
45–49	5,388,249	5,701,506	11,089,755	5,851,334	6,264,605	12,115,939	5,357,925
50–54	5,620,670	6,089,362	11,710,032	5,347,916	5,756,102	11,104,018	4,734,829
55–59	5,481,863	6,133,391	11,615,254	4,765,821	5,207,207	9,973,028	4,127,245
60–64	4,669,892	5,417,729	10,087,621	4,026,972	4,589,812	8,616,784	3,409,319
65–69	3,902,955	4,879,526	8,782,481	3,122,084	3,869,541	6,991,625	2,931,088
70–74	2,853,547	3,944,577	6,798,124	2,315,000	3,128,831	5,443,831	2,185,216
75–79	1,847,661	2,946,061	4,793,722	1,560,661	2,274,173	3,834,834	1,359,424
80–84	1,019,227	1,915,806	2,935,033	875,584	1,408,727	2,284,311	665,093
85–89	477,185	1,043,107	1,520,202	362,063	656,084	1,018,147	255,776
90+	204,340	515,525	719,865	180,316	312,438	492,754	106,500
Total of all age groups	110,053,161	116,492,644	226,545,805	98,912,192	104,299,734	203,211,926	88,331,494
Total persons aged 55+	20,456,670	26,795,632	47,252,302	17,208,501	21,446,813	38,655,314	15,039,661
Total persons aged 65+	10,304,915	15,244,512	25,549,427	8,415,708	11,649,794	20,065,502	7,503,097
Total persons aged 75+	3,548,413	6,420,409	9,968,822	2,978,624	4,651,422	7,630,046	2,386,793
Total persons aged 85+	681,525	1,558,542	2,240,067	542,379	968,522	1,510,901	362,276
Percentage of total population							
55+			20.9			19.0	
65+			11.3			9.9	
75+			4.4			3.7	
85+			1.0			0.7	

	Percentage Change			
	1970–1980	1960–1970	1950–1960	1940–1950
55+	22.2	20.3	25.4	30.7
65+	27.3	21.2	34.8	36.2

SOURCES: U.S. Bureau of the Census, 1943 (Table 1), 1953 (Table 94), 1964 (Table 156), 1972 (Table 50), and 1983 (Table 40).

ing and our ability to predict the demand for needs among the elderly. It is equally important to realize that a knowledge of demographic trends will also help us to better understand and predict the extent to which we will be able to supply these needs and the kinds of trade-offs that may be necessary in order to do so. Some of the subpopulation factors mentioned in the preceding paragraphs may influence supply-side considerations, but the more important factors in this sense will emerge from considering the elderly in relation to the total population. For example, fairly good evidence suggests that as federal monies for the elderly have increased, dollars for the youngest segment of the population have decreased. Similarly, the viability of the

		1950			1940		
Female	Totals by Age	Male	Female	Totals by Age	Male	Female	Totals by Age
5,521,560	10,879,485	4,545,606	4,556,172	9,101,778	4,209,269	4,045,956	8,255,225
4,871,125	9,605,954	4,142,277	4,153,303	8,295,580	3,752,750	3,504,096	7,256,846
4,302,620	8,429,865	3,639,761	3,612,763	7,252,524	3,011,364	2,832,501	5,843,865
3,733,133	7,142,452	3,047,212	3,027,151	6,074,363	2,397,816	2,330,524	4,728,340
3,326,822	6,257,910	2,431,035	2,582,455	5,013,490	1,896,088	1,910,569	3,806,657
2,553,716	4,738,932	1,633,382	1,785,826	3,419,028	1,270,967	1,298,565	2,569,532
1,694,135	3,053,559	992,645	1,157,730	2,150,375	723,680	780,302	1,503,982
914,834	1,579,927	500,345	624,225	1,124,570	359,011	415,380	774,391
392,805	648,581	177,760	251,845	429,605	121,455	155,557	277,012
174,171	280,671	56,670	91,175	147,845	34,919	52,821	87,740
90,991,681	179,323,175	74,833,239	75,864,122	150,697,361	66,061,592	65,607,683	131,669,275
17,092,236	32,131,897	12,478,810	13,133,170	25,611,980	9,815,300	9,776,219	19,591,519
9,056,483	16,559,580	5,791,837	6,493,256	12,285,093	4,406,120	4,613,194	9,019,314
3,175,945	5,562,738	1,727,420	2,124,975	3,852,395	1,239,065	1,404,060	2,643,125
566,976	929,252	234,430	343,020	577,450	156,374	208,378	364,752
	18.5			17.0			14.9
	9.2			8.1			6.8
	3.1			2.6			2.0
	0.5			0.4			0.3

current Social Security program is directly tied to the availability of workers and the ratio of workers to retirees.

This discussion, although general, should make it clear that demographic trends play a key role in shaping the social and built environment and can have an important influence on demographic trends. In the pages that follow, we will trace the evolution of the elderly population in the United States, giving particular attention to the emergence of the "oldest old" as a significant subpopulation and the "new aged" as a group that has emerged from different social and built environments. Both of these groups will pose new and different challenges to policymakers responsible for guiding the emergence of a social and built environment to meet their needs.

THE EVOLUTION OF THE OLDER U.S. POPULATION

By now, nearly everyone is aware, at least in a general way, of the rapid growth that has occurred in the nation's older population (Siegel and Davidson, 1984; Population Reference Bureau, 1975). The data in Table 1 allow us to detail some of the highlights of the recent changes in the size of this subpopulation. Perhaps one of the most important points to be made from these data is that both the size and the pace of change in size are strongly influenced by the age criterion employed to define the "older population." In the discussion that follows, we focus on the ages 55 and older and 65 and older because for most purposes these two ranges represent the lower and upper ages within which most persons have defined the older population.

In 1940 there were just over 20 million persons who were 55 years of age or older; just over 9 million of these were 65 or older. The number of persons above these ages has increased steadily during each successive decade and roughly doubled during each of the 30-year intervals within the 40-year period; that is, there were nearly twice as many older persons in 1970 as in 1940, and there were twice as many in 1980 as at midcentury. Indeed, by 1980 the number of persons aged 55 and older had passed the 47.25 million mark, and the number of persons aged 65 and older exceeded 25.5 million. These recent figures represent a 141 percent increase in the number of persons 55 and older during the 40-year period and a 183 percent increase in the number of persons 65 and older. To put the magnitude of these increases into proper perspective, we need only consider by way of contrast that the nation's total population increased by 72 percent (from around 132 million to 227 million) while the population under the age of 15 increased by just 55 percent (from about 33 million to 51 million persons).

Although the increase in the older population seems quite substantial, particularly when compared with the increase in the total population and its youngest dependent sector, the most substantial increases have actually occurred within the oldest age groups of the old. For example, the number of persons aged 75 and older was more than 275 percent higher in 1980 than in 1940. Yet even this increase seems small compared with the increase in the number of persons 85 and older, which went from 0.36 million in 1940 to over 2.2 million in 1980—an increase of nearly 515 percent and 10 times greater than the increase occurring within the group of individuals under the age of 15.

Components of Change

The number of elderly in the population can change from one decade to the next as a result of three basic processes. One of these processes, the aging of younger cohorts, is similar to fertility in the general population in the sense that it is the basic mechanism through which people are added to the ranks of the elderly. Mortality, on the other hand, is the basic mechanism by which people leave the population. Migration can make either a

TABLE 2 Components of Change (in millions) for the Population Aged 65 and Older, 1940–1980

Components	1970–1980	1960–1970	1950–1960	1940–1950
Population at end of decade	25,549	20,066	16,560	12,285
Population at beginning of decade	20,066	16,560	12,285	9,019
Net increase	5,483	3,506	4,275	3,266
Gains—persons reaching 65	17,455	14,242	12,396	9,776
Losses				
Death to 65+	12,265	11,027	8,623	6,713
Deaths to initial population	10,096	9,007	6,921	5,167
Deaths to remaining population	2,169	2,020	1,702	1,546
Gross change	29,720	25,269	20,619	16,489
Percentage of changes				
Rate of gross gain	87.0	86.0	100.1	108.4
Rate of gross loss	61.1	66.6	70.2	74.4
Rate of net gain	25.9	19.4	29.9	34.0
Total death rate	32.7	35.7	34.9	35.7
MRIP 65+	50.3	54.4	56.3	57.3
MRPR 65	12.4	14.1	13.7	15.8

NOTE: MRIP 65+ = Mortality rate for initial population 65 and over. MRPR 65 = Mortality rate for persons reaching 65.

SOURCE: Adapted from Siegel and Davidson, 1984.

positive or negative contribution to the growth of the elderly population. In Table 2 we present data that show the changes over decades in the number of persons aged 65 and older, along with estimates of the contribution of the components of change. In making these estimates, we have relied on basic census survival techniques, and we have made no effort to take account of migration or of the varying degrees of coverage or accuracy of reporting age between censuses. Although we want to emphasize that these estimates do contain errors, we are also confident that they are sufficient to capture the general trends in the components.

Between 1940 and 1950 the number of persons 65 and older increased by nearly 3.3 million from an initial population of just over 9 million. Achieving this net gain required the addition of nearly 10 percent more people to the 65-and-older group than were already part of it at the beginning of the decade because nearly 60 percent of the persons 65 and older in 1940 died during the decade, as did about 16 percent of those persons who aged to 65 and older during the decade. In other words, nearly 75 deaths occurred over the decade to persons who were 65 and older or who aged into this group for each 100 persons who were already this age at the beginning of the decade.

By the next decade (1950–1960) the number of deaths had declined to around 70 per 100 people at the beginning of the decade. Most of the improvement in this figure resulted from a decline in the deaths of persons reaching age 65 or older during the decade rather than a decline in deaths to persons already 65 at the start of the decade. At the same time, there was a substantial increase (3.5 million) in the number of persons who aged into the elderly group during this decade from the number who had done so during the previous decade. Thus, the resulting net increase in the number of persons aged 65 or older during the period can be thought of as resulting primarily from persons "aging in" and from a decline in the number of deaths in the group.

Had the trends of the 1950s continued, the elderly population would probably have begun to "young" eventually. That is, the average age of the elderly would have begun to decrease. This did not happen, however, and a number of changes in trends were initiated during the 1960s that reversed the potential direction of the 1950s. First, the death rate of persons reaching age 65 and older stabilized and was at nearly the same level during this decade as it had been during the previous decade. Second, the death rate for persons 65 and older began to decline rather substantially. Finally, this was the first decade during which the number of persons aging into the elderly population was considerably smaller than the number of elderly at the beginning of the decade. In this sense, it is important to note that the latter was not a function of a decline in the number of persons aging into the elderly population; this figure actually increased by nearly 2 million over the number aging in during the previous decade. Rather, the smaller number was a function of the increased chances of survival for those aging in during earlier decades and the increasing size of the cohorts supplying these individuals.

During the 1970s the trends that had emerged in the 1960s continued, and the result was the largest interdecade net increase in the number of elderly over the period being considered. The cohorts aging in were some 2.2 million persons larger than the cohorts that had aged in during the 1960s; they constituted roughly the same proportion (87 percent) of the population aged 65 and older at the beginning of the decade as was true of those aging in and those 65 and older during the 1960s. Whereas the mortality rate for those persons aging in was nearly stable between the 1950s and the 1960s, there was once again a substantial reduction between the 1960s and the 1970s. Even this reduction (1.7 deaths per 100 persons), however, was small compared with the reduction of 4.1 deaths per 100 population that occurred for persons who were 65 and older at the beginning of the decade.

Age Composition of the Elderly Population

Thus, over the whole period under consideration (1940–1950 to 1970–1980), the number of persons reaching age 65 and older during the last decade was some 78 percent larger than during the first, the mortality rate for persons 65 and older at the start of each decade decreased by more than 12 percent, and the mortality rate for those reaching age 65 and older during the decade decreased by over 21 percent. The percentage of the total population in this group increased steadily from just 6.8 percent in 1940 to 11.3 percent in 1980; the comparable change for the population aged 55 and older was from 14.9 percent to 20.9 percent.

The data presented earlier documenting the growth of the elderly population, and in particular those data dealing with the components of change, strongly suggest that there have been significant changes in the composition of this population. What is interesting in this sense is that many of these changes are not as dramatic as some people have believed whereas others are more dramatic than is usually thought. A clear example of the former can be seen in Table 3. Many people still believe that the average age of the elderly population has increased dramatically over the past few decades, but these data show that the mean age for persons 55 and older increased over the past five decades by just 2 years to 67.7 in 1980. Over the same period, the population aged 65 and older aged by 1.7 years to 74.4.

These averages, however, are strongly influenced not merely by the decreases in death rates discussed earlier, but also by the sharp increases that have occurred in the size of the cohorts entering the elderly ages between each decade; in other words,

TABLE 3 Age Composition (percentage) of the Population Aged 55 and Older and of the Population Aged 65 and Older, 1940–1980

Age	1980	1970	1960	1950	1940
Population groups aged 55 and older					
55–59	24.7	25.8	28.7	28.3	30.0
60–64	21.3	22.3	21.5	23.7	24.1
65–69	18.6	18.1	18.8	19.6	19.4
70–74	14.4	14.1	14.3	13.3	13.1
75–79	10.1	9.9	9.2	8.4	7.7
80–84	6.2	5.9	4.8	4.4	3.9
85–89	3.2	2.6	1.9	1.7	1.4
90+	1.5	1.3	.8	.6	.4
Mean	67.7	67.2	64.6	66.1	65.7
Population groups aged 65 and older					
65–69	34.4	34.8	37.8	40.8	42.2
70–74	26.6	27.1	28.6	27.8	28.5
75–79	18.8	19.1	18.4	17.5	16.7
80–84	11.5	11.4	9.5	9.1	8.6
85–89	5.9	5.1	3.9	3.5	3.1
90+	2.8	2.5	1.8	1.3	.9
Mean	74.4	74.1	73.4	73.0	72.7

SOURCE: Derived from Table 1.

the size of the cohorts tends to offset the "aging effect" of decreases in death rates when the averages are calculated. If we look at the age distributions of the elderly over the period, a different picture of change emerges. In 1940, 54 percent of the population aged 55 and older was under the age of 65; a full 30 percent was under the age of 60. As late as 1960 the corresponding figures were just over 50 percent and nearly 29 percent, but by 1980 the percentage of the population that was 55 and older but still under 65 had declined to 46 percent; less than 25 percent of the 55-and-older population was under the age of 60.

Although the decrease in the relative numbers of the elderly was heavily concentrated in the two youngest age groups, the increase in relative numbers was heavily concentrated in the age groups over 75. The age group 75–79 increased its share of the elderly population from 7.7 percent to over 10 percent; the age group 80–84 increased its share from just under 4 percent to over 6 percent. Persons aged 85 and older, who made up less than 2 percent of the population aged 55 and older in 1940, were 4.7 percent of that population by 1980. This shift in the age composition of the elderly population can also be highlighted by noting that the ratio of persons 55–59 to those 85 and older declined from 16:1 in 1940 to just over 5:1 by 1980.

We can observe similar compositional shifts for the population aged 65 and older in the sense that the share of the population in the two youngest age groups declines whereas that in the age groups over 75 increases. In addition, the largest proportional increase occurs in the population aged 85 and older, which saw its share of the 65-and-older population increase from 4 percent in 1940 to 8.7 percent in 1980.

Sex Composition

At the same time the elderly population has been increasing and undergoing a substantial shift in its age composition, its sex composition has also been changing dramatically, a trend that is highlighted in Table 4 by comparing the upper left cell of the first four rows with the lower right cell. This comparison shows that in 1980 the proportion of the 55-and-older population that was female was nearly the same as the proportion of the 85-and-older population that was female in 1940. In 1940 the proportion of females in both the population aged 55 and older

TABLE 4 Sex Differentials in the Elderly Population, 1940–1980

Differential	1980	1970	1960	1950	1940
Percentage of women in population by age group					
55+	56.7	55.5	51.4	51.3	49.9
65+	59.7	58.1	54.7	52.8	51.1
75+	64.4	61.0	57.1	55.1	53.1
85+	69.6	64.1	61.0	59.4	57.1
Percentage of change from previous decade					
Men 55+	18.9	14.4	20.5	27.1	
Women 55+	24.9	25.5	30.1	34.3	
Men 65+	22.4	12.2	29.5	31.4	
Women 65+	30.8	28.6	39.5	40.7	
Age composition by group					
Men					
65–69	37.9	37.1	39.0	42.0	43.0
70–74	27.7	27.5	29.1	28.2	28.8
75–79	17.9	18.5	18.1	17.1	16.4
80–84	9.9	10.4	8.9	8.6	8.1
85–89	4.6	4.3	3.4	3.1	2.8
90+	2.0	2.1	1.4	1.0	0.8
Women					
65–69	32.0	33.2	36.7	40.0	41.4
70–74	25.9	26.9	28.2	27.5	28.1
75–79	19.3	19.5	18.7	17.8	16.9
80–84	12.6	12.1	10.1	9.6	9.0
85–89	6.8	5.6	4.3	3.9	3.4
90+					
Average age of 65+ population					
Men	73.6	73.6	73.1	72.8	72.5
Women	74.8	74.4	73.6	73.4	72.8

SOURCE: Derived from Table 1.

and the population aged 65 and older was not substantially different from one-half, but at each census after this date females made up a larger share of each of these age groups. In fact, by 1970 they were nearly 57 percent of the 55-and-older population and 60 percent of the 65-and-older population.

Table 5 contains a more detailed account of the sex differential. The ratios in this table show the number of women to men at each census by 5-year age groups. The data clearly demonstrate the effects of differential survival by age and its cumulative effects as well as the difference in the relative improvements in survival for men and women. That is, at each point in time the excess of women in the population increases with age, and at each age the excess of women increases over time. In

TABLE 5 Ratios of Women to Men in the Population Aged 65 and Older by Age Group, 1940–1980

Age Group	1980	1970	1960	1950	1940
55–59	1.12	1.09	1.04	0.99	0.94
60–64	1.16	1.14	1.09	0.99	0.97
65–69	1.25	1.24	1.13	1.06	1.01
70–74	1.38	1.35	1.17	1.09	1.02
75–79	1.59	1.46	1.25	1.17	1.08
80–84	1.88	1.61	1.37	1.25	1.16
85–89	2.19	1.81	1.54	1.42	1.28
90+	2.52	1.73	1.63	1.61	1.51

SOURCE: Derived from Table 1.

1940 the age differential in the sex ratio increased from .94 at age 55–59 to 1.51 by age 90 and older; or one could say the range in this ratio was just 0.57. By 1950 and 1960 this range varied slightly at around 0.60 before increasing by 1970. By 1980 it had increased to 1.40 as the sex ratio at age 55–59 had increased to 1.12 and at age 90 and over reached 2.52. Indeed, by 1980 women outnumbered men by more than 2:1 in both age groups above 85 and by more than 1.5:1 at ages 75–79 and 80–84. Thus, the increase in the range was more the result of changes at the upper end of the age distribution or among the oldest of the old than the result of changes among the younger old.

Finally, going back to Table 4, we can see (as the sex ratios would suggest) that the older female population is older than the older male population. In 1940 nearly 72 percent of the male population aged 65 and older and more than 69 percent of the female population aged 65 and older was under the age of 75. Although by 1980 both sexes had experienced age compositional changes that were generally similar, the magnitude and timing of the changes were quite different. For example, over the five censuses the total shift up from the two combined age groups 65–74 for men was 6.2 percent; for females, it was nearly double at 11.6 percent. The percentage of the male population at these ages decreased at each census from 1940 through 1970 but actually increased from 1970 to 1980; the percentage of the female population at these ages decreased continuously from 1940 to 1980. The general shift from these younger old ages was, of course, a concomitant of a general shift toward the older old ages for both sexes with the majority of the gain occurring for the ages 80–89; but again, in both of the age groups in this range, the gain for women was about double that for men.

Ethnic or Racial Composition

Although it is generally believed that there are some major differences in population aging among ethnic or racial subgroups, these differences are difficult to track with confidence over time. For example, there are problems of coverage and age misreporting of varying degrees in nearly all of the censuses for blacks and some ethnic groups. These problems are compounded by differences in procedures for collecting and coding data in the different censuses. In censuses prior to 1960, race was determined by the interviewer, but with the introduction of self-enumeration in 1960, race came to be determined by the respondent. In 1980 coding and allocation procedures were altered in such a way that many Hispanics who were formerly classified as white were classified as nonwhite. Thus, data comparing whites and nonwhites are more useful for intercensal periods prior to 1970–1980; data for blacks are probably more useful for periods after 1960.

With these qualifications in mind, let us examine the data in Table 6. From 1940 to 1980 the nonwhite population increased its share of the total elderly from about 7 percent to over 10 percent. Even given the problems of comparing 1980 white/nonwhite data with white/nonwhite data for earlier periods, there is strong evidence in the table for an increasingly important role for the growth of the nonwhite elderly population in helping to shape the growth of the total elderly population. In the two decades 1940–1950 and 1950–1960, the nonwhite population contributed just over 8 percent to the total increase in the population aged 65 and older, but in the ensuing decade this figure increased to nearly 13 percent.

What these figures suggest is that the growth in the number of nonwhite elderly has been greater than the growth in the white elderly. Although this is true, it is also true that the nonwhite elderly population relative to the total nonwhite population has not grown at the same pace as the elderly population in general has grown relative to the country's total population. In the country as a whole the population aged 55 and older increased its share of the total population from 14.9 percent in

TABLE 6 Ethnic or Racial Differentials in the Elderly Population, 1940–1980

Differential	1980	1970	1960	1950	1940
Percentage of total 55+ nonwhite population	10.7	9.1	8.4	7.3	7.0
Percentage of total 65+ nonwhite population	10.2	8.6	7.7	7.4	7.1
Percentage of total nonwhite population					
55+	13.4	13.8	13.1	11.5	10.2
65+	6.8	6.8	6.1	5.6	4.8
Percentage change from previous decade					
Nonwhite					
55+	44.9	31.3	44.7	35.0	
65+	49.9	39.0	38.2	41.2	
White					
55+	20.0	20.1	24.1	29.4	
65+	26.8	22.3	32.0	35.5	
Composition by age group					
Nonwhite					
65–69	37.3	39.9	41.5	46.9	48.0
70–74	27.0	26.6	27.9	25.5	26.4
75–79	18.6	16.3	17.4	15.1	13.4
80–84	9.6	9.5	7.8	7.5	6.6
85–89	4.6	4.5	3.6	3.4	3.3
90+	2.9	3.2	1.8	1.6	2.3
White					
65–69	34.0	34.4	37.8	40.3	41.8
70–74	26.6	27.2	28.8	28.0	28.6
75–79	18.8	19.4	18.4	17.7	16.9
80–84	11.7	11.6	9.5	9.3	8.7
85–89	6.1	5.1	4.0	3.5	3.1
90+	2.8	2.3	1.5	1.2	0.9
Average age					
Nonwhite	73.8	73.8	73.0	72.3	72.4
White	74.4	74.1	73.4	73.0	72.7

SOURCES: U.S. Bureau of the Census, 1943 (Table 1), 1953 (Table 94), 1964 (Table 156), 1972 (Table 50), and 1983 (Table 40).

1940 to 20.9 percent in 1980; the population aged 65 and older increased its share from 6.8 percent in 1940 to 11.3 percent in 1980. For the nonwhite population the comparable figures were 10.2 percent to 13.4 percent for the population aged 55 and older and 4.8 percent to 6.8 percent for the population 65 and older. The nonwhite population is aging more slowly than the total population largely because its younger age groups are growing at a more rapid rate than are the younger age groups in the total population.

Whites aged 65 and older have had a higher mean age at each census than nonwhites, but nonwhites have had a higher proportion reporting age 90 and older at each census. This difference fluctuates considerably over the five censuses, however, and the variation is largely the result of variations in the nonwhite population. There can be no doubt that some of this fluctuation is the result of the reporting problems discussed earlier, but there is evidence to suggest that a mortality crossover effect does occur. That is, studies have shown that, although the chances of whites outliving nonwhites are better throughout most of the life span, at advanced ages the probabilities "cross over" and the chances of nonwhites living longer are better than those of whites. Nevertheless, the general trend for both whites and nonwhites is for their age compositions to be shifting toward the upper ages—to those age groups 80 and older.

The data in Table 7 are for the black population. In 1940 blacks made up just under 10 percent of the total population. During each decade from 1940 to 1980, blacks increased their representation in the total population, but these increases were marginal at best. Thus, as late as 1980, blacks still made up less than 12 percent of the total population. If we look only at older Americans, the picture of change is not radically different, but black representation is considerably less, making up just less than 7 percent of all persons aged 55 and older and 65 and older in 1940 and rising to 8.5 percent and 8.2 percent, respectively, by 1980. In short, blacks are a significant minority within the population generally and among the elderly specifically.

It is evident from the increasing percentage of the black population in the older ages that this subpopulation is aging in the same general manner as the total population. In 1940 slightly more than 10 percent of the black population was over the age of 55 compared with nearly 15 percent of the total population. By 1980 just over 15 percent of the black population was over the age of 55 compared with nearly 21 percent of the total population. Thus, aging within the black population has been occurring in the same general manner as in the total population, but it has occurred more slowly in the former as the gap between the percentage of the elderly in the two increased from 2 per-

TABLE 7 Characteristics of the Elderly Black Population, 1940–1980

Characteristic	1980	1970	1960	1950	1940
Percentage of total population that is black	11.7	11.1	10.5	10.0	9.8
Percentage of population 55+ that is black	8.5	8.2	7.7	6.9	6.7
Percentage of population 65+ that is black	8.2	7.8	7.0	7.1	6.8
Percentage of black population					
55+	15.1	14.0	13.1	11.8	10.2
65+	7.9	6.9	6.2	5.8	4.8
Percentage change from previous decade					
55+ Population	26.2	27.9	40.1	35.0	
65+ Population	33.9	33.5	34.8	40.7	
Composition by age group					
Total					
65–69	37.2	40.2	41.7	47.0	48.2
70–74	27.0	26.8	27.8	25.5	26.5
75–79	18.6	16.3	17.4	15.1	25.3 (75+)
80–84	9.6	9.2	7.7	7.5	
85+	7.6	7.5	5.4	5.0	
Sex ratios (F:M)					
65–69	1.34	1.26	1.13	1.13	0.95
70–74	1.40	1.26	1.15	1.01	0.94
75–79	1.54	1.31	1.16	1.01	1.14 (75+)
80–84	1.67	1.46	1.27	1.12	
85+	2.00	1.55	1.38	1.56	

SOURCES: U.S. Bureau of the Census, 1943 (Table 1), 1953 (Table 94), 1964 (Table 156), 1972 (Table 50), and 1983 (Table 40).

centage points in 1940 to 3.4 percentage points in 1980. The difference in aging within these two populations is the product of a combination of higher birth rates and lower rates of survivorship among blacks of most ages.

Data showing the age composition and sex ratios for the black population are also shown in Table 7. In general, these data reveal the same general trends as were discussed earlier for the total and nonwhite populations. The age composition of the older black population (as well as the changes in it) is approximately the same as for the nonwhite population. As was the case in comparing the nonwhite and white older age structure, the black elderly population is younger than the total elderly population, which results more from a concentration of blacks at the youngest old ages than from differences in their proportions at the oldest old ages.

Similarly, the sex ratio patterns are generally the same for blacks as for the total population in the sense that there is a general trend at each age for the imbalance to increase over time and at each date for it to increase with age. The two major exceptions to this pattern appear to be at ages 85 and older, for which problems of coverage and age misreporting were particularly acute during the earlier censuses examined here, and for 1950, for which the ratio is higher for those aged 65–69 than for the intermediate older ages. Nevertheless, for later census dates, there is a tendency for the black sex ratios to exceed the sex ratios for the total population at the younger old ages and for the sex ratios of the total population to exceed those for the black population at age 75 and older.

Regional Distribution of the Elderly

Table 8 focuses on the regional distribution of the elderly and the age composition of the elderly in each of the regions; separate data are presented for the total and black elderly populations. The first row of figures in this table shows the percentage of all persons in the United States who lived in each of the regions at each census. Basically, these data highlight the well-known regional shifts that have occurred to the West and South during the post-World War II period: the West and the South have increased their share of the population from just under 11 percent and 32 percent to about 19 percent and 33 percent, respectively; the Northeast and North Central regions have seen their shares decline from just over 27 percent and 30 percent, respectively, to about 22 percent and 26 percent. In 1940, 1950, and 1960, the largest plurality of older Americans lived in the North Central region; the Northeast, on the other hand, had the second largest concentration of elderly through 1950 and a proportion nearly equal to that of the South in 1960.

The regional redistribution of the elderly population, however, has followed the same general trend as the regional redistribution of all persons and in fact has been even more salient. For example, in 1940 the Northeast and North Central regions housed 57.8 percent of the total and 63 percent of the elderly population. Yet these percentages declined at each consecutive census, and by 1980 these regions had 47.7 percent of the total population and 49.9 percent of the elderly population. That is, although their share of the total population declined by 10.1 percent, their share of the elderly decreased by 13.1 percent. The overall trend in these redistributional changes in each region can be easily followed by looking at the index of redistribution, which is merely the ratio of the percentage of the population older than the specified age to the percentage of the total population in the region. A value greater than unity indicates a larger share of elderly than the total population; a value less than unity indicates a lower share of the elderly than the region's total population share. In 1940 only one region, the South, had a proportion of the elderly that was lower than its proportion of the total population; by 1980, however, the South and the North Central regions had nearly equal proportions of the country's total and elderly populations. The Northeast was the only region to have a greater proportion of the elderly than its share of the total population. The West, on the other hand, stood out as the only region to have a lower proportion of the elderly population than its total population share.

Measured in terms of the percentage of population aged 55 and older and the percentage of population aged 65 and older, each regional population has aged, but aging has occurred differently within each of the regions. The percentage of the regional population aged 65 and older is shown in tabular form in Table 8.

In 1940 each of the regions except the South had populations with between 7.2 percent and 7.6 percent aged 65 and older. The South, with only 5.5 percent of its population over 65, had the youngest regional population. Between 1940 and 1960 the rise in the percentage of population 65 and older was considerably more dramatic in the Northeast and the South than in the North Central region and the West. Indeed, by 1960 the Northeast, which had a lower percentage of the elderly in 1940 than either the North Central region or the West, had passed both of these regions, and the overall differential among regions was reduced to just 1.7 percentage points.

Between 1960 and 1970 the rise in the percentage of the population aged 65 and older was sharper in the South than in any

TABLE 8 Regional Distribution (percentage) of the Total Elderly and Black Elderly Populations and Regional Differences (percentage) in the Age Composition of the Elderly Population, 1940–1980

	1980				1970				1960				1950				1940			
Element	NE[a]	NC	S	W	NE	NC	S	W	NE	NC	S	W	NE	NC	S	W	NE	NC	S	W
Percentage of total U.S. population	21.7	26.0	33.3	19.0	24.1	27.8	30.9	17.1	24.9	28.8	30.7	15.6	26.1	29.6	31.4	12.9	27.3	30.5	31.6	10.6
Percentage of total population that is 55+	23.9	26.0	32.8	17.3	26.1	28.1	30.2	15.6	27.7	30.0	27.9	14.4	28.8	32.1	26.0	13.1	29.2	33.5	25.6	11.7
Percentage of total population that is 65+	24.6	25.9	32.9	16.6	25.9	28.5	30.1	15.5	27.4	30.5	27.6	14.5	28.2	32.3	26.5	13.0	28.8	34.2	25.5	11.5
Percentage 55+/ percentage of total population	1.10	1.00	0.98	0.91	1.08	1.01	0.98	0.91	1.11	1.04	0.91	0.92	1.10	1.08	0.83	1.01	1.07	1.10	0.81	1.10
Percentage 65+/ percentage of total population	1.13	1.00	0.99	0.87	1.08	1.03	0.97	0.91	1.10	1.06	0.90	0.93	1.08	1.09	0.84	1.01	1.06	1.12	0.81	1.09
Percentage 55+	22.2	20.9	20.5	18.9	20.5	19.2	18.6	17.4	19.8	18.6	16.2	16.4	18.6	18.4	14.0	17.0	15.9	16.3	12.0	16.6
Percentage 65+	12.9	11.4	11.3	9.9	10.6	10.1	9.6	8.9	9.9	9.6	8.2	8.4	8.8	8.9	6.9	8.2	7.2	7.6	5.5	7.5
Age groups																				
65–69	32.5	33.2	35.1	35.2	34.7	33.4	36.5	34.5	38.9	37.5	38.6	37.1	39.4	39.7	41.8	41.1	42.2	40.2	45.3	41.3
70–74	25.0	26.0	27.5	26.4	27.6	26.8	27.2	26.8	28.7	28.6	28.5	29.1	27.8	27.7	27.9	27.9	29.0	28.7	27.5	28.7
75–79	17.9	18.9	18.9	18.3	19.2	19.8	18.4	19.0	17.6	18.7	18.4	18.8	18.0	17.9	17.4	17.2	16.8	17.7	14.9	17.3
80–84	11.4	12.21	10.7	11.2	11.3	12.0	10.7	11.8	9.0	9.7	9.2	9.6	9.7	9.7	8.6	9.1	8.3	9.2	8.0	8.7
85–89	5.9	6.6	5.3	5.9	4.8	5.5	4.8	5.3	3.8	4.2	4.0	4.0	3.5	3.8	3.1	3.6	2.9	3.2	3.1	3.0
90+	2.7	3.1	2.5	2.9	2.4	2.5	2.4	2.6	1.9	1.4	1.3	1.3	1.1	1.2	1.3	1.2	0.9	0.9	1.2	0.9

Black population																				
Percentage of total population that is black	18.3	2.01	53.0	8.5	19.2	20.2	53.1	7.5	16.0	18.3	60.0	5.7	13.4	14.8	68.0	3.8	10.7	11.0	77.0	1.3
Percentage of total black population that is 55+	18.0	19.0	55.8	7.2	16.9	18.6	58.6	5.9	15.1	17.6	63.0	4.3	12.2	15.2	69.6	3.0	10.0	12.6	78.6	1.7
Percentage of total black population that is 65+	16.4	18.1	58.9	6.6	15.9	18.2	60.6	5.3	13.4	16.3	66.5	3.8	10.5	13.4	73.4	2.7	8.2	11.5	78.6	1.7
Percentage 55+	14.8	14.2	15.9	12.7	12.3	12.9	15.5	11.1	12.4	12.6	13.8	9.8	10.7	12.1	12.0	9.4	9.6	11.6	10.0	14.1
Percentage 65+	7.1	7.1	8.7	6.1	5.7	6.2	7.9	4.9	5.2	5.5	6.9	4.1	4.5	5.2	6.2	4.2	3.7	5.0	4.9	6.0
Age groups																				
65–69	38.7	37.4	36.5	39.8	41.9	50.3	39.6	41.9	44.1	43.1	40.8	43.7	47.3	47.6	46.7	49.0	48.7	47.7	48.1	50.6
70–74	26.9	26.9	27.1	27.1	27.5	27.5	26.2	26.3	28.2	27.7	27.7	27.3	26.8	25.5	25.3	32.6	27.0	26.6	26.4	26.1
75–79	18.3	18.5	18.8	17.4	15.6	16.4	16.6	15.8	16.0	17.0	17.8	17.0	14.2	14.9	15.2	15.2	24.3	25.7	25.5	23.3
80–84	9.4	9.8	9.7	8.7	8.5	8.8	9.6	8.7	7.3	7.5	7.9	7.0	6.8	7.2	7.8	6.3				
85+	6.7	7.4	7.9	7.0	6.5	7.0	8.0	7.3	4.4	4.7	5.8	5.0	4.9	4.8	5.0	5.9				

[a]NE = Northeast; NC = North Central; S = South; W = West.

SOURCES: U.S. Bureau of the Census, 1943 (Table 26), 1953 (Table 145), 1964 (Table 232), 1972 (Table 56), and 1983 (Table 50).

of the other regions; by the end of this decade the percentage aged 65 and older in this region surpassed that in the West. During the 1970s the population aged 65 and older increased in all regions more dramatically than it had since the 1940s; however, it increased more sharply in the Northeast and South than in the North Central region and West with the result that by 1980 the Northeast had a full 3 percent more of its population aged 65 and older than did the West and the South and the North Central region had nearly identical shares of their population aged 65 and older.

The age composition of the elderly population in each of the regions has also changed significantly over time. For example, the 65-and-older population in each of the regions has aged as indicated by the fact that in no region was there less than an 8 percent decline in the proportion of this population between ages 65 and 74 from 1940 to 1980. Nevertheless, there was substantial variation in the extent of aging; this decline was just over 8 percent in the West, but it was just under 14 percent in the Northeast. In the Northeast the decline occurred mainly in the decade from 1940 to 1950 and in the two decades from 1960 to 1980. In the West, it was largely concentrated in the two decades from 1950 to 1970. In the North Central region and the South the decline in the percentage of population aged 65 and older that is 65 to 74 is similar and intermediate to that in the other two regions. In both of these regions the major proportion of the decline occurred from 1940 to 1970; the largest decline occurred from 1960 to 1970.

Urban–Rural Differences

Table 9 shows the level of urbanization of the total population and the 65-and-older population for the nation and for each of its regions from 1950 to 1980. During this period the definition of urban and rural changed slightly with respect to the way in which unincorporated places were treated; consequently, although the distribution of population at each date reflects a difference at that point in time, changes over time are also influenced by definitional change. None of these changes was major, however, and we are of the opinion that the data do capture the trend of distributional change.

With these considerations in mind, the observer is immediately struck by the extent to which the total population and the elderly population are equally urbanized and the extent to which there has been little difference in the level of urbanization over time. At midcentury, both the total and the elderly populations had about 64 percent of their numbers residing in urban areas; and the level of urbanization of both populations increased considerably during the 1950s and the 1960s but little during the 1970s. By 1980 the level of urbanization for both populations was approaching 75 percent, and at no point did the difference exceed 0.8 percent. These national patterns, however, do mask some interesting and substantial differences that exist across and within regions.

The level of urbanization has been consistently higher in the Northeast and the West than in the North Central region and the South for both the total and elderly populations. In 1950 the largest differences in level of urbanization between the total and elderly populations could be found in the West, where the elderly population was more urbanized than the total population, and in the North Central region, where the total population was more urbanized than the elderly. By 1980 there was still a substantial differential in level of urbanization for both populations across regions, but within regions the differential between the total and elderly populations had virtually disappeared in all of the regions except the Northeast, where the total population was actually slightly less urbanized than it had been in 1950 and the elderly population was nearly 4.5 percent more urbanized than it had been in 1950. In other words, within all regions the urban elderly population has been increasing at a faster rate than either the rural elderly population or the total urban and rural population except in the West (this statement is not true for the total urban population there) and the Northeast (there, it is not true for the rural elderly during the 1970s).

The age composition data for the urban and rural elderly populations both nationally and regionally show that, in general, the urban elderly were somewhat younger in 1950 than the rural elderly in all areas except the West. The magnitude of this differential varied across regions, but over time the dominant trend has been for the rural elderly populations to "become" younger at a faster rate than the urban elderly. Indeed, by 1980 the rural elderly of each region were younger than their urban counterparts. This trend has probably been influenced consid-

TABLE 9 Total and Elderly Urban Populations in the United States and by Region (percentage) and Regional Differences in the Urban and Rural Age Composition of the Elderly, 1950–1980

	United States		Northeast		North Central		South		West	
Decade	Total	65+	Total	65+	Total	65+	Total	65+	Total	65+
1980	73.7	74.5	79.1	82.1	70.5	70.4	66.9	67.3	83.9	84.5
1970	73.5	72.9	80.4	82.6	71.6	69.3	64.6	63.0	82.9	82.8
1960	69.9	69.6	80.2	81.5	68.7	66.6	58.5	57.2	77.7	79.6
1950	64.0	63.8	79.5	77.7	64.1	60.6	48.6	47.8	69.8	74.0

	United States		Northeast		North Central		South		West	
Age Group	Urban	Rural	Urban	Rural	Urban	Rural	Urban	Rural	Urban	Rural
1980										
65–69	33.7	36.3	33.7	35.8	32.6	34.4	34.2	37.0	34.3	39.6
70–74	26.6	27.3	26.3	26.8	26.2	26.4	27.4	28.0	26.4	28.0
75–79	19.0	18.2	19.0	18.0	19.1	18.6	19.2	18.3	18.6	17.1
80–84	11.8	10.4	12.1	10.9	12.4	11.6	11.1	9.8	11.6	8.9
85+	8.9	7.8	8.9	8.5	9.7	9.0	8.1	6.9	9.1	6.4

1970										
65–69	34.5	35.6	34.7	34.7	33.4	33.4	36.1	37.2	33.8	38.1
70–74	27.2	26.9	27.8	26.9	26.9	26.8	27.3	27.0	26.7	26.9
75–79	19.2	18.8	19.3	18.9	19.8	19.7	18.5	18.3	19.2	17.9
80–84	11.5	11.2	11.2	11.5	12.0	12.1	10.8	10.5	12.1	10.4
85+	7.6	7.5	7.0	8.0	7.9	8.0	7.3	7.0	8.2	6.7
1960										
65–69	38.2	36.9	39.7	36.7	38.1	36.2	38.7	38.3	36.6	39.2
70–74	28.8	28.3	29.1	28.2	28.7	28.5	28.6	28.4	29.1	29.3
75–79	18.2	18.9	17.5	18.6	18.4	19.2	18.3	18.7	19.1	18.0
80–84	9.4	10.0	8.8	10.2	9.4	10.2	9.1	9.3	9.8	8.7
85+	5.4	5.9	4.9	6.3	5.4	5.9	5.3	5.3	5.4	4.8
1950										
65–69	41.4	39.7	41.7	37.6	40.8	38.0	42.1	41.7	40.6	42.5
70–74	27.8	27.9	28.0	27.9	27.5	27.9	27.7	27.8	28.1	27.7
75–79	26.3	27.3	25.9	29.0	26.8	28.8	25.9	26.1	26.5	25.2
80–84 } 85+ }	4.5	4.9	4.4	5.5	4.9	5.3	4.3	4.4	4.8	4.6

SOURCES: U.S. Bureau of the Census, 1953 (Table 145), 1964 (Table 233), 1972 (Table 57), and 1983 (Table 50).

TABLE 10 Marital Composition (absolute number and percentage) of the Elderly Population by Age Group and Sex, 1940–1980

Decade and Age Group	Men								Women							
	Single		Married		Widowed		Divorced		Single		Married		Widowed		Divorced	
	No.	%	No.	%	No.	%	No.	%	No.	%	No.	%	No.	%	No.	%
1980																
65–69	208,751	5.4	3,220,514	83.0	282,545	7.3	168,814	4.4	287,669	5.9	2,679,906	54.8	1,651,807	33.8	267,953	5.5
70–74	156,171	5.5	2,277,135	79.6	320,245	11.2	105,979	3.7	262,012	6.6	1,690,340	42.7	1,830,220	46.2	180,047	4.5
75–79	104,110	5.6	1,356,101	73.6	323,432	17.6	59,051	3.2	205,390	7.0	870,270	29.5	1,770,105	60.0	106,586	3.6
80–84	57,253	5.7	651,876	64.4	276,386	27.3	26,227	2.6	138,827	7.3	338,278	17.7	1,379,391	72.3	52,316	2.7
85+	37,665	5.6	323,457	48.4	292,825	43.8	14,031	2.1	119,987	7.9	127,726	8.4	1,246,552	81.8	30,436	2.0
Total	563,950	5.5	7,829,083	76.3	1,495,433	14.6	374,102	3.6	1,013,885	6.7	5,706,520	37.5	7,878,075	51.7	637,338	4.2
1970																
65–69	221,999	7.1	2,511,965	80.6	273,861	8.8	108,523	3.5	289,111	7.4	2,026,280	52.0	1,420,898	36.5	161,075	4.1
70–74	169,511	7.3	1,762,886	75.8	320,653	13.8	71,277	3.1	241,493	7.8	1,244,819	40.0	1,525,353	49.0	104,072	3.3
75–79	115,116	7.3	1,087,208	68.8	334,647	21.2	42,944	2.7	190,934	8.4	636,342	27.9	1,395,378	61.1	61,647	2.7
80–84	66,914	7.6	508,525	58.0	280,008	32.0	10,611	2.4	123,463	8.8	240,526	17.2	1,006,613	71.9	29,172	2.1
85+	58,228	10.8	232,742	43.4	232,780	43.4	12,932	2.4	102,685	10.7	103,305	10.8	739,395	76.8	15,934	1.7
Total	631,768	7.5	6,103,326	72.4	1,441,949	17.1	256,287	3.0	947,686	8.1	4,251,272	36.5	6,087,637	52.2	371,900	3.2

1960																
65–69	222,027	7.7	2,289,201	79.4	294,901	10.2	77,304	2.7	260,368	7.9	1,703,279	51.6	1,250,898	37.9	88,785	2.7
70–74	167,016	7.8	1,562,813	73.1	358,546	16.8	50,602	2.4	212,109	8.4	986,041	39.1	1,271,577	50.4	52,432	2.1
75–79	104,233	7.9	852,659	64.7	33,550	25.3	27,586	2.1	145,853	8.8	455,313	27.4	1,032,827	62.2	25,326	1.5
80–84	47,313	7.4	340,886	53.7	236,303	37.2	10,662	1.7	84,116	9.5	143,128	16.2	645,702	73.1	10,096	1.1
85+	23,784	7.1	129,076	38.7	175,885	52.8	4,638	1.4	50,972	9.6	43,487	8.2	431,536	81.4	4,407	0.8
Total	564,373	7.7	5,174,635	70.8	1,399,185	19.1	170,792	2.4	753,418	8.5	3,331,248	37.4	4,632,540	52.1	181,046	2.0
1950																
65–69	209,960	8.7	1,776,810	74.0	358,880	15.0	53,995	2.3	218,510	8.4	1,270,475	48.9	1,068,905	41.1	40,255	1.5
70–74	133,945	8.3	1,085,310	67.5	357,560	22.2	30,370	1.9	162,460	9.0	658,660	36.6	958,730	53.3	19,630	1.1
75–79	80,110	8.1	585,475	59.0	312,160	31.4	14,900	1.5	109,390	9.4	285,610	24.7	754,200	65.1	8,530	0.7
80–84	37,090	7.4	240,970	48.2	216,625	43.3	5,660	1.1	58,375	9.4	88,625	14.2	474,045	75.9	3,180	0.5
85+	18,050	7.7	78,735	33.6	135,710	57.9	1,935	0.8	33,195	9.7	23,965	7.0	284,350	82.9	1,510	0.4
Total	479,155	8.3	3,767,300	65.7	1,380,935	24.1	106,860	1.9	581,930	8.9	2,327,335	35.7	3,540,230	54.3	73,105	1.1
1940																
65–69	195,007	10.3	1,363,456	71.9	308,000	16.2	29,623	1.6	179,086	9.4	88,691	46.5	823,196	43.1	19,396	1.0
70–74	126,322	9.9	825,326	64.9	302,921	23.8	16,398	1.3	123,512	9.5	445,966	34.3	720,414	55.5	8,673	0.7
75–79	68,573	9.5	406,148	56.1	241,285	33.3	7,674	1.1	72,036	9.2	179,353	23.0	525,501	67.3	3,412	0.4
80–84	31,333	8.7	164,315	45.8	160,311	44.7	2,732	0.8	38,064	9.2	55,985	13.5	320,184	77.1	1,147	0.3
85+	12,406	7.9	51,582	33.0	91,448	58.5	938	0.6	16,665	8.0	13,907	6.7	177,413	85.1	393	0.2
Total	433,641	9.8	2,810,827	63.8	1,103,965	25.1	57,365	1.3	429,363	9.3	783,892	34.4	2,566,708	55.6	33,021	0.7

SOURCES: U.S. Bureau of the Census, 1943 (Table 6), 1953 (Table 102), 1964 (Table 176), 1973 (Table 203), and 1984a (Table 264).

erably by elderly mobility patterns operating on both ends of the age distribution—that is, by young elderly moving in greater numbers from urban to rural areas than from rural to urban areas and older elderly moving from rural to urban areas.

Marital Composition and Living Arrangements

Age and sex differences in mortality as well as rates and patterns of remarriage in the elderly population strongly suggest the value of examining patterns of marital composition separately by sex. The extent to which these factors operate is clearly revealed in Table 10 in which recent changes in the marital composition of the elderly can be traced. Among men aged 65 and older, nearly 64 percent were married in 1940, and this proportion increased steadily to just over 76 percent by 1980. Among women of the same age, only 34 percent were married in 1940, and although this proportion increased to 37 percent by 1960, it changed little after this time. By way of contrast, some 55 percent of women aged 65 and older were widowed in 1940, and this proportion decreased to only about 52 percent by 1980; for comparable men, however, the proportion of men 65 and older who were widowed decreased from 25 percent in 1940 to about 15 percent by 1980.

There is an inverse relationship between age and the percentage of the population who are married and a direct relationship between age and the percentage of the population who are widowed for each sex at each point in time. Among men, the proportion married varied from nearly 72 percent for those aged 65–69 to 33 percent for those 85 and older in 1940; for women the comparable figures were 46 percent and about 7 percent. Thus, the age differential for both men and women in 1940 was about 39 percent. Between 1940 and 1980 the proportion of men married at each specific age increased, but because it increased somewhat more rapidly at the upper ages than it did at the lower, by 1980 the differential for men had decreased to about 35 percent. Among women the general pattern of improvement in the proportion of women married at each date for each age is also evident, with one minor exception. In the case of women, however, the levels of improvement are much smaller at each age than those for men, and they are relatively much smaller at the older than at the younger ages. In fact, by 1980 the differential between those women aged 65–69 and those 85 and older actually increased to more than 46 percent.

Knowing this, what happens to the age differential in the percentage of the population who are widowed is not surprising. For both men and women, the differential was about 42 percent in 1940; it decreased to about 37 percent for males in 1980. For women, the differential increased to 48 percent in 1980 largely because improvements in the proportion of those widowed at the oldest ages came much more slowly than improvements at the younger ages.

Data on living arrangements are particularly useful for telling us something about the daily environment in which the elderly function. Yet putting together a historical series of data on living arrangements, even for the short period under observation here, is difficult because of changes in tabulation procedures and concepts (e.g., the transition from head of a household to a householder from one census to the next). Nevertheless, it is possible to identify how each person in a household relates to the head/householder in rather broad terms (Table 11). Again, for largely the same reasons, it is important to look at changes in living arrangements separately for men and women.

In 1940, 79 percent of the men living in households were heads, and another 11 percent were members of households headed by one of their children. The remaining men (10 percent) were either members of households headed by other relatives or members of households headed by nonrelatives. The percentage of men heading households increased at each census, reaching nearly 91 percent by 1970 (the last census before the change to the householder concept). Even after this change in 1980, 90 percent of the men aged 65 and older were identified as householders; at the same time, about 3 percent were identified as spouses of householders. The percentage of men living in households in which the head/householder was a child decreased to just over 3 percent; those living in households in which the head/householder was another relative or nonrelative decreased to less than 5 percent.

Thus, the dominant trend among men has been for the percentage of men who are heads/householders to increase at each successive census and for the percentage in each of the other relationship categories to decrease. Indeed, this trend is so salient that it is not merely the relative numbers that have declined

TABLE 11 Living Arrangements of the Population Aged 65 and Older by Sex (absolute number and percentage), 1940–1980

Decade and Sex	Head/ Householder	Spouse	Child	Parent	Brother/ Sister	Other Relative	Non-relative	Total in Household	Total 65+	Percentage Not in Household
Men										
1980	8,868,946	334.753	15,270	305,886	135,576	59,994	128,507	9,848,932	10,304,915	4.4
	90.0	3.4	0.2	3.1	1.4	0.6	1.3			
1970	7,328,143		48,419	353,811	134,131	59,485	149,461	8,073,450	8,415,708	4.1
	90.8		0.6	4.4	1.7	0.7	1.8			
1960	6,063,161		8,946	478,890	137,089	103,283	193,736	6,985,105	7,503,097	6.9
	86.8		0.1	6.9	2.0	1.5	2.8			
1950	4,353,425		4,780	538,345		222,345	258,130	5,377,025	5,791,837	7.2
	81.0		0.1	10.0		4.1	4.8			
1940	3,324,838			456,954		171,210	248,302	4,201,304	4,406,120	4.4
	79.1			10.9		4.1	5.9			
Women										
1980	7,262,123	5,027,963	28,939	1,213,053	343,797	144,730	153,559	14,174,164	15,244,512	7.0
	51.2	35.5	0.2	8.6	2.4	1.0	1.1			
1970	4,934,811	3,862,136	61,880	1,390,722	360,787	132,091	182,827	10,925,254	11,649,794	6.2
	45.2	35.3	0.6	12.7	3.3	1.2	1.7			
1960	3,228,881	3,001,349	19,110	1,422,422	331,039	222,871	216,076	8,441,748	9,056,483	6.8
	38.3	35.6	0.2	16.9	3.9	2.6	2.5			
1950	2,074,195	2,023,155	9,585	1,348,665		452,980	269,460	6,178,040	6,493,256	4.9
	33.6	32.7	0.2	21.8		7.3	4.4			
1940	1,509,424	1,372,811		995,513		318,733	219,585	4,416,066	4,613,194	4.2
	34.2	31.1		22.5		7.2	5.0			

NOTE: Blanks indicate that data were not available.

SOURCES: U.S. Bureau of the Census, 1943 (Table 10), 1953 (Table 107), 1964 (Table 181), 1973 (Table 204), and 1984a (Table 265).

but also the absolute numbers: in each relationship category except that of child this number has so decreased that by 1980 there were fewer men in households headed by each type of individual than there were in 1940.

A similar pattern can be observed for women aged 65 and older: the number of heads/householders increased steadily from 1.5 million in 1940 to 7.3 million in 1980, and their share of all women in households rose from 34 percent to 51 percent. The number of women identified as spouses increased from one census to the next, but the percentage of women in households who were identified as spouses stabilized at the 1960 level of 35 percent. The number of women aged 65 and older living in a household headed by one of their children or their spouse increased through 1960 but has declined since then; on the other hand, the percentage of women living under this arrangement has decreased steadily since 1940. The number of women living with other relatives and nonrelatives has been smaller, and the relative number living under these arrangements has decreased with each successive census.

Thus, although the overall trend for both men and women living in households has been for an increasing proportion to live in households they are heading, there are also some important sex differentials. Continuously since 1940, women have been about twice as likely as men to live in a household headed by another relative. In 1940 nearly 30 percent of women aged 65 and older who were members of households were in households headed by some relative; this same statement was only true of about 15 percent of the comparable men. By 1980 the comparable figures were just over 12 percent and 5 percent, respectively.

There have also been markedly different patterns for men and women in the growth of the nonhousehold population. In 1940 and 1950 there were actually more men than women in the nonhousehold population, but by 1960 there were 1.19 women for each man, and this ratio has increased steadily since then, reaching 2.35 by 1980. To some degree, these ratios merely reflect the growth differential between older men and women, but they have undoubtedly also been influenced by the greater likelihood that women will live in households with relatives as heads during the early part of the period and the greater availability of nonhousehold facilities such as homes for veterans.

The reversal of the ratio in later years probably reflects the differential by sex in increased longevity and the greater availability to women of nonhousehold care. For example, in 1980, there were nearly 1.5 million persons aged 65 and older in nonhousehold settings. Of this group, 1.2 million were in homes for the aged, and nearly 75 percent of those in such facilities were women.

THE "OLD OLD"

That segment of the elderly population about which the least is known is the "old old" or the oldest of the old. It is generally believed that in recent years this population segment has been growing more rapidly than any other, and we have presented data earlier in this paper that confirm this notion. We do not, however, know a great deal about how this growth has come about or about the composition and distribution of this population (Rosenwaike, 1985). Unfortunately, demographers have been unable to explore these issues in much depth because of tabulation constraints in the data published by the Census Bureau. As a general rule, compositional information has been aggregated for the population aged 65 and older and, in some instances, for that aged 75 and older.

The availability of public-use data tapes makes it possible for the researcher to overcome many of these problems, and projects that use these data sources are currently under way at the University of Pennsylvania and Florida State University. Eventually, these projects will provide detailed data and analyses of the emergence of this population and its changing composition, but until they are further along, we can examine only the basic information about this population with any kind of historical perspective.

Earlier, we noted the rapid rate at which the population aged 85 and older has been increasing. The data in Table 12 show that this is not as recent a phenomenon as is frequently thought and that the rate of increase for the population aged 90 and older has actually been greater than that for the conventionally defined old old aged 85 and older. During each decade since 1940 the 85-and-older population has increased by about 60 percent, except for the last decade (1970–1980), during which the increase was nearly 50 percent. In the three decades from 1940 through 1970, the population aged 90 and older increased by 68 percent, 90 percent, and 75 percent, respectively, before increasing by just 45 percent in the decade from 1970 to 1980. In this sense, it is important to realize that the attention given to the 85-and-older population in recent years is probably due more to its growth to a significant number than to its rate of growth per se. Indeed, what might be more important in the future is that, over this period, the population aged 90 and older increased its share of the old old population, growing from less than one in four individuals to nearly one in three.

For both the population aged 85 and older and that aged 90 and older, women increased in numbers at a more rapid rate than men. Over time, the sex differential has tended to increase in both ages, but it was particularly salient in the decade from 1970 to 1980 during which the male population aged 85 and older increased by only 25 percent and the male population aged 90 and older increased by only 13 percent. The comparable figures for women were 61 percent and 65 percent. These growth differentials have produced an increasingly unbalanced sex ratio. Among the population aged 85 and older, the sex ratio increased from 1.33 (women per man) in 1940 to 1.56 in 1960. By 1970 the ratio had reached 1.79, and by 1980 it had increased to 2.29. In other words, in the single decade from 1970 to 1980, the increase in the sex ratio was greater than it had been over the previous 30 years. Similarly, among the population aged 90 and older the sex ratio increased by 0.22 from 1940 to 1970; it increased 3½ times this during the 1970s.

The growth of the old old population and its increasingly large sex ratio are the result of two basic trends. First, the cohorts that have reached the threshold ages to become eligible to move into the old old ages have been increasingly large. For example, it is members of the cohorts that are aged 75–84 at the beginning of each decade who become the "new old old" over the course of the decade. In 1940 there were 2.3 million such people, whereas by 1960 their number had doubled. By 1970 there were 2.7 persons in this cohort for each person in it in 1940. By 1980 the number of persons aged 75–84 increased to more than 7.7 million, which represents some 3.4 persons in this cohort for each person in it in 1940.

A substantial amount of the increase in the size of the cohorts reaching these ages is the result of reduced risks of mortality at

TABLE 12 Age and Sex Composition of the Old Old (number and percentage), 1940–1980

Year	Sex	85–89	90+	85+	85–89	90+	65+ to 85+	Ratio of Women to Men 85–89	90+	85+
1940								1.28	1.51	1.33
	Male	121,455	34,919	156,374	77.7	22.3	3.5			
	Female	155,557	52,821	208,378	74.7	25.3	4.5			
	Total	277,012	87,740	364,752	75.9	24.1	4.0			
1950								1.42	1.61	1.46
	Male	177,760	56,670	234,430	75.8	24.2	4.0			
	Female	251,845	91,175	343,020	73.4	26.6	5.3			
	Total	429,605	147,845	577,450	74.4	25.6	4.7			
1960								1.54	1.64	1.56
	Male	255,776	106,500	362,276	70.6	29.4	4.8			
	Female	392,805	174,171	566,976	69.3	30.7	6.3			
	Total	648,581	280,671	929,252	69.8	30.2	5.6			
1970								1.81	1.73	1.79
	Male	362,063	180,316	542,379	66.8	33.2	6.4			
	Female	656,084	312,438	968,522	67.7	32.3	8.3			
	Total	1,018,147	492,754	1,510,901	67.4	32.6	7.5			

1980								2.19	2.52	2.29
	Male	477,185	204,340	681,525	70.0	30.0	6.6			
	Female	1,043,017	515,525	1,558,542	66.9	33.1	10.2			
	Total	1,520,202	719,865	2,240,067	67.9	32.1	8.8			
Percentage of Change										
1940–1950	Male	46.4	62.2	49.9						
	Female	61.9	72.6	64.6						
	Total	55.1	68.5	58.3						
1950–1960	Male	43.9	87.9	54.5						
	Female	56.0	91.0	65.3						
	Total	51.0	89.8	60.9						
1960–1970	Male	41.5	69.3	49.7						
	Female	59.0	79.4	70.8						
	Total	57.0	75.6	62.6						
1970–1980	Male	31.8	13.3	25.7						
	Female	59.0	65.0	60.9						
	Total	49.3	46.0	48.3						

SOURCE: Derived from Table 1.

TABLE 13 Life-Table Death Rates and Survivors to Each Age Group from Age 55–84 per 1,000 Persons Aged 55–59, 1940–1980

	Death Rates					Survivors to Each Age of 1,000 Persons Aged 55–59		
Age Group	1980	1970	1960	1950	1940	1980	1960	1940
Total								
55–59	.0530	.0660	.0683	.0783	.0908	947	932	909
60–64	.0794	.0956	.1041	.1150	.1299	872	835	791
65–69	.1165	.1386	.1531	.1664	.1904	770	707	640
70–74	.1694	.1976	.2267	.2519	.2894	640	547	455
75–79	.2427	.2885	.3437	.3829	.4445	485	359	253
80–84	.3554	.4035	.5485	.5708	.6609	313	162	88
Male								
55–59	.0707	.0890	.0912	.0992	.1073	929	909	893
60–64	.1061	.1306	.1383	.1433	.1522	830	783	757
65–69	.1571	.1872	.2004	.2035	.2175	700	626	592
70–74	.2259	.2573	.2829	.2947	.3214	542	449	402
75–79	.3149	.3563	.4080	.4322	.4833	371	266	208
80–84	.4354	.4688	.6204	.6243	.7073	209	101	61
Female								
55–59	.0369	.0444	.0462	.0573	.0733	963	954	927
60–64	.0558	.0639	.0726	.0864	.1078	909	885	827
65–69	.0828	.0974	.1110	.1206	.1632	834	787	692
70–74	.1261	.1506	.1781	.2125	.2581	729	647	513
75–79	.1937	.2382	.2917	.3395	.4082	588	458	304
80–84	.3088	.3596	.4955	.5270	.6204	406	231	115

SOURCES: Grove and Hetzel, 1968; National Center for Health Statistics, 1975, 1985.

the younger old ages. These reductions can be followed in Table 13, which contains the life-table death rates of persons aged 55 and older by 5-year age groups for each decade from 1940 to 1980. We could discuss the reductions in these mortality rates in detail, but the easiest way to illustrate their consequences in this context is to assume their effect by asking the following question: If a cohort aged 55–59 had 1,000 people in it and was subject to each of these schedules, how many people would survive to age 85 and older?

By the 1940 mortality schedule, nearly 100 of the original 1,000 persons would have died before reaching age 60, and 360 would have died before age 70. From this point on, deaths would increase, and by the time the cohort reached age 85, only 88 persons would survive. By the 1960 mortality schedule, the number of survivors to age 85 nearly doubles to 162, but the sharpest contrast occurs when the effects of the 1940 schedule are compared to those of the 1980 schedule. By the 1980 schedule, just 50 people would die before age 60, and 230 would die before age 70. By age 85, the 1980 mortality schedule produces 313 survivors or 3.6 survivors for each 1 survivor by the 1940 schedule.

The lower panels of the table show the same data separately for men and women. The same general pattern of survivorship for the artificial cohorts operates for men and women as it did for the general population except that the rates of mortality are higher for men than for women and the improved risk of death at the middle old ages (65–79) is considerably better for women than for men. Thus, the increased number of survivors from 1940 to 1980 for men aged 65–69, 70–74, and 75–79 is 108, 140, and 163, respectively; for females the comparable numbers are 142, 216, and 284. Put another way, the mortality saved by the 1980 schedule over the 1940 schedule is about the same for women at age 65–69 as it is for men at age 70–74. After these points, women continue to gain through age 80–84; men, on the other hand, peak at 163 at age 75–79 before dropping back to 148 at age 80–84.

Nevertheless, it is obvious that both men and women reaching the young old ages have considerably better chances of reaching the old old ages in 1980 than they did in 1940. For each male who was age 55–59 in 1940 and lived to age 85, there were 3.4 comparable men in 1980 (the ratio for women was 3.5). Indeed, by the 1980 mortality schedule, more than 40 percent of the women reaching age 55–59 would survive to reach the old old ages, whereas this was true of only about 20 percent of the men. In 1940, only 6 percent of the men and 12 percent of the women aged 55–59 would survive to reach the old old ages. Clearly, mortality reductions in the old ages have significantly contributed to the growth of the old old population.

THE NEW AGED

It is our contention that changes in the composition, behavior, and needs of future generations of the elderly can best be foreseen by a consideration of how newly entering cohorts differ from their immediate predecessors. Thus, the purpose of this section is to explore the differences over time and across cohorts between that group of the older population considered in the preceding section—the old old—and the group at the opposite end of the spectrum—those who have just entered the ranks of the older population. We have already discussed the fact that in recent censuses the new aged constitute smaller proportions of the entire older population than had been true previously, primarily because of reductions in mortality among those already aged 65 and older. Consequently, in 1980 those aged 55–64 accounted for only 46 percent of the entire 55-and-older population, whereas in 1940 this age group represented 54 percent.

Our purpose here will be first to explore how the most recent cohort of the new aged differs in important ways from the remainder of the elderly. In particular, we will argue that the group aged 55–64 in 1980 represents the cutting edge of critical differences in the composition and life-course experiences of the elderly of yesterday and the elderly of tomorrow. Table 14 illustrates one aspect of such differences: median years of education completed by birth cohorts prior to 1865 through those born from 1955 to 1960. The data are arranged so that the reader can consider differences in educational attainment by age, cohort, and period, and this threefold consideration will set the model for the analytical approach we follow throughout this section. The table can be read three ways:

1. by row (horizontally) showing median educational attainment for a stated birth cohort;
2. by column (vertically) showing median educational attainment for successive cohorts in a given age group; and
3. diagonally, showing the age structure of educational attainment for a given period.

The 1980 groups aged 55–59 and 60–64 show 12.3 and 12.1 median school years completed, respectively. These rates are, on the one hand, anywhere from 1.1 to 3.9 years greater than those attained by other members of the older population and, on the other hand, a maximum of 0.6 years less than those attained by any other cohort. In other words, the 1980 "new aged" have educational experiences that are generally similar in duration to those of all segments of the population younger than themselves but that are substantially greater than those of all seg-

TABLE 14 Educational Attainment (median years) by Age Group, 1940–1980

Birth Period	20–24	25–29	30–34	35–39	40–44	45–49	50–54	55–59	60–64	65–69	70–74	75+	Decade
1955–1959	12.8												
1950–1955		12.9											
1945–1950	12.7		12.9										
1940–1945		12.5		12.7									
1935–1940	12.3		12.4		12.6								
1930–1935		12.3		12.3		12.5							
1925–1930	12.1		12.2		12.3		12.4						
1920–1925		12.1		12.1		12.2		12.3					
1915–1920	11.2		11.6		11.8		12.1		12.1				
1910–1915		10.3		10.5		10.6		10.9		11.0			
1905–1910			9.5		9.8		9.7		10.0		10.3		
1900–1905				8.8		8.9		8.8		9.0		8.4	1980
1895–1900					8.6		8.7		8.6		8.7		
1890–1895						8.5		8.5		8.4		8.5	1970
1885–1890							8.4		8.4		8.3		
1880–1885								8.3		8.2		8.2	1960
1875–1880									8.3		8.2		
1870–1875										8.2		8.1	1950
1865–1870												8.0	
Before 1865											8.1		1940

SOURCES: U.S. Bureau of the Census, 1943 (Table 18), 1953 (Table 16), 1964 (Table 173), 1973 (Table 199), and 1984a (Table 262).

ments older than themselves. In 1970 the position of these age groups was intermediate between those younger and older (second diagonal), but in 1960, 1950, and 1940, there was very little difference in educational attainment within the older population. There were successively greater differences between the younger and older populations as a whole, however. Thus, those cohorts born after 1915 differ from those born before that year in terms of the length of their education. The current cohort of the new aged and all successive cohorts who will become part of the older population (at least through the year 2015) will have, at the midpoint, completed high school and will have some postsecondary education. Although we certainly do not wish to claim that education is a panacea for all social ills, there is little doubt that greater educational attainment will have subsequent effects on individuals' tastes and expectations. It is certainly conceivable that this greater degree of "sophistication" will affect the nature and type of services that will be demanded by these cohorts.

Higher levels of education might be expected to have additional influences on the life-course experiences of the new aged within the older population. In general, there is a positive influence of education on earning power, although the actual level of earnings will also depend on the overall rate of labor force participation. Tables 15 and 16 show median income by age for men and women relative to overall income levels for persons of the gender. (The data presented here pertain only to those individuals with income.) Once again, the data are presented in such a way as to permit full consideration of age, period, and cohort effects.

Turning first to the experience of men (Table 15), the age effects are quite clear: men at either end of the age spectrum tend to earn relatively less than those in the middle. Generally, the income of persons aged 25 to 64 is higher than that for persons under 24 and over 65. At a given point in time, peak income comes somewhere in the middle of the 25–64 age span. For 1950, 1960, and 1970 (no data are available for 1940), the peak income age was 35–39 and/or 40–44; in 1980 it had moved to 45–49. From a cohort perspective, a similar phenomenon—that is, the peak income years coming slightly later in middle age—also seems to be emerging.

The limited data available suggest that cohorts born prior to

TABLE 15 Income for Men by Age, Relative to the Median, 1950–1980

Birth Year	20	25	30	35	40	45	50	55	60	65	70	75	Decade
1955	0.59204												
1950		1.02830											
1945	0.54178		1.31811										
1940		1.15811		1.51241									
1935	0.60742		1.33941		1.56150								
1930		1.18687		1.41099		1.58481							
1925	0.66782		1.18687		1.43705		1.51319						
1920		1.14868		1.35054		1.41505		1.39158					
1915			1.14868		1.35054		1.33524		1.11838				
1910				1.30255		1.24789		1.21142		0.71364			
1905					1.30255		1.24789		1.03146		0.57984		
1900						1.24228		1.05369		0.56336		0.45830	1980
1895							1.24228		1.05369		0.43169		
1890								1.04369		0.49128		0.32892	1970
1885									1.04369		0.49128		
1880										0.41347		0.28158	1960
1875											0.41347		
Pre-1870												0.41347	1950

SOURCES: U.S. Bureau of the Census, 1953 (Table 139), 1964 (Table 219), 1973 (Table 245), and 1984a (Table 293).

TABLE 16 Income for Women by Age, Relative to the Median, 1950–1980

Birth Year	20	25	30	35	40	45	50	55	60	65	70	75	Decade
1955	1.04339												
1950		1.42600											
1945	1.28001		1.34014										
1940		1.30972		1.29481									
1935	1.30437		1.12386		1.32548								
1930		1.08237		1.21257		1.29368							
1925	1.47498		1.08237		1.36480		1.23199						
1920		1.18661		1.30121		1.45628		1.13432					
1915			1.18661		1.30121		1.45344		0.93302				
1910				1.28071		1.52082		1.36319		0.85786			
1905					1.28071		1.52082		1.06463		0.85655		
1900						1.26532		1.13896		0.83443		0.79846	1980
1895							1.26532		1.13896		0.81132		
1890								0.89318		0.77367		0.74307	1970
1885									0.89318		0.77367		
1880										0.71368		0.66642	1960
1875											0.71368		
Pre-1870												0.71368	1950

SOURCES: U.S. Bureau of the Census, 1953 (Table 139), 1964 (Table 219), 1973 (Table 245), and 1984a (Table 293).

1920 enjoyed their peak income years before age 45; those born more recently seem to be reaching the income peak in their late forties or early fifties.

Finally, and perhaps most important for present purposes, let us consider the period effects. The 1980 data (first diagonal) show much higher relative income after age 35 than was true in previous years. For those out of the labor force, this trend may well be attributable to the significant increases in the real value of Social Security retirement benefits during the 1970s. Yet relative income, not only for the "new aged" of 1980 but also for those who will be the new aged in 1990 and 2000, was also greater than had been the case in prior census years—for both the 45–54 and 35–44 age groups, income was 50–60 percent above the overall average, in rather sharp contrast to the experience of older cohorts as they passed through the same age range. The experience of the new aged is similar, with relative income for those aged 55–64 in 1980 being appreciably greater than for previous cohorts when they were aged 55–64.

The pattern among women (Table 16), however, is much different; a pronounced downward shift toward higher relative income by age has occurred between 1970 and 1980. Prior to 1980 the age pattern among women had been similar to that of men: peak income came in the 40–44 and 45–49 age groups, and there was some increase in this age over time. Yet in 1980, peak income occurred at age 25–29, and the highest relative income groups were entirely under the age of 45. The reason for this change may be seen in the pronounced changes in female labor force participation rates, which are shown in Table 17.

The remarkable increases in labor force participation among American women during the 1970s is well known. For all ages from 20–24 through 55–59, the level of participation by age was higher in 1980 than it had been at any time since 1940. The largest absolute and relative increases occurred among women aged 25–34 and 35–44; as a result, peak labor force participation among women, which had previously been found for women in their late forties and early fifties (after age 20–24), occurred throughout the early forties. For those women who entered the ranks of the older population between 1970 and 1980, labor force participation had been relatively constant compared with earlier cohorts but was much lower than their own experience in 1970. Among men (Table 18), labor force participation declined

TABLE 17 Women in the Labor Force by Age, 1940–1980

Birth Year	20	25	30	35	40	45	50	55	60	65	70	75	Decade
1955	67.8												
1950		66.3											
1945	56.1		63.2										
1940		45.4		64.4									
1935	44.8		44.2		65.0								
1930		35.1		50.3		61.5							
1925	43.2		35.5		50.3		56.3						
1920		32.6		40.2		53.0		48.4					
1915	45.1		30.9		45.3		52.0		34.0				
1910		35.2		33.9		47.4		47.4		15.0			
1905			30.4		36.2		45.8		36.1		7.8		
1900				28.0		34.8		39.7		17.2		3.2	1980
1895					25.6		30.8		29.5		9.1		
1890						23.2		25.9		16.6		4.7	1970
1885							20.8		20.5		9.6		
1880								17.7		12.8		4.2	1960
1875									14.4		6.6		
1870										9.3		3.6	1950
1865											4.9		
Pre-1865												2.1	1940

SOURCES: U.S. Bureau of the Census, 1943 (Table 24), 1953 (Table 156), 1964 (Table 194), 1973 (Table 215), and 1984a (Table 272).

TABLE 18 Percentage of Men in the Labor Force by Age, 1940–1980

Birth Year	20	25	30	35	40	45	50	55	60	65	70	75	Decade
1955	82.7												
1950		91.8											
1945	80.9		94.0										
1940		92.9		94.5									
1935	86.1		95.0		93.7								
1930		93.9		94.8		92.0							
1925	81.9		95.8		94.8		88.5						
1920		90.3		95.8		93.5		80.6					
1915	88.0		93.9		95.4		91.4		60.4				
1910		94.9		94.6		94.5		86.8		29.2			
1905			95.6		94.3		92.2		73.0		18.3		
1900				95.3		93.2		87.7		39.0		9.1	1980
1895					94.1		90.6		77.6		22.4		
1890						92.9		86.7		43.9		12.0	1970
1885							91.1		79.4		28.7		
1880								87.8		59.8		15.5	1960
1875									78.9		38.7		
1870										59.2		18.6	1950
1865											38.2		
Pre-1865												17.8	1940

SOURCES: U.S. Bureau of the Census, 1943 (Table 24), 1953 (Table 156), 1964 (Table 194), 1973 (Table 215), and 1984a (Table 272).

at all ages in 1980 relative to 1970 (and earlier years), with the most pronounced reductions occurring at ages 55–69 and especially at age 60–64.

In short, the life-course pattern of participation in the labor force among coming cohorts of the new aged is likely to be much different than the experiences of current and previous cohorts. Among men, some combination of institutional factors (pushing for earlier retirement) and possibly higher earnings earlier in the life cycle (affording the possibility of more leisure rather than more work in the late middle years) may have the effect of creating cohorts of new aged who are in the labor force to a relatively small extent. Among women, future cohorts of the new aged are likely to enter this phase with considerable experience in working for pay throughout their life. Although it is unlikely that their labor force participation at ages 55–64 would be higher than the current level, it is important to note that they will be entering their retirement years with their own pension and Social Security entitlements. This trend should have two effects: (1) it should increase the level of income among future generations of new aged married couples, and (2) it should also have quite favorable consequences for the economic status of future cohorts of older widows.

Another issue related to the support, financial and otherwise, of future generations of older persons is the number of family members available to provide such support. Women who were aged 55–59 and 60–64 in 1980 had borne, on the average, 2.9 and 2.6 children, respectively, over the course of their reproductive lifetimes (Table 19). These levels are greater than those of women aged 65–79 (2.3-2.4) but lower than those of women older than 80 (3.0-3.1). For the younger women, there is, of course, a greater probability that their children are still living and that they would still be approaching their own peak income years. There are fewer children of the extreme aged still alive, and they themselves are or will soon be entering the older population. Those women who will be the next generation of the new aged will have even more surviving children because their lifetime fertility has been 3.1 to 3.2 children ever born. For younger women (i.e., for women born after 1935), however, a sharp drop in the probable number of surviving children is likely. Although these women have not yet finished with childbearing, completed fertility to date for all women born prior to 1965 is lower for

TABLE 19 Actual and Projected (values within parentheses) Completed Fertility by Age for Women Born Between 1885–1965

Birth Period	Age 15	20	25	30	35	40	45	Age in 1980
1960–1965	77.7	(451.2)	(919.0)	(1,216.9)	(1,320.8)	(1,348.3)	(1,353.0)	15–19
1955–1960	87.4	507.5	(1,033.8)	(1,368.8)	(1,485.7)	(1,516.7)	(1,522.0)	20–24
1950–1955	84.4	559.7	1,140.1	(1,509.6)	(1,638.5)	(1,672.7)	(1,678.5)	25–29
1945–1950	93.8	684.3	1,369.2	1,813.0	(1,967.7)	(2,008.9)	(2,015.8)	30–34
1940–1945	110.8	880.2	1,725.3	2,212.2	2,401.0	(2,451.2)	(2,459.7)	35–39
1935–1940	106.3	955.9	2,073.6	2,651.4	2,879.9	2,940.1	(2,950.3)	40–44
1930–1935	94.8	848.2	2,005.5	2,781.8	3,099.6	3,190.1	3,201.2	45–49
1925–1930	67.7	693.9	1,698.8	2,493.2	2,921.2	3,060.6	3,078.7	50–54
1920–1925	64.3	569.9	1,439.1	2,182.3	2,639.0	2,826.2	2,856.2	55–59
1915–1920		503.7	1,241.6	1,906.5	2,334.7	2,534.3	2,572.9	60–64
1910–1915			1,132.9	1,709.8	2,123.5	2,312.4	2,352.7	65–69
1905–1910				1,704.5	2,055.4	2,246.1	2,284.4	70–74
1900–1905					2,229.7	2,397.5	2,439.6	75–79
1895–1900						2,632.7	2,673.5	80–84
1890–1895							2,929.6	85+
1885–1890							3,136.8	

SOURCE: Heuser, 1976.

each successive age and for each successive cohort. Important changes in the timing of reproductive activity among American women are still under way, but it seems unlikely that the average completed family size for any cohort born after 1945 will greatly exceed 2 children. In a real sense, it could be argued that smaller families are the other side of the increased labor force participation discussed earlier. In effect, future generations of women will enter their later years with greater financial resources but fewer familial resources to provide necessary support.

The potential implications of this sort of change are profound. With fewer familial resources available, the responsibility for the provision of long-term care is likely to continue shifting away from the family and toward society as a whole. Conversely, we might also expect that older individuals will have greater command over resources and will be able to meet a larger share of the pecuniary costs of this care.

This mention of health-related issues brings the present discussion back to the overall question of the health of the older population and, in particular, the extent to which the new aged will differ from the present population over the age of 65 in terms of health characteristics. In the introductory section of this paper, we noted the changing pattern of mortality by age in the older population. In the context of health, we can now consider the role that other variables, especially income, might play in affecting the relative health status of future generations of older Americans. We have already noted several reasons for expecting higher levels of income among future members of the older population; there will be higher relative income among men while working and the greater labor force participation of women will not only increase current income but also tend to build up assets for use in retirement. Income levels among the older population, regardless of age, tend to interact with various measures of health status in more or less predictable ways. Table 20 illustrates that, in general, for each age group (55–64, 65–74, and 75+) within the older population, as the level of income increases, the fewer the number of chronic conditions limiting activity; the lower the percentage of people assessing their health as "poor" or "fair"; and the fewer the number of days spent on average per year in short-stay hospitals.

Within income groups, it is often the case that the number of

TABLE **20** Selected Indicators of Health Status by Age and Income, 1979–1980

		Income						
Age	Total	Less than $2,999	$3,000–4,999	$5,000–6,999	$7,000–9,999	$10,000–14,999	$15,000–24,999	More than $25,000
Activity limitations per person								
55–64	3.0	6.0	5.7	4.5	3.8	3.1	2.3	1.8
65–74	4.1	5.9	5.3	4.7	4.4	3.7	3.2	2.9
75+	5.3	6.0	5.4	5.1	5.4	5.1	5.3	5.5
Percentage in fair or poor health								
55–64	26	57	50	44	37	29	18	13
65–74	32	48	43	38	33	25	21	18
75+	31	35	33	32	31	30	27	27
Physician visits per person								
55–64	5.5	6.2	8.7	5.9	5.5	5.6	5.1	5.4
65–74	6.3	6.9	6.6	6.4	6.2	6.3	6.1	6.6
75+	6.6	6.2	6.1	5.9	6.1	7.2	8.3	7.2
Short-stay hospital days, per person								
55–65	1.8	3.3	2.4	3.1	2.6	2.0	1.4	1.1
65–74	2.4	3.1	3.2	2.7	2.2	2.2	1.9	2.2
75+	3.6	4.0	3.1	3.5	3.1	4.3	3.7	4.0

SOURCE: Ries, 1985.

limiting conditions and average hospital days increase with age, but this is not the case for self-assessed health status for which this relationship holds only for the two highest income categories. In fact, for family income levels below $10,000, fair or poor health is reported less frequently among persons aged 75 and older than among persons aged 55–74. Perhaps it may be fairly said that persons in the oldest age group survive to that age precisely because they are comparatively healthy. The average number of physician visits per year generally bears no relationship to income but generally shows a pattern of increasing frequency of visits as a function of age. In brief, the data shown here as well as the demographic trends operating within the older population suggest two counterbalancing tendencies:

1. increased income, especially among the new aged, which has been associated with lower levels of chronic, activity-limiting conditions, lower levels of self-assessed poor health, and fewer days, per capita, of hospital usage; and
2. the continued aging of the older population, which has been

associated with greater levels of chronic conditions and greater use of health care facilities and providers.

As noted earlier, much of the underlying cause of the continued aging of the older population lies in declining mortality. One of the critical issues that will arise in conjunction with this aging and that is of particular relevance to the social and built environment is the question of long-term care needs. Ries (1985) recently prepared projections of total population and nursing home residents, by age, for the year 2003 under conditions of constant and declining mortality (Table 21). Even in the unlikely event that there would be no changes in mortality between the years covered by this study (1978–2003), Ries projects that the number of nursing home residents will increase by nearly 60 percent, from 1.2 million to 1.9 million. If, however, age- and sex-specific mortality continues to decrease, as it did during the period from 1966 to 1976, then the number of nursing home residents would rise by more than 100 percent to 2.6 million.

THE FUTURE OLDER POPULATION

In the first three sections of this paper, we examined (1) the basic demographic structure of the older population and how this structure has changed from 1940 to 1980; (2) the dramatic effects that reductions in mortality at the older ages have had on the growth of the elderly population and its changing age and sex composition; and (3) the emergence of the new old, illustrating how cohorts entering the other end of the elderly age distribution (its new births) would influence its composition and structure.

Now, we want to draw from each of the three previous sections and consider what we can expect in the future. To some extent, these issues have already been touched on. The mortality schedules discussed earlier portend that new cohorts entering the older ages will live under considerably lower risks of death until much later in life. The data we presented on education, earnings, labor force participation, and family size suggest the potential for a more heterogeneous life-style among the elderly in the future. What is important to realize is that we can identify such trends, but we cannot necessarily extrapolate them to the future

TABLE 21 Nursing Home Population (in thousands) by Age, 1978–2003

	Persons in Nursing Homes		Constant Mortality			Declining Mortality		
Age	%	No.	Population, 2003	Number in Nursing Homes	Percentage Change	Population, 2003	Number in Nursing Homes	Percentage Change
65–74	1.5	200	17,130	200	15	18,451	300	24
75–84	6.8	500	11,134	800	62	12,814	900	86
85+	21.7	500	3,932	900	84	6,684	1,400	213
Total		1,200	32,196	1,900	58	37,919	2,600	117

SOURCE: Ries, 1985.

and know what to expect. For example, future cohorts that enter the older ages may be more healthy than past cohorts and more able to provide for themselves, but if they live longer, their savings and income may actually become less adequate than those of many elderly today. Indeed, it is even possible that their better physical condition and their expectations of a different life-style may lead them to dispose of savings at a greater rate at the very time that they are expected to live longer.

Nevertheless, an understanding of future trends in the growth and structure of the elderly population is necessary if we are even to assess the alternative futures. The projections most frequently used for planning and policy purposes are the Series 14 middle-mortality/middle-fertility projections of the Bureau of the Census. These projections, which roughly assume a continuation of current fertility trends, forecast that life expectancy at birth will increase to 76.7 years by the year 2000 and continue to increase gradually to 81 years by 2080. The corresponding figures for men are 72.9 years in 2000 and 76.7 years in 2080; for women, the expectancy is 80.5 years in 2000 and 85.2 years in 2080 (U.S. Bureau of the Census, 1984b).

The projections (Table 22) also indicate that the total population of the country will increase to nearly 250 million in 1990 and 268 million by the turn of the century. By the year 2020, there would be some 296 million people in the country. The proportion of persons aged 55 and older will not change radically from its 1980 level (21 percent) through the turn of the century, even though the absolute number of persons 55 and older will have increased from 47 million in 1980 to nearly 59 million in the year 2000. Over the next 20 years, however, as the first of the baby boom cohorts enters the 55-and-older age group, both the proportion and number of older persons will rise sharply. The percentage of the total population that is 55 and older will pass 26 percent by the year 2010, and it will approach 31 percent by the year 2020 when the number of persons aged 55 and older will be nearly 92 million. Of particular significance in this growth is the increasing size of the cohorts entering these ages. Note, for example, that between 1990 and 2020, the two cohorts making up the ages 55–64 double in size.

The population aged 65 and older will follow roughly the same path in the sense that its absolute numbers will continue to increase but its proportion of the total population will increase

TABLE 22 Bureau of the Census Middle-Level Projections of the Total and Elderly Population (in thousands) by Age, 1990–2020

	1990			2000			2010			2020		
Age	No. of Persons	% 55+	% 65+	No. of Persons	% 55+	% 65+	No. of Persons	% 55+	% 65+	No. of Persons	% 55+	% 65+
Total	249,657			267,955			283,238			296,357		
55–59	10,433	19.8		13,280	22.6		18,825	25.4		20,507	22.4	
60–64	10,618	20.1		10,487	17.9		16,023	21.6		19,791	21.6	
65–69	9,996	19.0	31.6	9,096	15.5	26.0	11,703	15.8	29.9	16,620	18.1	32.3
70–74	8,039	15.2	25.4	8,581	14.7	24.6	8,615	11.6	22.0	13,235	14.4	25.7
75–79	6,260	11.8	19.7	7,295	12.4	20.9	6,782	9.2	17.3	8,824	9.6	17.2
80–84	4,089	7.8	12.9	5,023	8.6	14.4	5,544	7.5	14.1	5,662	6.2	11.0
85–89	2,157	4.1	6.8	3,025	5.1	8.7	3,756	5.1	9.6	3,587	3.9	7.0
90+	1,156	2.2	3.6	1,901	3.2	5.4	2,795	3.8	7.1	3,494	3.8	6.8
55+	52,748			58,688			74,043			91,720		
65+	31,697			34,921			39,195			51,422		
% 55+	21.1			21.9			26.1			30.9		
% 65+	12.7			13.0			13.8			17.3		
85+	3,313			4,926			6,551			7,081		
% 85+	1.3			1.8			2.3			2.4		
% 55–85+	6.2			8.3			8.8			7.7		
% 65–85+	10.4			14.1			16.7			13.8		

NOTE: "% 55+" = projected percentage of the population that is 55 years old and older.

SOURCE: U.S. Bureau of the Census, 1984b.

only moderately. The larger increase in the proportion of the population aged 65 and older will lag 10 years behind the larger increases in the 55-and-older population; thus, they will not begin to appear until the year 2020. Nevertheless, according to the projections, the population aged 65 and older will increase from its 1980 level of 26 million to 39 million in the year 2010; it will grow to 51 million by 2020. In other words, nearly one-half of the expected growth in the population aged 55 and older between 1980 and 2020 will occur in the single decade from 2010 to 2020, during which the size of the 65-and-older population will increase by some 12 million persons.

The projected reductions in mortality will ensure the continued growth of the old old (aged 85 and older) population. Its numbers will increase from their 1980 level of 2.2 million to nearly 7.1 million by the year 2020. By that time, they will constitute nearly 2.5 percent of the total population.

Although the projections described in the preceding paragraphs are those that are most frequently cited, this does not mean that the picture they portray will materialize. In fact, it is important to note that a major shortcoming of the Census Bureau middle-range projections in the past has been their underestimates of reductions in mortality. In the two sets of projections released prior to those discussed above, the mortality error accounted for over 40 percent of the 6-year aggregate error, and in the projections made since 1960, 8 percent too many deaths were predicted by only the sixth year of the projection period. Clearly then, previous Census Bureau projections have erred in a manner that most strongly affects the older ages. What can we expect if this type of error is similarly reflected in the current middle-range projections?

To help answer this question, Table 23 presents data for an alternative set of projections that assumes a life expectancy at birth in the year 2000 that is 2 years greater than in the previously discussed set and a life expectancy that will rise to 85.9 years in the year 2080.

These assumptions result in total population increases (over the middle-level projections) that range from nearly 360,000 in 1990 to more than 5.4 million by the year 2020. What is even more important for our purposes, however, is that the majority of these gains would occur in the population aged 55 and older. For example, by the year 2000, about 1.3 million of the total

TABLE 23 Bureau of the Census Low-Mortality Projections of the Total and Elderly Population (in thousands) by Age, 1990–2020

	1990			2000			2010			2020		
Age	No. of Persons	% 55+	% 65+	No. of Persons	% 55+	% 65+	No. of Persons	% 55+	% 65+	No. of Persons	% 55+	% 65+
Total	250,016			269,576			286,721			302,015		
55–59	10,452	19.7		13,369	22.3		19,042	24.8		20,803	21.6	
60–64	10,643	20.1		10,582	17.6		16,281	21.2		20,201	21.0	
65–69	10,026	18.9	31.4	9,206	15.3	25.5	11,962	15.5	28.7	17,106	17.7	30.9
70–74	8,073	15.2	25.3	8,722	14.6	24.2	8,878	11.5	21.3	13,776	14.3	24.9
75–79	6,300	11.8	19.7	7,467	12.4	20.7	7,077	9.2	17.1	9,340	9.7	16.9
80–84	4,136	7.8	12.9	5,220	8.7	14.5	5,926	7.7	14.2	6,172	6.4	11.1
85–89	2,205	4.2	6.9	3,247	5.4	9.0	4,215	5.5	10.1	4,151	4.3	7.5
90	1,201	2.3	3.8	2,182	3.7	6.1	3,553	4.6	8.6	4,827	5.0	8.7
55+	53,036			59,996			76,934			96,376		
65+	31,941			36,045			41,611			55,372		
% 55+	21.2			22.3			26.8			31.9		
% 65+	12.8			13.4			14.5			18.3		
85+	3,406			5,429			7,768			8,978		
% 85+	1.4			1.9			2.7			3.0		
% 55–85+	6.4			9.0			10.1			9.3		
% 65–85+	10.8			15.1			18.7			16.2		

NOTE: "% 55+" = projected percentage of the population that is 55 years old and older.

SOURCE: U.S. Bureau of the Census, 1984b.

increase of 1.6 million (or about 81 percent) occurs in the population aged 55 and older. By the year 2020, nearly 4.7 million of the total increase of 5.4 million (or about 86 percent) occurs in the population aged 55 and older. If we make these comparisons on the basis of the population aged 65 and older, we can see that the majority of deaths saved would actually be concentrated in this age range. That is, with the low-mortality projections, there would be 1.1 million more persons aged 65 and older than there would be for the middle-level projections by the year 2000, and nearly 4 million more by the year 2020.

As the data imply, these alternative sets of projections produce substantially different age compositions of the elderly over time. The proportion of the 65-and-older population aged 65–74 (which was 61 percent in 1980) will drop to about 57 percent in 1990 by both sets of projections, and it will continue to decline over the next two decades. According to the middle-level projections, it will increase again to 58 percent by the year 2020; yet according to the low-mortality projections, it will reach only 55 percent by this time. The reasons for this pattern center around the different sizes of the newly entering cohorts and the extent to which their fluctuations in size will be offset by the enhanced survival chances of those already in the older ages. These factors can be highlighted by looking at the other end of the elderly age distribution. The proportion of persons aged 85 and older will increase with both sets of projections for each of the first three decades of the projection period, reaching 17 percent for the middle-level projections and 19 percent for the low-mortality-level projections. By the end of the projection period (the year 2020), the respective shares of the 65-and-older population that will be aged 85 and older are 14 percent and 16 percent, but it should be noted that with the low-mortality projections, we are estimating an increase of nearly 2 million more persons aged 85 and older than with the middle-level projections.

Although it is clearly impossible to state definitively that the low-mortality projection ultimately will prove closer to reality than the middle-level alternative, the weight of recent experience certainly favors this conclusion. Such an outcome will clearly have profound effects on the social and built environment, both as it relates to the needs of the older population and as it tempers the overall quality of life for the entire population.

The limitations of both space and time preclude a detailed

elaboration of the entire realm of such effects. We prefer to consider the issue we deem to be potentially of the greatest import, namely, the need for long-term care. Probably the most striking difference between the two sets of population projections shown in Tables 22 and 23 is the difference in the size of the very old population—that is, the population aged 85 or older. We have already noted the much greater probability that this segment of the population resides in a nursing home or similar facility. At this writing, it is far from certain whether reductions in mortality will increase or decrease the level of morbidity and the presence of chronic, potentially disabling conditions among the older population (Feldman, 1985; Fries, 1985; Schneider, 1985). Of course, the worst-case scenario would be that increases in life expectancy at the older ages would result in additional years of life characterized by affliction with such conditions. Thus, we would argue that the demand for congregate living facilities and long-term care facilities would rise as a result of a diminution in mortality. Furthermore, we could extend the argument to note that considerably greater resources will be required to construct such facilities, to train more personnel to staff them, and to pay the costs of their operation.

Given the present role of the public sector, through Medicaid, of bearing a large proportion of these latter costs (in addition to the costs of increased short-term hospitalization and medical treatment through Medicare), we could easily arrive at some rather sobering conclusions regarding the impact of reductions in mortality on the social and built environment, not only for aged individuals and their families but also for society at large. Even if the age-specific proportions of older persons residing in long-term care facilities do not increase, the number of persons so residing must inexorably rise with the increase in the size of the population at risk. Any increases in the size of the 85-and-older population, such as that arising from reduced mortality, will increase the number who will ultimately require such a living arrangement. And any increases in the demand for such care will lead to increases in the demand for the resources to underwrite these costs.

Such resources presumably will continue to come from the aged individuals themselves, from their families, and from society as a whole, embodied in the public sector. As we have previously noted, there is some reason to believe that future generations of the elderly, especially women, will command more resources than is true of present generations. Yet these resources cannot be regarded as infinite and, indeed, will have to be stretched over a long life span. These individuals will have fewer surviving children on whom to rely for financial and other support, and, as life expectancy rises, the children of the oldest old will more and more be counted among the youngest (and even among the intermediate) old. The children of the oldest old will themselves be concerned with providing for their own impending care needs and may be unable to provide both financial and personal support to their oldest old parents. One might argue that it is the proper role of society to provide the necessary resources, but the allocation of additional scarce resources for these purposes means that fewer resources are available for other needs, that additional resources will have to be transferred from the private to the public sector, or that continued borrowing by the public sector will ensue. Thus, under this worst-case scenario, the social and built environment would deteriorate for all parties.

Few persons look forward to spending their last years in an institutionalized setting. Unless policies are altered to permit societal funding for home-based care, however, this prospect becomes increasingly likely. The children of the potentially institutionalized will be fewer in number, relatively, and it is possible that they will be unable to provide home-based care even if it were affordable. If society as a whole chooses to underwrite the resource costs of such care, it may have to face the choice of doing without resources for other socially defined purposes, subjecting itself to greater taxation (and, therefore, to less disposable income), or witnessing the continued growth of the nation's budgetary deficit, which will ultimately destroy the health of the nation's economy.

REFERENCES

Coale, A. J. 1964. "How a Population Ages or Grows Younger." In R. Freedmen (ed.), *Population: The Vital Revolution,* New York: Doubleday & Company.

Cowgill, D. O. 1974. "The Aging of Populations and Societies." *Annals of the American Academy of Political and Social Science* 415:1–18.

Feldman, J. 1985. "Demography of Aging." Paper presented at the annual meeting of the Gerontological Society of America, New Orleans.

Fries, J. 1985. "Evidence for Compression of Morbidity." Paper presented at the annual meeting of the Gerontological Society of America, New Orleans.

Grove, R., and A. Hetzel. 1968. *Vital Statistics Rates in the United States, 1940–1960.* Hyattsville, Md.: National Center for Health Statistics, Table 48.

Hermalin, A. 1966. The effect of changes in mortality rates on population growth and age distribution in the United States. *Milbank Memorial Fund Quarterly* 44: 451–69.

Heuser, R. 1976. *Fertility Tables for Birth Cohorts by Color: United States, 1917–1973.* Hyattsville, Md.: National Center for Health Statistics.

Keyfitz, N. 1968. "Changing Vital Rates and Age Distribution." *Population Studies* 22:235–251.

Lopez, A., and K. Hanada. 1982. "Mortality Patterns and Trends Among the Elderly in Developed Countries." *World Health Statistics Quarterly* 35:203–224.

Manton, K. 1982. "Changing Concepts of Morbidity and Mortality in the Elderly Population." *Milbank Memorial Fund Quarterly* 60:183–244.

Myers, G. C. 1985a. "Aging and Worldwide Population Change." In *Handbook of Aging and the Social Sciences,* R. Binstock and E. Shanus, eds., New York: Van Nostrand Reinhold.

Myers, G. C. 1985b. "Demographic and Socio-Economic Aspects of Population Aging." In *Population Aging.* Paris: CICRED.

National Center for Health Statistics (and predecessor agencies). 1940–1980. *Vital Statistics of the United States.*

National Center for Health Statistics. 1975. *U.S. Decennial Life Tables for 1969–1971.* Hyattsville, Md.: National Center for Health Statistics.

National Center for Health Statistics. 1985. *U.S. Decennial Life Tables for 1979–1981.* Hyattsville, Md.: National Center for Health Statistics.

Pearl, R. 1940. "The Aging of Populations." *Journal of the American Statistical Association* 209:277–297.

Population Reference Bureau. 1975. "The Elderly in America." *Population Bulletin* 30(3).

Ries, P. 1985. "Health Characteristics According to Family and Personal Income." Data from the National Health Survey, Series 10, No. 147. Hyattsville, Md.: National Center for Health Statistics.

Rosenwaike, I. 1985. "Implications for Aging and Diseases of Aging." Paper presented at the annual meeting of the Gerontological Society of America, New Orleans.

Schneider, E. 1985. "Implications for Aging and Diseases of Aging." Paper presented at the annual meeting of the Gerontological Society of America, New Orleans.

Siegel, J. S. 1980. "On the Demography of Aging." *Demography* 17:345–364.

Siegel, J. S., and M. Davidson. 1984. "Demographic and Socioeconomic Aspects of Aging." *Current Population Reports,* Series P-23, No. 138. Washington, D.C.: U.S. Government Printing Office.

U.S. Bureau of the Census. 1943. Sixteenth Census of the United States: Population. Volume IV: Characteristics by Age, Part 1, U.S. Summary. Washington, D.C.: U.S. Government Printing Office, Tables 1, 6, 10, 18, 24, 26.

U.S. Bureau of the Census. 1953. Census of Population: 1950. Volume II: Characteristics of the Population. Part 1, U.S. Summary, Chapter C. Washington, D.C.: Government Printing Office, Tables 94, 102, 107, 116, 139, 145, 156.

U.S. Bureau of the Census. 1964. Census of Population: 1960. Volume I: Characteristics of the Population. Part 1, U.S. Summary, Chapter D. Detailed Characteristics. Washington, D.C.: U.S. Government Printing Office, Tables 156, 173, 176, 181, 194, 219, 232, 233.

U.S. Bureau of the Census. 1972. Census of Population: 1970. Volume I: Characteristics of the Population. Part 1, U.S. Summary, Chapter B. General Population Characteristics. Washington, D.C.: U.S. Government Printing Office, Tables 50, 56, 57.

U.S. Bureau of the Census. 1973. Census of Population: 1970. Volume I: Characteristics of the Population. Part 1, U.S. Summary, Chapter D. Detailed Characteristics. Washington, D.C.: U.S. Government Printing Office, Tables 199, 203, 204, 215, 245.

U.S. Bureau of the Census. 1983. Census of Population: 1980. Volume I: Characteristics of the Population. Part 1, U.S. Summary, Chapter B. General Population Characteristics. Washington, D.C.: U.S. Government Printing Office, Tables 40, 50.

U.S. Bureau of the Census. 1984a. Census of Population: 1980. Volume I: Characteristics of the Population. Part 1, U.S. Summary, Chapter D. Detailed Characteristics. Washington, D.C.: U.S. Government Printing Office, Tables 262, 264, 265, 272, 293.

U.S. Bureau of the Census. 1984b. "Projections of the Population of the United States by Age, Sex and Race; 1983 to 2080." *Current Population Reports,* Series P-25, no. 952. Washington, D.C.: U.S. Government Printing Office.

Social and Physical Environments for the Vulnerable Aged

Beth J. Soldo and Charles F. Longino, Jr.

NOTIONS OF VULNERABILITY

Human aging encompasses much more than physiologic change over the life course. Age-related changes are manifest across all aspects of life including physical, environmental, economic, and social aspects and mental well-being. Yet change along any dimension is not simply, or irrevocably, correlated with chronological age.

The serious loss or compromise of capacity in one area, however, can accelerate the rate of decline in others. Such interactions are often complex. Poor health, for example, can require increased medical expenditures that divert income from other essential areas such as home upkeep or the purchase of food. Over time, such interactions can result in further erosion of functional capacity in the aging. Alternatively, a supportive social or physical environment may retard the rate of functional loss to some degree.

Clinical assessment and care plan protocols for the elderly

Beth Soldo is an associate professor in the Department of Demography, Georgetown University, Washington, D.C. Charles Longino, Jr., is the director of the Center for Social Research in Aging at the University of Miami, Coral Gables, Florida. The research reported in this chapter was supported by National Institute on Aging Grant no. R01 AG05153, The Commonwealth Fund Grant no. 7405, and Public Health Service Grant no. 507 RR 07136-15.

typically reflect this multidimensional understanding of the human aging process. But the same perspective does not consistently guide national planning and policy development. With the exception of a limited number of local-area demonstrations (see, e.g., Carcagno and Kemper, 1983; Hicks et al., 1981; U.S. Comptroller General, 1978), assessments of the care requirements of a population often take into consideration only the quantitative aspects of aging, such as rapid increases in both the absolute and relative numbers of the elderly and the unprecedented growth of the oldest old proportion of the population. Demographic analyses also call attention to other important planning variables such as key compositional factors (e.g., the predominance of women in older populations) and the uneven tempo of growth in various segments of the elderly population (Manton and Soldo, 1985b). Yet the study of the quantitative features of population aging can provide only limited information on the status or needs of the elderly. In fact, the diversity of the elderly population undermines the simple logic of extrapolating from the observed age structure to estimates of need. Even among those persons aged 85 and older, there is a subgroup of hardy survivors who are physically and mentally intact. Recent analyses have also isolated a subgroup of the young old (those aged 65–74) who evidence substantial co-morbidity (Soldo and Manton, 1985c).

Effective planning for an aging society clearly requires attention to the qualitative aspects of aging as well as to the quantitative features. Such factors largely define the quality of life at any age and include not only health status but also financial status and aspects of both the social and physical environment. For the frail elderly, however, these same factors are also markers of vulnerability. By this we mean that these factors have the innate potential to mediate—positively or negatively—the behavioral and life-style consequences of chronic ill health (Soldo, 1986). When qualitative factors coalesce into natural coping resources, they can often blunt the demand for formal services, services that are usually financed by the public sector. But when these same factors are deficient or absent, the demand on societal resources can be exacerbated. Thus, the total volume of resources necessary to sustain the elderly depends on the joint distribution of both the quantitative and qualitative features of aged populations.

In this paper, we attempt to integrate a qualitative emphasis that follows from biomedical research and service delivery experience with the quantitative insights of demography. We do so in order to broadly assess (1) the vulnerability of the elderly; (2) the supportive quality of the social and physical environment they occupy; (3) the potential for further environmental amelioration of disability; and (4) potential changes in the mix and distribution of markers of vulnerability over time. In our discussions and analyses, we have restricted our attention to the community-based elderly even while acknowledging the survivorship bias that confounds this approach. That is, the elderly who retain their community residences, even in the wake of substantial disability, are the select survivors of their initial cohorts from which mortality has claimed the less hardy and institutionalization the most vulnerable.

We begin our inquiry by documenting the functional dependencies of the aged and the extent to which the frail elderly of today are also vulnerable financially, socially, and environmentally. Next, we consider service and environmental responses to dependency, distinguishing between formally and naturally organized services. We conclude by identifying some of the specific implications of our analysis for planning efforts—for example, the issues involved in creating environments for "successful" aging.

THE VULNERABLE AGED

Functional Dependency

Our point of departure for examining dimensions of vulnerability among the aged is to consider the health status of the elderly. This is a difficult task if only because the "health" of even a single older person, assessed at but one point in time, summarizes the operation of multiple age- and time-dependent processes, both physiologic and pathologic, that differ in terms of duration, severity, and trajectory (Soldo and Manton, 1985a).

Our main concern, however, is with the health of the population of individuals aged 65 and older. From this perspective, there are two basic assessment strategies. The first requires an examination of the distribution and mix of diseases within the population. In an older population, this approach focuses primarily on the chronic diseases that affect four out of every five of the elderly in the community and nearly all of those in long-term care facilities (Soldo and Manton, 1985b). The disease-specific approach, while offering distinct advantages for epidemiological forecasting, is unwieldy for cross-sectional analysis because neither care needs nor disease severity are uniquely identified with the simple presence or absence of pathology. Of greater utility for our purposes is a functional assessment that examines the behavioral consequences of chronic morbidity. In this approach, deficient functional capacities are viewed as relating directly to the need for assistance, usually from another person, in carrying out such basic functions as eating, bathing, and dressing (Becker and Cohen, 1984; Katz, 1983).

Data from the 1982 National Long-Term Care Survey (NLTCS) offer the opportunity to assess the functional capacity of aged noninstitutionalized persons in considerable detail. This survey, which was sponsored jointly by the Health Care Financing Administration (HCFA) and the assistant secretary for planning and evaluation, was fielded by the U.S. Bureau of the Census.[1] Approximately 36,000 persons from a listing of Medicare enrollees were screened by phone to identify 6,340 noninstitutionalized elderly who reported having a limitation in either the "instrumental activities of daily living" (IADL)[2] or the "activities of daily living" (ADL)[3] that lasted 3 months or longer. A personal review confirmed the presence of such limitations in 5,582 cases (87 percent of those who qualified on the screener). These 5,582 cases represented approximately 4.6 million persons aged 65 and older who live in the community with either IADL or ADL dependencies. The number of cases corresponds to approximately 18.9 percent of all noninstitutionalized elderly.

Table 1 shows estimates of functional dependency by age and sex using two scales of functional disability: the IADL and the ADL. Limitations in the activities of daily living (ADL) are broadly accepted by gerontologists as indexing incapacities for self-care. The 1982 NLTCS assesses performance in six activities: eating, toileting, bathing, bed transference, dressing, and continence. Because these activities scale in the order in which they are lost, a simple count of the number of ADL limitations is a useful summary index of functional incapacity. The instrumental activities of daily living (IADL) scale refers to the capac-

TABLE 1 Percentage of Persons 65 Years of Age and Older Living in the Community with Functional Disabilities, by Age and Sex, 1982

Age and Sex	Type of Dependency				
	Only IADL Limited[a]	ADL Score[b]			
		1–2	3–4	5–6	Total
65–74	4.5	4.2	1.8	2.1	12.6
Male	4.2	3.4	1.7	2.4	11.7
Female	4.8	4.7	1.9	1.9	13.3
75–84	7.9	9.0	3.6	4.5	25.0
Male	7.1	6.5	2.5	4.6	20.9
Female	8.5	10.3	4.3	4.4	27.6
85+	10.2	17.4	7.8	10.4	45.8
Male	9.9	15.7	7.7	7.5	40.8
Female	10.3	18.2	7.9	11.8	48.2
Total 65+	6.0	6.6	2.8	3.5	18.9
Male	5.4	5.1	2.3	3.3	16.0
Female	6.4	7.7	3.2	3.6	20.9

[a]Such individuals need assistance with the instrumental activities of daily living (IADL): managing money, shopping, light housework, meal preparation, making a phone call, and taking medication.
[b]The ADL score is the number of activities of daily living with which the respondent requires assistance.

SOURCE: Tabulations from the 1982 National Long-Term Care Survey.

ity to perform basic but noncare activities, such as managing money or making a phone call. To a large extent the IADL summarize cognitive functioning. Even those elderly individuals with severe physical disability should still be able to use the phone or manage their own money if they are not cognitively limited as well (Manton and Soldo, 1985b).

The data in Table 1 indicate that, although rates of functional dependency increase with age and are typically higher for women than for men, functional loss is not an inevitable consequence of aging. Even at age 85 and older, over half of all those who remain in the community have no measurable loss in their basic capacities. Related analyses of these same data indicate that, among the noninstitutionalized elderly, the loss of functional capacity at the younger ages (65–74 years of age) is associated with life-threatening diseases such as malignant neoplasms; at the extremes of old age, disability is usually related to the chronic degenerative diseases such as senility or arteriosclerosis (Soldo and Manton, 1985c).

The high rates of functional disability at the extreme ages—coupled with unprecedented and largely unanticipated improvements in life expectancy at ages 65 and 85—are often interpreted as implying dramatic increases in the number of the frail elderly (National Center for Health Statistics, 1984; New York State Office for the Aging, 1983; Rice and Feldman, 1983). Although both the existence and magnitude of morbidity–mortality link-

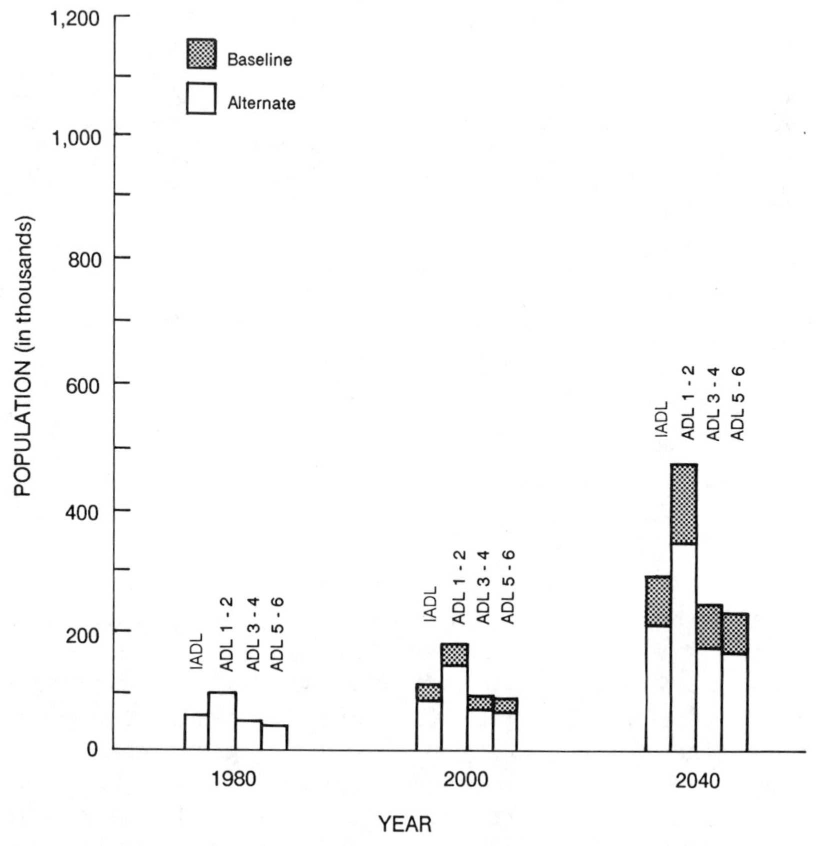

FIGURE 1 Baseline and alternate projections for men aged 85 and older, 1980, 2000, and 2040. Note: Baseline and alternate figures for 1980 are the same. ADL = activities of daily living; IADL = instrumental activities of daily living. SOURCE: Reprinted from Manton and Soldo (1985a).

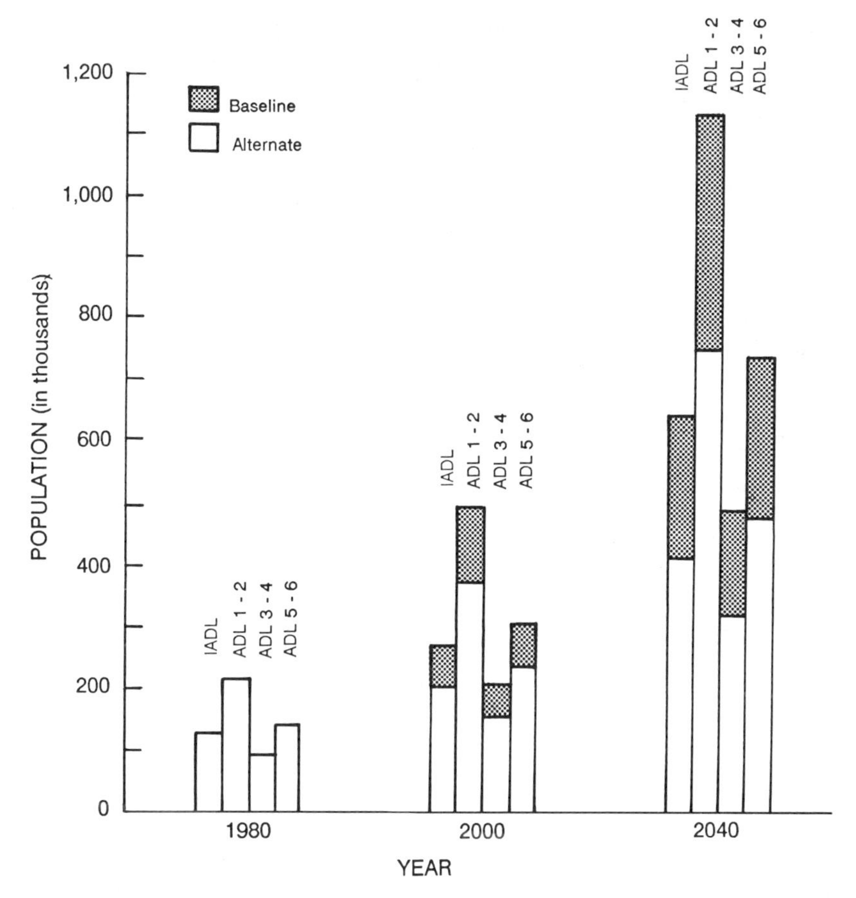

FIGURE 2 Baseline and alternate projections for women aged 85 and older, 1980, 2000, and 2040. Note: Baseline and alternate figures for 1980 are the same. ADL = activities of daily living; IADL = instrumental activities of daily living. SOURCE: Reprinted from Manton and Soldo (1985a).

ages have been the subject of recent and intense debate, we believe it is reasonable to assume that those same factors that have produced increases in old-age life expectancy have also modified the disease and disability profile of the elderly (Feldman, 1982; Fries, 1980, 1983; Gruenberg, 1977; Manton, 1982; Manton and Soldo, 1985a, 1985b; Riley and Bond, 1983; Verbrugge, 1984; and Walford, 1983). This issue is no mere academic debate; as an illustration of this point, consider Figures 1 and 2, reprinted from Manton and Soldo (1985a). These figures show, for men and women, respectively, the projected growth in the absolute number of the frail elderly, aged 85 and older, under alternative assumptions.

The baseline projections assume no improvements in the rates of disability consequent to modest gains in old-age life expectancy; that is, current age–sex specific rates of disability, by type, were superimposed on the age–sex structure implied by projections prepared by the Social Security Administration (1981). These baseline projections can be compared with those prepared under the assumption that age–sex specific disability rates will be reduced in proportion to projected mortality declines. Because of the simple demographic imperative of increasingly larger cohorts entering old age, the number of the frail elderly aged 85 and older increases in either scenario. Yet by allowing for the interdependence of morbidity, disability, and mortality, there is a 27 percent reduction for men and a 39 percent reduction for women in disability rates by the year 2040. Assuming perfect interdependence, there would be approximately 1.4 million fewer disabled persons 85 years of age and older in the year 2040 than if rates of disability are assumed to be independent of mortality declines.

These two scenarios probably represent the best- and worst-case projections in that additional years of life expectancy are unlikely to translate directly into additional disability-free years of life (Wilkins and Adams, 1983). Thus, the two projections may be thought of as indicating the upper and lower bounds on the number of community-based disabled elderly in the future. These projections also suggest the potential role of health care policy in shaping the disability profile of the elderly in the future. Changes in the health status of the elderly are caused by and, in turn, cause major shifts in both the composition of the U.S. population as a whole and in the needs profile of the older ages. In the long run, however, the health care requirements of an aged population also respond to the amount of resources allocated to disease prevention and treatment (Manton and Soldo, 1985a). Yet in the short run as well, the course of disability for individuals and the aggregate volume of demand on the public sector depends, in part, on the "natural" resources available to the disabled elderly, that is, the qualitative aspects of population aging.

Disability and Other Markers of Vulnerability

With the progression of disability, the social world of the elderly often contracts. The social world of the most disabled, for example, may be fully defined by the housing space they occupy. Cross-sectional data offer persuasive but not definitive evidence for the changing utility the frail elderly assign to different household structures, particularly the utility of living alone. The presence of a "caring unit" within a household, for example, often allows the functionally impaired to continue to reside in the community (Branch and Jette, 1982; Brody et al., 1978; Weissert and Scanlon, 1982).

Within a community's population of the frail elderly, there also appears to be a natural sorting-out process that operates, through which the disabled elderly associate themselves with

TABLE 2 Percentage Distribution of Disability Among Community Long-term Care Elderly by Type of Living Arrangement

Type of Living Arrangement	Disability Level				
		ADL Score			
	IADL Only	1–2	3–4	5–6	Total[a]
Alone	34.4	44.5	14.7	6.4	100.0 (1,434)[b]
With spouse[c]	32.1	30.8	15.7	21.4	100.0 (1,918)
With other relations[d]	28.5	30.6	14.1	26.7	100.0 (1,175)
With nonrelative	22.9	34.5	13.6	29.0	100.0 (121)
Total	31.7 (1,472)	35.1 (1,631)	14.9 (694)	18.3 (851)	100.0 (4,648)

NOTE: ADL = activities of daily living; IADL = instrumental activities of daily living.

[a]Totals may reflect rounding.
[b]Weighted base count in thousands.
[c]Includes those who live only with a spouse and those who live with a spouse and others.
[d]Includes those who live only with relatives (not a spouse) and those who live with both relatives and nonrelatives.

SOURCE: Tabulations from the 1982 National Long-Term Care Survey.

living arrangements consistent with the degree of support they require from their immediate environment (Lawton, 1981). Such a gradient of need across types of living arrangements is evident in the data presented in Table 2. Clearly the "luxury of living alone" is reserved for those who can meet the physical demands of household independence (Tissue and McCoy, 1981).

Very few of the severely disabled elderly (i.e., those whose functional self-care capacities are limited in five or six areas) live alone. The different types of shared living arrangements, however, vary in their supportive quality, as indicated by the percentage distribution of "unmet" IADL and ADL dependencies shown in Table 3.

TABLE 3 Percentage Distribution of Unmet Functional Needs Among Community Long-term Care Elderly by Type of Living Arrangement

	Unmet Functional Dependencies			
Type of Living Arrangement	No Unmet Needs	Unmet IADL Needs Only[a]	Unmet ADL Needs[b]	Total[c]
Alone	86.8	9.8	3.4	100.0 (1,434)[d]
With spouse[e]	95.5	3.4	1.1	100.0 (1,918)
With other relatives[f]	93.4	4.1	2.5	100.0 (1,175)
With nonrelatives	91.6	5.5	2.9	100.0 (121)
Total	92.2	5.6	2.2	100.0 (4,648)

[a]Respondents reporting that they need but do not receive help with doing housework/laundry, preparing meals, going grocery shopping, managing money, or managing medications.
[b]Respondents reporting that they need but do not receive help with eating, bed transference, inside mobility, dressing, bathing, and toileting. This group included those who had unmet activities of daily living (ADL) needs with or without unmet instrumental activities of daily living (IADL) needs.
[c] Totals may reflect rounding.
[d]Weighted base counts in thousands.
[e]Includes those who live only with a spouse and those who live with a spouse and others.
[f] Includes those who live only with relatives (not a spouse) and those who live with both relatives and nonrelatives.

SOURCE: Tabulations from the 1982 National Long-Term Care Survey.

In this analysis, persons with care needs are those who did not receive assistance with at least one of the IADL or ADL tasks in which they are dependent. Defined in this way, the prevalence of unmet care needs is not substantial, a circumstance that may reflect underreporting as a result of the long-standing accommodations many frail elderly persons make to the gradual loss of capacity. Nonetheless, approximately 364,000 disabled but noninstitutionalized elderly report at least one neglected aspect of personal care.

Of most interest to the present discussion is not the magnitude of unmet needs as such but rather the systematic differentials in the prevalence of unmet need across types of shared households. The likelihood of unmet care needs varies inversely with the closeness of the bond that relates the disabled elder to other members of the household. Functionally limited elderly persons who live with spouses are the least likely to report areas of unmet need; those living with nonrelatives are the most likely to have unattended areas of care.[4] Related analyses have also shown that those who live with nonrelatives, and particularly those whose care needs are not fully satisfied, are the most likely to be on a waiting list for nursing home admission (Soldo and Manton, 1985c).

The evidence presented in our discussion thus far suggests that the vulnerability of the frail elderly is primarily a reflection of their morbidity and disability and not of inadequate social environments. Apart from obvious measurement problems, the concept of vulnerability as discussed in the preceding paragraphs directs attention to additional aspects of the social and physical world of the disabled. Thus, to consider vulnerability, it is necessary to examine evidence that relates disability to multiple aspects of the environment occupied by the frail elderly.

For this purpose, a simple quality-of-life deficiency index was created by summing respondent reports of deficiencies in five aspects of their social, economic, and physical environments:

- *Financial*—Monthly personal income is less than the 25th percentile of the income distribution, or about $325 per month (25.2 percent).
- *Service*—At least one IADL or ADL care need is neglected in the current care-giving arrangement (7.8 percent).
- *Social*—Contact is not maintained with family or friends

through personal visits or telephone calls, or the current level of contact is reported to be less than desired (49.2 percent).

- *Housing*—There is a perceived but unmet need for special housing modifications such as ramps, grab bars, raised toilets, hand rails, an elevator, or a stair lift (32.9 percent).
- *Neighborhood*—Global dissatisfaction is expressed with the neighborhood or there are perceived problems with local crime or the inconvenient location of food or drug stores (58 percent).

The proportion of older disabled persons affected by each of these deficiencies is shown in parentheses.[5] By these standards, more than half of those with functional limitations live in neighborhoods that they themselves consider to pose serious problems. Nearly half have less social contact with family and friends than they would like, and about a third perceive a need for modifications that would enhance their mobility within their dwelling units. It should be noted that the proportion with inadequate financial resources is fixed by definition. In combination, the most frequent pairings were those in which perceived deficiencies in the neighborhood were augmented by social or housing problems or both.

To consider the extent to which social, economic, and environmental needs tend to cluster within the older population, the tabulation of quality-of-life deficiencies by age and level of disability is shown in Table 4.

Defining vulnerability multidimensionally, we see that nearly 90 percent of the frail elderly are not simply disabled but also socially, economically, or environmentally impoverished as well. Nearly two-thirds are deficient in at least two areas, and slightly more than one-fifth have problems in three or more areas. These data suggest that, for a sizable number of the frail elderly, "natural resources" have not fused into an environment supportive of optimal functioning or well-being. This pattern is true even for those who are able to sustain their community residences in spite of extreme disability. It is also of interest to note that the number of quality-of-life deficiencies varies only slightly with either age or disability. Although any diachronic interpretation, particularly in the absence of a nonfrail comparison group, is problematic, the findings discussed earlier are nonetheless consistent with the interpretation that environmental deficiencies predate frailty. To the extent that such environmental problems

TABLE 4 Percentage Distribution of the Number of Quality-of-Life Deficiencies Among the Functionally Limited Elderly by Age and Level of Disability

Age and Disability Level	Number of Qualify-of-Life Deficiencies[a] 0	1	2	3	4+	Total
65–74						
IADL only	16.6	31.4	33.1	15.1	3.8	100.0
ADL 1–2	11.8	30.6	30.7	20.9	6.1	100.0
ADL 3–4	11.1	28.6	34.1	19.1	7.1	100.0
ADL 5–6	9.8	28.1	33.7	23.2	5.3	100.0
Total	13.1	30.2	32.6	18.9	5.3	100.0 (1,948)[b]
75–84						
IADL only	19.0	28.7	34.0	15.6	2.8	100.0
ADL 1–2	12.2	31.6	32.8	18.1	5.4	100.0
ADL 3–4	11.0	27.6	38.1	16.5	6.9	100.0
ADL 5–6	9.1	33.0	32.6	20.3	5.0	100.0
Total	13.6	30.3	33.9	17.5	4.7	100.0 (1,821)
85+						
IADL only	11.6	32.3	38.3	14.1	3.7	100.0
ADL 1–2	11.7	34.3	30.4	17.1	6.6	100.0
ADL 3–4	11.8	30.3	31.3	23.1	3.5	100.0
ADL 5–6	10.2	30.3	31.5	24.4	3.6	100.0
Total	11.3	32.3	32.6	19.1	4.7	100.0 (879)
65+						
IADL only	16.9	30.4	34.2	15.2	3.4	100.0
ADL 1–2	11.9	31.8	31.5	19.0	5.9	100.0
ADL 3–4	11.2	28.6	35.0	19.0	6.3	100.0
ADL 5–6	9.6	30.5	32.8	22.4	4.8	100.0
Total	13.0	30.6	33.1	18.4	4.9	100.0 (4,648)

NOTE: ADL = activities of daily living; IADL = instrumental activities of daily living.

[a]Summary index indicating deficiencies in five areas: financial, service, social contact, modified housing, and neighborhood. Consult text for complete definitions.
[b]Weighted base counts in thousands.

SOURCE: Tabulations from the 1982 National Long-Term Care Survey.

are also markers of risk for the onset or rapid progression of chronic morbidity, improving the quality of the social and economic environment in which aging occurs may not only improve the quality of life for the already frail but may also retard rates of transition from the well to the disabled state.

In an era of fiscal austerity, the targeting of limited public resources emerges as an important policy issue. The data presented in Table 4, however, provide little guidance for identifying the age or disability groups that would most benefit from programs to enhance environmental quality. In contrast, the distribution of the quality-of-life deficiency index by living arrangements, shown in Table 5, can be used to identify the most vulnerable segments within the older, frail population.

These data indicate that the disabled elderly who live with relatives or nonrelatives have the greatest chance of having at least one environmental deficiency and also are the most likely to have multiple deficiencies in their immediate environment.

TABLE 5 Percentage Distribution of the Number of Quality-of-Life Deficiencies Among the Functionally Limited Elderly by Type of Living Arrangement

Type of Living Arrangement	Number of Quality-of-Life Deficiencies[a]					Total[b]
	0	1	2	3	4+	
Alone	12.1	29.3	34.0	18.7	5.9	100.0 (1,434)[c]
With spouse[d]	15.4	32.5	32.3	16.3	3.5	100.0 (1,918)
With relative[e]	10.3	28.6	33.9	21.4	5.9	100.0 (1,175)
With nonrelative	9.5	30.6	33.1	18.4	4.9	100.0 (121)
Total	13.0	30.6	33.1	18.4	4.9	100.0 (4,648)

[a]Summary index of deficiencies in five areas: financial, service, social contact, modified housing, and neighborhood. Consult text for complete definitions.
[b]Totals may reflect rounding.
[c]Weighted base counts in thousands.
[d]Includes those who live only with a spouse and those who live with a spouse and others.
[e]Includes those who live only with relatives (not a spouse) and those who live with both relatives and nonrelatives.

SOURCE: Tabulations from the 1982 National Long-Term Care Survey.

TABLE 6 Percentage of Functionally Limited Elderly with Housing Adaptations by Level of Disability and Type of Living Arrangement

Type of Living Arrangement	Percentage with Housing Adaptations[a] IADL Only	ADL Score 1–2	3–4	5–6	Total
Alone	20.2	40.4	58.5	56.4	37.1 (1,434)[b]
With spouse[c]	12.1	29.3	39.2	43.1	28.3 (1,918)
With other relatives[d]	10.3	26.1	37.3	32.6	24.9 (1,175)
With nonrelatives only	13.8	49.3	62.5	38.3	34.1 (121)
Total	14.4 (1,472)	33.0 (1,631)	45.2 (694)	40.4 (851)	30.3 (4,648)

NOTE: ADL = activities of daily living; IADL = instrumental activities of daily living.

[a]Installation of ramps, stair lift, elevator, grab bars, handrails, raised toilet, push bars on doors, or widening of door or hallways.
[b]Weighted base counts in thousands.
[c] Includes those who live only with a spouse and those who live with a spouse and others.
[d]Includes those who live only with relatives (not a spouse) and those who live with both relatives and nonrelatives.

SOURCE: Tabulations from the 1982 National Long-Term Care Survey.

Approximately 27 percent of those who live with relatives and 25 percent of those living with nonrelatives have three or more environmental deficiencies. Because each of these arrangements has the built-in potential for social interaction, multiple deficiencies summarize economic and housing/neighborhood inadequacies—areas of need that are most amenable to program intervention. These data also suggest that, even among the frail elderly, coresiding with others may be, in part, motivated by economic reasons (Soldo et al., 1984).

additional insights into the environmental quality associated with different types of living arrangements are offered in Table 6, which displays the percentage of the elderly, within each type of living arrangement and at each level of disability, who live in a household in which environmental modifications have been made. Although approximately one-third of the frail elderly live in households with housing adaptations, the incidence of such modifications is greatest for those living alone, particularly those with high levels of disability. Over half of the elderly who live alone and are limited in three or more activities of daily living have made housing modifications. Undoubtedly, such adaptations in the built environment are essential to avoid institutionalization in the absence of a live-in care provider.

The elderly who live with others may trade off personal assistance for environmental compensation. For nearly half of the extremely disabled who live with spouses, however, housing modifications would appear to supplement rather than replace in-home care giving. In contrast, the very frail elderly who live with other relatives are less likely to live in homes in which environmental features reduce the care-giving demands and burdens. The NLTCS is not sufficiently detailed to determine whether this pattern reflects financial constraints operating in multigenerational households or a less durable commitment of nonspousal care givers to home care (Hess and Soldo, 1985). Nonetheless, these data suggest that modifications to the built environment may be an important strategy for reducing the care-giving burden, particularly in dwelling units in which a relative is the primary care giver. Further research is required to determine whether such adaptive housing modifications are generally cost effective in extending the care-giving commitment and thereby delaying nursing home admissions. The effectiveness of such environmental strategies is most likely to be greatest in situations in which personal care dependencies are not complicated by cognitive impairment.

The evidence presented in this section has two significant implications for the analysis of the needs of the frail elderly. First, in the vast majority of cases, the needs of the elderly are not discrete but appear as a cluster. Disability is often linked with multiple deficiencies in the social and economic resource base of the frail elderly. Thus, the preceding analysis provides empirical support for Lawton's (1978) argument that the number of truly independent elderly is very small, indeed. Viewed longitudinally, the number of persons whose total resources across all dimensions are sufficient to sustain them over a lifetime is even smaller.

This finding also indicates that effective planning and program development must address varying sets of needs. Yet integrated service delivery systems are much more the exception than the rule. In part, this is because the federal infrastructure (i.e., the committee system within Congress and the departmental structure within the executive branch) is not naturally organized to foster integrated program planning or implementation. As a result, eligibility standards are not uniform, assessments of need are seldom coordinated, and orchestrating the necessary service bundle usually falls to the older person or his/her family.

Second, the preceding analysis also demonstrates the heterogeneity of the older population. Whereas differences by age within the older population are routinely documented by demographers (Myers, 1985), the diversity within levels of disability has only recently come to be fully appreciated (Manton and Soldo, 1985a). Within the community long-term care population, there exist individuals at all levels of disability whose care needs are augmented by inadequacies in numerous other aspects of the social and physical environments they occupy. Contrasts between the long-term care populations in the community and those in the nursing home have demonstrated significant differences between the two groups in terms of social support networks and prior living arrangements (see, e.g., Weissert and Scanlon, 1982). Nevertheless, such findings cannot be allowed to overshadow the need for incorporating notions of heterogeneity into national planning efforts for the noninstitutionalized but frail elderly.

Intercohort differences, and the heterogeneity to which these differences give rise, must also be factored into national planning efforts, particularly with respect to the prevalence of disease and associated health care needs. There are, for example, significant differences across cohorts in the prevalence of various chronic diseases—for example, cardiovascular disease (Patrick et al., 1982). Such differences suggest that, apart from changes in the volume of health and personal care services required in the future, there will also be significant differences in the mix of care services required by the population at any point in time. Forecasts of need based only on period data will not accurately reflect health-status changes that are driven by cohort differences.

RESPONSES TO DEPENDENCY

Just as there are differences in the types and clusters of needs that are manifest among the elderly at any single point in time, so too is there considerable variability in the style and mix of responses made to dependency. In this section, we consider two generic strategies for accommodating dependency: service responses and environmental responses. We make this distinction only for the ease of discussion. In practice, the two approaches are not mutually exclusive. Community programs, for example, may link relocation to upgraded housing units with increased access to supportive services (Lawton, 1980b). Regardless of how compensation strategies are structured, the implicit common denominator is an understanding of behavior within a person–environment interaction framework (Lawton, 1980a; Nahemow and Lawton, 1973). The degree of functional capacity is seen as being jointly determined by individual characteristics and the multidimensional nature of the social and physical environment.

Although it would be desirable to parallel our discussion of multidimensional vulnerability with an examination of response clusters, existing data bases provide little opportunity for each analysis.[6] Hence, in the following discussion, we confine our attention to responses to personal care dependencies. We exclude medical care services because these are assumed to be provided by a health care worker, usually in a health care facility.[7]

Service Responses

Service responses to frailty can be arrayed across at least two continua. One continuum is defined in terms of the relationship of the care provider to the frail older person. This continuum is anchored at one end by an exclusive reliance on family and friends—the informal support network—and on the other end by the receipt of formally organized services. The second continuum is defined in terms of frequency and regularity of service receipt. In general, those elderly persons who require only periodic assistance, such as help with grocery shopping, rely on family and friends, whereas those whose needs are complex and unrelenting are likely to depend on a mix of formal and informal services in the community (Soldo, 1985; Doty, 1986).

Table 7 presents data on community care patterns. Over 90 percent of the frail elderly receive nonmedical care service from their informal support networks. In three-quarters of these cases, the family is the sole provider. Only 7.5 percent of the frail elderly rely exclusively on formal community services. The data shown in this table also indicate that the boundaries of the informal support network extend beyond the household of the frail elderly—nearly one-third of the frail elderly receive assistance from friends and relatives with whom they do not live. Thus, the social world of the disabled often extends, albeit indirectly, outside the immediate household.

Under current health care financing arrangements, it is clear that the informal support network provides the bulk of personal care assistance. Related research testifies to the extent of family involvement (Manton and Soldo, 1985b), the effectiveness of such care in delaying institutionalization (Brody et al., 1978), and the extent to which informal care giving reduces the demand for formal care services (Soldo, 1985). Perhaps of most interest for anticipating the service requirements of aged populations are the differences in the probability of formal service receipt by type of living arrangement. At any level of need, the probability

TABLE 7 Percentage of Functionally Limited Elderly with Housing Modifications Differentiated by Whether or Not Such Modifications Would Make Life Easier

	Percentage with Housing Modifications[a]	
Disability Level	Would Be Easier	Would Not Be Easier
IADL limit only	15.3	14.2
ADL 1–2	28.6	35.1
ADL 3–4	41.8	47.5
ADL 5–6	37.8	42.5
Total	30.9	30.0
	(1,482)[b]	(3,167)

NOTE: ADL = activities of daily living; IADL = instrumental activities of daily living.

[a]Installation of ramps, stair lift, elevator, grab bars, handrails, raised toilet, push bars on doors, or widening of doors or hallways.
[b]Weighted base counts in thousands.

SOURCE: Tabulations from the 1982 National Long-Term Care Survey.

of formal service is lowest for the frail elderly who live either with spouses or other relatives (Soldo, 1985).

These findings, in conjunction with the data presented in Table 5, suggest that the volume of demand for publicly financed services will be greatly influenced by the distribution of the disabled elderly across different types of living arrangements. In anticipating future service demands, a number of other factors must be considered as well: changes in intergenerational attitudes, the increasing incidence of divorce, and the course of sex differentials in old-age mortality. Yet allowing only for changes in the age structure, Glick (1979) has projected continued increases in the number of elderly persons, particularly older women, who live alone. His projections indicate that the demand for community long-term care will far outpace the growth of even the disabled portion of the elderly. Barring changes in service delivery approaches, these projections also suggest that the relative number of older persons with unmet care needs or with multiple social and environmental deficiencies may increase over time.

In addition to strengthening the arguments for integrated long-range planning, the data considered in this section highlight the difficult policy choices involved in accommodating a rapidly growing population. Current long-term care policy directives are oriented toward reducing the rates of nursing home admissions by encouraging home-based care. Whether this policy proves to be a cost-effective strategy remains to be seen (Weissert, 1981), but this potential shift in policy is already raising questions concerning the limits of our collective and filial responsibility to the dependent elderly (Soldo et al., 1985). As the pace of population aging quickens, such value-based dilemmas will undoubtedly assume greater urgency. They are discussed more fully in the next sections.

Environmental Responses to Dependency

Environmental responses to dependency are seldom independent of service responses, and the two overlap nearly completely in the extreme response of institutionalization. Our concern, however, is with the more commonplace responses that occur in the community. We have noted the propensity of the disabled elderly to accommodate their limitations by making explicit changes in the physical space they occupy. Care-giving households often make less dramatic and permanent changes as when the "sick" room is relocated to the dining room for the convenience of both the care provider and the care receiver (Noelker, 1982).

Yet changes in the structure or organization of dwelling units do not encompass the vast array of environmental responses to dependency. Often, the environmental context of disability is involuntarily defined in the case in which an older person continues to maintain a long-standing and familiar residence even as the social world of the neighborhood deteriorates. In this section, however, we focus more narrowly on the ways in which disability is accommodated through residential relocation.

Our knowledge of the prosthetic effect of the immediate housing environment for the frail elderly is informed primarily by studies of "special populations"—for example, elderly persons who relocate to age-segregated buildings, service-saturated demonstration projects, or wealthy retirement communities.[8] Such individuals are self-selected and hardly represent the vast majority of elderly who age in place or move from one private dwelling to another. Nonetheless, prior research tends to demonstrate the positive effects on global or subjective markers of well-being that can result from improved housing environments. For this reason, we examine next the process by which supportive environments are sought out as an accommodation to age-related changes in personal needs.

Retirement Communities

When the Social Security Administration initially funded the Comparative Study of Midwestern Retirement Communities a decade ago, its focal interest was a comparative evaluation of the costs and benefits of living in age-focused housing (Peterson et al., 1979). Study settings were chosen to represent a range of types of niches or localized living environments whose costs, degrees of service, and natural settings differed considerably. The sites chosen for this study included high-rise, central-city public housing developments for the aged, a large suburban life-care village, and small towns in the Ozarks region of Southern Missouri that had essentially become retirement communities through the in-migration and dense concentration of recently retired people. Each community attracted a different mix of residents.

Although the residents of the public housing site had appreciably lower incomes than the residents of the life-care community, older persons in both of these planned environments were more likely than those who lived in nonstructured communities to describe their health as "good." Such preliminary findings would seem to imply that the residents of housing developments for the elderly are better off than they would be in other environments. Yet almost all voluntary movers evidence higher levels of satisfaction in their new surroundings than at their former address. In addition, retirement communities are specialized living environments and do not attract a representative cross section of the older population.

The problem of assessing the prosthetic effects of the housing environment occupied by an elderly person independent of the effects of self-selection was addressed by drawing a shadow sample of matching controls from a national opinion survey (Longino et al., 1981). Researchers then administered an instrument to residents of the study sites that contained many of the attitudinal items from the national survey. In this way, self-selection (at least on background variables) was controlled for in the analysis of relative benefits. It was possible, therefore, to assess environmental effects with some confidence by comparing the quality of life of residents in the study communities with similar people in the general population.

The results of the study indicated that the life-care community provided measurable benefits to residents in the areas of medical care, freedom from the fear of crime, and loneliness and boredom. The cost-of-housing benefit was negative; the same tangible housing and services could have been purchased more cheaply in suburban areas elsewhere. The intangibles of life-care community living, however, seemed to make a substantial difference to the residents. They felt that they were getting a "good deal"; their morale was higher than that of their counterparts elsewhere.

Yet it appeared from the study results that beneficial living environments are not reserved solely for the affluent. People in the shadow sample were far more likely to complain about insufficient medical care than were the residents of the public housing site for the elderly. Residents also benefited from a reduced fear of crime. (Many of the residents had moved from high crime areas into the public housing units, whose security guards and exclusively elderly residents made them feel safer.)

Similar conclusions were drawn, with one key exception, when rural retired migrants were compared with their shadow sample from the general population. The Ozarks residents, while feeling safer from crime and more socially adequate in every way than their counterparts in the general population, were much more likely to complain about insufficient medical care.

Although we might expect those elderly persons who selected more supportive environments to show improved functional capacity, such improvement is not always the case. In comparing several groups of such residents with stationary community controls, Lawton (1980b) reported a relative and substantial decline in functional capacity among the frail elderly who moved into five different housing projects. Because factors that generally have a positive bearing on health (morale, social behavior, and leisure-time activity) were negatively correlated with functional capacity in the 12-month follow-up assessment, Lawton speculates that the net effect of programmatically improved housing may be to "buffer the individual against a decline in health, so that attitudes, affect, and even some forms of social involvement, could remain at relatively favorable levels" (1980b). Consequently, elderly public housing residents may consider their medical care to be more adequate than that of their community counterparts, but this belief does not necessarily translate into improved functional capacity. However, several other markers of vulnerability are lessened in this type of housing environment.

The Comparative Study of Midwestern Retirement Communities indicated that the factors motivating a change of housing environments were predictably related to the likely outcome of a residential move. Resource deficits in the face of declining functional capacity can trigger a change in residential location. Both subsidized and nonsubsidized planned communities are service-enriched living environments, designed with the needs of older residents in mind. The people who move to such places tend to be motivated by perceived deficiencies in their previous housing and community environments; in their reasons for moving, they tend to emphasize those very areas of support that are the strengths of the planned community. Thus, people who are attracted to such communities tend to have characteristics that imply greater need and vulnerability. The fit between living environment and individual needs would seem to be reasonably good in such settings. Persons with a greater need for support in the instrumental activities of daily living tend to be attracted to communities built to meet those needs, and support seems to flow from within the community to the persons who move there (Longino, 1986; Longino and Lipman, 1981, 1986, Peterson et al., 1979).

Indirect Environmental Influences

Preliminary evidence also suggests that aspects of the built environment can influence, both positively and negatively, not only disability itself but also the ease with which care services are provided (Newman, 1985). Noelker (1982), for example, has recently reported on an innovative study of the environmental impediments to care in households shared by the care provider and his or her relative. Both spatial barriers (e.g., inadequate number of bedrooms) and navigational barriers (e.g., interior stairs) were found frequently. Spatial barriers were most highly correlated with tension among household members, perhaps stemming from a lack of privacy; navigational barriers were positively correlated with the number of personal care tasks with which the elderly person required assistance and the care provider's perception of the difficulty in providing such care.

Although most home care programs emphasize service delivery, modifications of the built environments in which care is provided may also be effective in preventing or postponing institutional placements. Because housing seems to affect the style, intensity, durability, and tolerability of care giving, it is fair to conclude that, in this context, housing characteristics function as important intermediate variables. The size, condition, and location of the involved households all indirectly affect the degree of fit between the elderly person's needs and the available compensating social resources.

FUTURE CONSIDERATIONS

In this paper, we have presented a wide array of data relating the disability of the elderly to markers of vulnerability in other areas and finally to a range of both service and environmental adaptations. Yet despite the range of information we have assembled, it is clear that we lack the detailed data necessary to the simultaneous examination of all of the quantitative and qualitative dimensions of population aging. As a result, many of our comments have been speculative, drawing particular attention to the gaps in our knowledge of how different types of people actually live in natural environments and why they function as they do (Parr, 1980).

We are impressed by the magnitude of change projected in the number of the frail elderly, even under the most optimistic of scenarios. To respond to this volume of demand, it is clear that our society cannot afford to dismiss out of hand any strategies that have the potential to be both cost effective and efficient. This imperative includes leveraging certain aspects of the social and built environments to enhance their functional capacity.

In the past decade, we have seen the development of a widespread community awareness of the needs of handicapped persons. This awareness derives from and perhaps has contributed to the parking and building regulations that have helped to eliminate barriers to the activities of the handicapped, thereby increasing their independence and productivity. The possibility of adapting our built environment for the disabled is no longer a novel idea. As the U.S. population ages, community awareness and acceptance of environmental modifications are likely to continue and expand.

Creating environments that are more supportive of older, functionally limited persons is not the exclusive purview of the public sector, however. Building codes and zoning regulations can obligate builders to add features that make new construction less hostile to persons who are restricted in their mobility. The private sector already is vigorously marketing planned, supportive housing for the marginally disabled. These efforts are likely to intensify as long as the number of old persons who can afford such environments increases. Even under the assumptions of modest economic growth, we can anticipate further increases in at least the absolute number of the future elderly with the financial wherewithal to "buy into" planned communities.

Despite the likely improvements in the financial profile of each new cohort, however, there will continue to be sizable numbers of older persons who will not be able to compete effectively for the prosthetic goods and services they will require. Meeting the needs of the low-income elderly will most likely remain the responsibility of the public sector while the private sector pursues the more affluent segment. Policymakers and planners concerned with the well-being of the elderly thus will be faced with two issues: one old and one new.

The perennial question in a pluralistic society such as ours is how to provide for the elderly—the poor and wealthy alike—in a manner that is "just" and "equitable." Given the rate at which the number of elderly persons and the volume of their needs are increasing, we must put aside any thought of meeting all the needs of all the elderly. Even taking as an objective a level of service far short of that goal, few societies can provide for even the minimal needs of their elderly populations without compromising some other social good, such as education, security, transportation, or environmental protection, goods that benefit young and old alike. Thus, the overarching issue in planning for an aged population is one of resource allocation, which subsumes, albeit implicitly, concerns for distributive justice.

Let us consider the implications of the allocation question even at the service delivery level. As noted earlier, the social and environmental resources available to an impaired older person are often reviewed in developing a care plan. It is not clear, however, how this information should be used in assigning service priorities. Tentative evidence, including some of the data presented earlier in this paper, suggests, for example, that a spouse's commitment to noninstitutional care is more durable than that of adult children, other relatives, or friends. Should other research confirm this finding, equity questions would arise concerning the appropriateness of concentrating public expenditures on elderly persons who are cared for by individuals other than spouses—that is, the equity of concentrating public monies on elderly persons whose resources for accommodating dependency are constrained and whose risk of a nursing home placement would appear to be greatest.

The Tawlsean principle of justice would require that society benefit those who are least advantaged socially or environmentally. But other understandings of justice may mandate that all of the frail elderly and their care providers, regardless of income, have an equal claim on available resources or an equal claim to a minimum level of assistance.

Similar questions may arise around the issue of providing

intensive care services to kinless elderly. Conventional service delivery wisdom is to focus service provision on such individuals. The materials presented earlier in this paper suggest that environmental modifications in the immediate household should also be considered to facilitate the optimal functioning of those with an inadequate support network. It seems clear, however, that the most technically advanced modifications, even in combination with intensive home care services, can elevate functioning only so much and sustain it only so long. For such individuals, institutionalization may be all but inevitable in the long run. This argument suggests that the most efficient and effective strategy of allocation might be to concentrate public resources on those whose nexus of private resources are most conducive to noninstitutional care.

We certainly do not claim to have the answers to these difficult questions. But when resources are finite, difficult choices must be made that may benefit one group at the expense of another. It is clear that, no matter how seemingly objective our attempts to construct the process of choice in formulating a national policy on aging, in the end, we must still confront value questions—and we must confront them directly in an orderly, critical, and reasonable way (Soldo et al., 1985).

A relatively new issue on the planning horizon is how to "create" environments that are conducive to successful aging. The solution to this question is not likely to be found in a unitary master plan generated either by the public or the private sector. It is more likely that a diverse array of "building blocks" will be made available to the disabled elderly and their care providers. These components will include increased and varied opportunities for adaptations to existing housing units, home-delivered services, and planned living environments that offer different mixes of ancillary services. Individuals may then choose from among the components of their expanding opportunity set the environmental, service, and health care service bundle that best balances needs with resources.

We believe that public policy is far less likely to create new environments for the vulnerable elderly in this century than it is to encourage the production of new "building blocks" with which people can create their own customized environments. Whereas this prophecy would seem to be a direct translation of contemporary political attitudes, we maintain that our rationale reflects an awareness of the heterogeneity of the elderly population as a whole and of the frail elderly in particular. Taking account of this heterogeneity in the formulation of public policy may be the hallmark of new initiatives that struggle, in a relatively short time, to accommodate the large baby boom cohorts and differing mixes of needs and resources.

NOTES

1. The methods and procedures of this survey are described in detail by Macken (1986).
2. The instrumental activities of daily living (IADL) scale measures the performance of the following tasks: managing money, shopping, light housework, laundry, meal preparation, making a phone call, and taking medication.
3. The activities of daily living (ADL) scale measures the unassisted performance of the following tasks: eating, bed/chair transference, indoor and outdoor mobility, dressing, bathing, and toileting. Respondents reporting incontinence problems also qualified for survey participation.
4. Other analyses indicated that the prevalence of unmet need decreases slightly with age and is greater for women than for men at any age or for any type of living arrangement.
5. Although it would be desirable to disaggregate this summary index to show patterns of deficiency, the unweighted sample size was sufficient to support this level of detail. This claim also applies to the statements in the next two paragraphs.
6. Newman (1985) also reports that, although rates of mobility limitations increase with age among the elderly, the prevalence of substandard housing conditions (defined in terms of the U.S. Department of Housing and Urban Development's [HUD's] criteria for physically adequate dwelling units) was fairly constant across age groups.
7. The recently released Survey of Income and Program Participation (SIPP), however, will provide data on the benefits individuals receive from a number of publicly financed programs.
8. In 1982 only about 9 percent of all community elderly with functional limitations received care at home from a visiting nurse. Approximately 2 percent received a home visit from a physician (Soldo and Manton, 1985c).

REFERENCES

Becker, P. M., and H. J. Cohen. 1984. "The Functional Approach to the Care of the Elderly: A Conceptual Framework." *Journal of the American Geriatric Society* 32:923–929.

Branch, L. G., and A. M. Jette. 1982. "A Prospective Study of Long-term Care Institutionalization Among the Elderly." *American Journal of Public Health* 72:1373–1379.

Brody, S., S. W. Poulshock, and C. F. Masciocchi. 1978. "The Family Caring Unit: A Major Consideration in the Long-term Care System." *Gerontologist* 18:556–561.

Carcagno, G. J., and P. Kemper. 1983. "The National Long-term Care Demonstration: Operational Issues in Developing the Research Design." *Home Health Care Services Quarterly* 4:31–46.

Doty, P. 1986. "Family Care of the Elderly: The Role of Public Policy." *Milbank Quarterly* 64:34–75.

Feldman, J. J. 1982. "Work Ability of the Aged Under Conditions of Improving Mortality." Statement before the National Commission on Social Security Reform, Washington, D.C. June 21.

Fries, J. F. 1980. "Aging, Natural Death and the Compression of Morbidity." *New England Journal of Medicine* 303:130–135.

Fries, J. F. 1983. "The Compression of Morbidity." *Milbank Memorial Fund Quarterly/Health and Society* 61:397–419.

Glick, P. C. 1979. "The Future Marital Status and Living Arrangements of the Elderly." *The Gerontologist* 19:301–309.

Gruenberg, E. M. 1977. "The Failures of Success." *Milbank Memorial Fund Quarterly/Health and Society* 55:3–24.

Hess, B. B., and B. J. Soldo. 1985. "Husband and Wife Networks." In *Social Support Networks and the Care of the Elderly: Theory, Research, Practice and Policy,* W. J. Sauer and R. F. Coward, eds. New York: Springer.

Hicks, B., H. Raisz, J. Segal, and N. Dohery. 1981. "The Triage Experiment in Coordinated Care for the Elderly." *American Journal of Public Health* 71:991–1003.

Katz, S. 1983. "Assessing Self-Maintenance: Activities of Daily Living, Mobility, and Instrumental Activities of Daily Living." *Journal of the American Geriatric Society* 31:721–727.

Lawton, M. P. 1978. "The Housing Problems of Community-Resident Elderly." Occasional Papers in Housing and Community Affiars, no. 1. Washington, D.C.: U.S. Department of Housing and Urban Development.

Lawton, M. P. 1980a. *Environment and Aging.* Monterey, Calif.: Brook/Cole.

Lawton, M. P. 1980b. *Social and Medical Services in Housing for the Aged.* Washington, D.C.: Government Printing Office.

Lawton, M. P. 1981. "An Ecological View of Living Arrangements." *Gerontologist* 21:59–66.

Longino, C. F., Jr. 1986. "Personal Determinants and Consequences of Independent Housing Choices." In *Housing an Aging Society,* R. Newcomber, M. P. Lawton, and T. Byert, eds. New York: Van Nostrand Reinhold.

Longino, C. F., Jr., and A. Lipman. 1981. "Married and Spouseless Men and Women in Planned Retirement Communities: Support Network Differentials." *Journal of Marriage and the Family* 43:169–177.

Longino, C. F., Jr., K. A. McClelland, and W. A. Peterson. 1981. "The Aged Subculture Hypothesis: Social Integration, Gerontophilia and Self-Conception." *Journal of Gerontology* 35:758–767.

Macken, C. L. 1986. "A Profile of Functionally Impaired Persons Living in the Community." *Health Care Financing Review* 7:33–49.

Manton, K. G. 1982. "Changing Concepts of Morbidity and Mortality in the Elderly Populations." *Milbank Memorial Fund Quarterly/Health and Society* 60:183–243.

Manton, K. G., and B. J. Soldo. 1985a. "Dynamics of Health Changes in the Oldest Old: New Perspectives and Evidence." *Milbank Memorial Fund Quarterly/Health and Society* 63:206–285.

Manton, K. G., and B. J. Soldo. 1985b. "Long-range Planning for the Elderly: An Integrated Policy Perspective." Paper prepared for the U.S. Senate Special Committee on Aging.

Myers, G. C. 1985. "Aging and Worldwide Population Change." In *Handbook of Aging and the Social Sciences,* R. H. Binstock and E. Shanas, eds. New York: Van Nostrand Reinhold.

Nahemow, L., and M. P. Lawton. 1973. "Toward an Ecological Theory of Adaptation and Aging." In *Environmental Design Research,* vol. 1, W. Priesen, ed. Stroudsburg, Pa.: Dowden, Hutchinson, and Ross.

National Center for Health Statistics. 1984. "Changes in Mortality Among the Elderly: United States, 1970–78, Supplement to 1980." *Vital and Health Statistics,* series 3, no. 22a. Rockville, Md.

New York State Office for the Aging. 1983. *Family Caregiving and the Elderly.* Albany, N.Y.

Newman, S. J. 1985. "Housing and Long-term Care: The Suitability of the Elderly's Housing to the Provision of In-home Services." *Gerontologist* 25:35–40.

Noelker, L. 1982. "The Impact of Environmental Problems on Caring for Impaired Elders in a Home Setting." Paper presented at the 35th Annual Scientific Meeting of the Gerontological Society of America, Boston, Mass.

Parr, J. 1980. "The Interactions of Persons and Living Environments." In *Aging in the 1980s: Psychological Issues,* L. W. Poon, ed. Washington, D.C.: American Psychological Association.

Patrick, C. H., Y. Y. Palesch, M. Feinleib, and J. A. Brody. 1982. "Sex Differences in Declining Cohort Death Rates from Heart Disease." *American Journal of Public Health* 72:161–166.

Peterson, W. A., C. F. Longino, Jr., and L. W. Phelps. 1979. *A Study of Security, Health and Social Support Systems and Adjustments of Residents in Selected Congregate Living and Retirement Settings.* Washington, D.C.: Social Security Administration.

Rice, D. P., and J. J. Feldman. 1983. "Living Longer in the United States: Demographic Changes in Health Needs of the Elderly." *Milbank Memorial Fund Quarterly/Health and Society* 61:393–396.

Riley, M. W., and K. Bond. 1983. "Beyond Ageism: Postponing the Onset of Disability." In *Aging in Society: Selected Reviews of Recent Research,* M. W. Riley, B. B. Hess, and K. Bond, eds. Hillsdale, N.J.: Lawrence Erlbaum Associates.

Social Security Administration. 1981. "Social Security Area Population Projections." Office of the Actuary, Actuarial Study no. 85. SSA Pub. No. 11-11532. Washington, D.C.: Government Printing Office.

Soldo, B. J. 1985. "In-home Services for the Dependent Elderly: Determinants of Current Use and Implications for Future Demand." *Research on Aging* 7:281–304.

Soldo, B. J. 1986. "Household Types, Housing Needs, and Disability." In *Housing an Aging Society,* R. J. Newcomer, M. P. Lawton, and T. O. Byerts, eds. New York: Van Nostrand Reinhold.

Soldo, B. J., and K. G. Manton. 1985a. "Demographic Challenges for Socioeconomic Planning." *Journal of Socioeconomic Planning Sciences* 19:227–247.

Soldo, B. J., and K. G. Manton. 1985b. "Health Status and Service Needs of the Oldest Old: Current Patterns and Future Trends." *Milbank Memorial Fund Quarterly/Health and Society* 63:286–319.

Soldo, B. J., and K. G. Manton. 1985c. "Heterogeneity Within the Population of Functionally Limited Elderly: Differences by Medicaid Status." Paper prepared under a subcontract to Systemetrics and LaJolla Management Corporation for a project funded by the U.S. Department of Health and Human Services, Health Care Financing Administration.

Soldo, B. J., E. D. Pellegrino, and J. T. Howell. 1985. "Epilogue: Confronting the Age of Aging." *Journal of Socioeconomic Planning Sciences* 19:289–293.

Soldo, B. J., M. Sharma, and R. T. Campbell. 1984. "Determinants of Community Living Arrangements of Older Unmarried Women." *Journal of Gerontology* 39:492–498.

Tissue, T., and J. L. McCoy. 1981. "Income and Living Arrangements Among Poor Aged Singles." *Social Security Bulletin* 44:3–31.

U.S. Comptroller General. 1978. "The Well-Being of Older People in Cleveland, Ohio." Report to Congress. Washington, D.C.: Government Printing Office.

Verbrugge, L. M. 1984. "Longer Life But Worsening Health? Trends in Health and Mortality of Middle-Aged and Older Persons." *Milbank Memorial Fund Quarterly/Health and Society* 62:475–519.

Walford, R. 1983. "Testimony Before the Subcommittee on Savings, Pensions, and Investment Policy of the Committee on Finance, U.S. Senate." Senate Hearing Document no. 98-359. Washington, D.C.: Government Printing Office.

Walter, A. R. 1985. "The Mediating Role of Social Networks in the Housing Decisions of the Elderly." In *Social Bonds in Later Life: Aging and Interdependence,* W. A. Peterson and J. Quadagno, eds. Beverly Hills, Calif.: Sage.

Weissert, W. 1981. "Long-term Care: Current Policy and Directions for the 1980s." Paper presented at the 1981 White House Conference on Aging, Washington, D.C.

Weissert, W., and W. Scanlon. 1982. "Determinants of Institutionalization of the Aged." Working Paper no. 1466-21 (rev.). Washington, D.C.: The Urban Institute.

Wilkins, R., and O. Adams. 1983. *Healthfulness of Life.* Montreal: Institutes for Research on Public Policy.

Current and Emerging Issues in Housing Environments for the Elderly

Raymond J. Struyk

The dominant issue in the debate surrounding the housing environment of the elderly is how to construct public assistance to support those housing transitions that are necessary to allow community-based housing to become an active and integral element in the overall long-term care system.

Two attributes in particular should affect the way we think about housing interventions for the elderly population. First, as people reach retirement age, they experience numerous changes, sometimes in rapid succession: incomes fall from preretirement levels, children leave home, health problems and activity limitations emerge, a spouse requires institutionalization or dies. Such a variety of life events means that any public policy to help with housing problems of such individuals must be flexibly designed; it should range from rent supplements to counseling homeowners about various housing options to the provision of support services to compensate for the inability to perform key activities of daily living.

Second, the elderly cannot be viewed as a monolithic group. As has just been suggested, they have widely different housing-related problems. What is at least as important is that individuals in the elderly population differ in three fundamental ways

---

Raymond J. Struyk is with the Urban Institute.

that must be taken into account in designing public policy: (1) health status (including activity limitations), (2) economic resources, and (3) householding status—whether they are homeowners or renters. Again, the resultant emphasis is on policies that are flexible enough to accommodate the elderly in these various circumstances.

The balance of this essay is in six main sections. It begins with a general inventory of the housing problems of the elderly that considers dwelling-specific items as well as the need for supportive services. The second section reviews current federal housing assistance programs for the elderly; the third presents a framework for thinking about housing policy that goes considerably beyond the present programmatic structure. The fourth section describes three specific federal housing interventions that could meet the requirement of being an element in a long-term care system. The next section gives some idea of the possible consequences of adopting such interventions, and the final section provides conclusions.

HOUSING AND HOUSING-RELATED NEEDS

This section, which draws heavily on an earlier paper (Struyk and Katsura, 1985), inventories the current housing needs of the elderly to provide an idea of the extent of the need for various types of housing assistance. The inventory is not extrapolated into the future because making such estimates is a highly complicated task, the outcomes of which are dependent on broad economic and housing market developments, trends in pension payments, and changes in the incidence and severity of health problems and activity limitations.

In considering the housing needs of the elderly, it is useful to make a distinction between traditional housing "problems" and the particular needs that arise from the health problems and activity limitations that are frequently the lot of elder citizens. The housing problems of the elderly (called dwelling-specific problems hereafter) include deficiencies in the dwelling, the high price of housing relative to income, and overcrowded conditions. All of these are problems that can be measured in fairly straightforward ways and whose definition does not generally have a special dimension for the elderly. Other, more general aspects of the housing environment—for example, conditions in the neighborhood, the convenience and quality of local shopping and medical services—are also relevant. These latter aspects are not as well measured in the available data, however, and are not treated further here.[1]

Housing problems associated with activity limitations or so-called dwelling-use problems are much less precisely defined. Indeed, activity limitations, which are used here as a shorthand label for the larger set of health-related problems, are better thought of as an indicator of a potential housing problem. Limitations on the activities of the elderly can mean that they are unable to use their dwelling fully. For example, they may be unable to use the kitchen and bathroom without assistance (possibly because the rooms are inconveniently located in relation to living and sleeping areas), clean and maintain their home properly, or go shopping without help. On the other hand, these limitations may be effectively offset by the assistance provided by other family members or neighbors or by modifications to the dwelling itself. Unfortunately, the only general measures of housing needs arising from activity limitations focus on the limitations themselves and not on the services the household must do without because of them.

Thus, to determine the number of elderly persons with housing-related problems, we must combine reasonably rigorous estimates of traditional dwelling-specific problems with less direct estimates of dwelling-use problems. One major difficulty—this time because of data limitations—is calculating the joint occurrence of dwelling-specific and supportive service needs. The apparent needs for support services are sharply reduced by the assistance (intervention) of family and friends.

Dwelling-specific Needs

Our focus in this section is on the incidence of physical deficiencies and excessive housing expenditure burdens in 1979[2] (Table 1). Moreover, we limit the population considered to those households that in 1979 were not participating in federal or state housing programs—some 14 million elder-headed households.

Among the elderly, a fairly clear ranking emerges, running from those with the worst housing situation to those with the best. Impoverished renters and impoverished owners with mortgages are at the low end of the ranking, and nonpoverty owners

TABLE 1 Incidence (percentage) of Housing Deficiencies and Excess Expenditures by Population Group, 1979[a]

Group	Physically Deficient[b]	Excess Expenditures[b]	Deficient and Excess Expenditures
Nonelderly			
Total	7.6	15.2	2.1
Renters	13.2	33.4	5.3
Owners with mortgages	3.1	7.9	0.5
Owners without mortgages	7.9	1.7	0.3
In poverty	26.3	70.8	16.6
Renters	28.7	86.5	22.5
Owners with mortgages	17.1	73.2	10.1
Owners without mortgages	26.2	18.2	3.0
Elderly (65+)			
Total	11.5	18.4	2.4
Renters	17.2	55.3	7.8
Owners with mortgages	6.5	25.3	2.9
Owners without mortgages	10.1	4.5	0.4
In poverty	29.0	41.0	8.7
Renters	31.0	74.9	17.7
Owners with mortgages	33.6	74.9	21.0
Owners without mortgages	27.4	17.7	2.3
Renters[c]			
Metropolitan	12.1	58.8	6.9
Nonmetropolitan urban	21.6	54.6	7.3
Nonmetropolitan rural	40.1	37.3	13.3
Black	46.0	57.8	20.9
Other	13.3	55.0	6.0
Owners with mortgages[c]			
Metropolitan	4.3	25.7	1.3
Nonmetropolitan urban	8.4	18.9	5.8
Nonmetropolitan rural	14.2	29.6	7.2
Black	24.7	44.3	12.5
Other	3.8	22.6	1.6
Owners without mortgages[c]			
Metropolitan	6.8	5.1	0.4
Nonmetropolitan urban	8.4	4.4	0.0
Nonmetropolitan rural	18.3	3.4	0.8
Black	36.5	7.2	2.0
Other	8.3	4.4	0.3

[a]Only unassisted households are included in these figures; see Appendix for definitions.
[b]The definitions of these needs are consistent with those used by the U.S. Department of Housing and Urban Development (HUD). See Appendix.
[c]These figures are only for households headed by elderly persons.

SOURCE: Struyk and Turner (1984), Table 3.

with mortgages and without mortgages are at the higher end. Differences by location exhibit a familiar pattern; the incidence of deficiencies rises steadily as we examine successively more rural locations. In addition, this pattern holds across all tenure groups. The incidence of excessive expenditures is more varied but generally tends to be lower in rural areas.

The relative disadvantages of black households are strikingly clear. Their units continue to exhibit extremely high levels of deficiencies, and the incidence of excessive expenditures is also higher for black than for other households, especially among renters. The differences among black households are generally small, however, in comparison to the divergence in dwelling deficiency rates between the races. Finally, although it is not shown in the table, it is worth noting that there is little difference in the rate of deficiencies among the elderly aged 65–74 and those 75 years of age and older (Struyk and Soldo, 1980, Table 3-6).

To summarize, in 1979 there were about 1.61 million elder-headed households in dwellings that would be characterized as physically deficient and about 2.58 million households spending an excessive share of income on housing.[3] Because only about 340,000 of the households have these problems in common—meaning that many are spending a large fraction of their incomes to live in decent housing—a total of about 3.85 million, or 28 percent of all elder-headed households, have a dwelling-specific housing problem. The incidence among those below the poverty line is much greater: of the 2.66 million elder-headed households in this group, 61 percent have at least one of these problems.

Dwelling-use Problems

Although it has long been recognized that those whose activities are limited by health problems or disabilities are less able to function effectively in their homes without assistance, national housing policy has accepted this fact only to a limited extent. In considering policy options for helping those persons with such problems, clearly, we must know the size of the population that needs assistance. A key point to note at the outset of this discussion is that dwelling-use problems can be alleviated by supportive services, by modifications made to the unit that facilitate its use, or by both of these methods.

Following are two estimates of the number of households with dwelling-use problems; these estimates are intended to bracket the actual number of those needing help. The more generous definition is one that counts as needing assistance all of those who have a functional impairment as a result of disability or health problems. Applying this type of criterion to data from the 1979 National Health Interview Survey, we find that about 12 percent of persons age 65 and older have a need for some form of supportive services in their homes; the figure is 7 percent of those aged 65–74 and 21 percent of those aged 75 and older. If we apply the same rate to elder-headed households, about 2 million households are in this category.[4]

The incidence of need defined in this way is greater for women than for men (in both age groups), greater for blacks than for other ethnic groups, and apparently (because it is possible that many of those with low incomes in 1979 had spent their way down to this level through expenditures for medical and supportive care) greater for those with lower incomes.

A more conservative (and possibly more accurate) estimate of the number needing supportive services can be obtained if we look at the share of those who have a functional limitation and who are receiving formal care services—that is, services provided by an agency, whether they are paid for by the recipient or not. This type of calculation has the advantage of deleting those who receive essential services only from family members, neighbors, and friends. Nationally, about 25 percent of the elderly who report a functional limitation are receiving formal services. Applying this rate to the 2 million households noted in the earlier paragraph yields about 500,000 households who require support services provided by a formal agency.

Yet this figure is probably too low—for two reasons. First, it is virtually certain that not all of those who need such services are receiving them. Second, some persons are now in long-term care institutions who would not be there if such services had been available to them. The evidence for this last statement appears in the analysis of the determinants of institutionalization. Those elderly persons who live alone are institutionalized at higher rates than the elderly in multiperson households, even after controlling for health status and activity limitations (Weissert and Scanlon, 1983).

All in all, we might take as fairly accurate an estimate on the order of 750,000 elder-headed households that need formal supportive services. Additionally, half again that number now need and receive informal services, either from sources within the households or from outside. Public policy should be so structured as to complement informal services rather than replace them.

It is also important to note that, when we examine the determinants of the likelihood of a person receiving formal supportive services, the dominant factors are the extent of the person's disability and the absence of informal services. After controlling for these conditions, income by itself is not an important factor, which suggests that, over some range, public programs and informal assistance are reaching many of those in the greatest need of supportive services (for details, see Soldo, 1983). Thus, service recipiency seems to be largely determined by incapacity, a lack of informal assistance, the availability of formal services, and, in some cases, the ability to pay for them.

In general, then, the patterns of dwelling-specific and dwelling-use needs are quite different. Whereas dwelling-specific problems are strongly related to income and little associated with age, dwelling-use problems are related to age and physical impairments but not particularly to income.

Dwelling Modifications

The need for some types of supportive services can be eliminated by various changes to an elderly person's dwelling, changes that can compensate for particular functional impairments. Such modifications range from the installation of grab bars and easy-to-grasp doorknobs and other hardware to specially equipped telephones to bathrooms and kitchens that have been remodeled to accommodate wheelchair use. In other cases, these changes can reduce the need for supportive services and thus complement their provision. The best estimate of the probable need for modified dwellings—beyond those already occupied by some 700,000 elder-headed households—is on the order of 1 million units (Struyk, 1982). As indicated earlier, these households are not in addition to the number of those needing some type of support services. If we assume that the needed modifications are concentrated among those with the greatest impairments (who are also most likely to be receiving formal supportive services), then approximately 250,000 households that are not also receiving formal supportive services need to occupy units with some special features. (Unit modifications are discussed further in a later section.)

Overlap Between Dwelling Problems

Newman (1985) has used 1978 data taken from a supplement to the annual housing survey to estimate that about 17 percent of the elder-headed households with a person having an activity limitation reside in a unit that is physically deficient. (Newman uses the same definition of dwelling deficiencies used earlier in this paper.) Note that this rate is substantially higher than the 10 percent rate for elder-headed households with no members with such limitations, suggesting that households with an impaired member have greater difficulty maintaining or affording decent housing.[5] This rate implies that in 1979 there were some 340,000 households in the group with both dwelling deficiencies and dwelling-use problems.

Similar calculations can be performed for the overlap between those households with excessive housing expenditures and those with a member with an activity limitation. This calculation yields an estimate of 540,000 households with the combined problems.[6]

Summary

The figures in Table 2 summarize the information compiled on the number of elder-headed households with various housing-related needs. As implied earlier in this section, these are order-of-magnitude estimates designed to give a general picture of the current situation. The first point is that those households with dwelling-specific needs far outnumber those with dwelling-use needs, which points to the necessity of continued action in this area. An encouraging point is that probably less than a million households are characterized as having both dwelling-specific and dwelling-use needs. This figure is only about 6 percent of all elder-headed households in 1981, suggesting that it is a group for which assistance should be possible.

TABLE 2 Summary of Housing Needs of Elder-headed Households, 1979

Type of Need	Households Number (000s)	Percentage[a]
Dwelling specific		
Deficient dwelling	1,610	11.5
Excessive housing expenditures	2,580	18.4
Dwelling use		
Supportive services		
Generous estimate	2,000	14.3
Stringent estimate	750	5.4
Dwelling modifications		
Including those needing supportive services—stringent definition	1,000	7.2
Excluding those needing supportive services—stringent definition	250	1.8
Overlap between dwelling-specific and dwelling-use problems		
Supportive services (generous definition) and:		
Deficient dwelling	340	2.4
Excessive housing expenditures	540	3.8
Supportive services (stringent definition) and:		
Deficient dwelling	128	0.9
Excessive housing expenditures	140	1.0

[a]Households not receiving housing assistance.

SOURCE: Struyk, 1985.

On the other hand, on the order of 5 percent to 14 percent of elderly households do have dwelling-use needs (or up to 9 percent of the population without dwelling-specific needs). These households are prime candidates for the shifting of elderly persons into institutions.

Finally, a cautionary note: these figures are for 1979. The sharp increases in the number of elderly that will occur in the years ahead, as well as the greater share of the older and more frail in this population, is well known and should be kept in mind when considering possible policy interventions.

CURRENT FEDERAL HOUSING POLICIES

How has the federal government organized its available resources to assist the elderly with their housing? This section presents an inventory of current federal programs. An overview of these programs from the perspective of dwelling-use and dwelling-specific problems provides a useful initial orientation.

Figure 1 is a simplified depiction of the arrangement of current federal policies for meeting the housing-related needs of the elderly. The central point is the essentially independent administration of programs dealing with housing problems and those providing support services. The joint provision of services is largely "unexplored territory," with the exceptions being the fledgling congregate housing program and some local efforts in which federal resources are effectively coordinated. Conspicuous gaps in coverage are evident—such as the absence of dwelling-specific aid for homeowners (except for home purchasing assistance provided by the Farmers Home Administration) and a lack of programs to help with dwelling modifications related to activity limitations. Likewise, the targeting of resources to lower income groups is mixed; it is probably good in the housing area and much weaker in the area of support services.[7] In short, the present system is a patchwork and one that only infrequently provides the right aid to persons who need both housing assistance and supportive services.

Current federal housing programs that assist the elderly can be divided into broad categories: (1) those that facilitate the operation of the private market and (2) those that provide some housing assistance, sometimes accompanied by support services but generally without them. The private market-facilitating programs that are relevant to this discussion are a set of insurance programs operated by the Federal Housing Administration (FHA). By agreeing to insure certain mortgages, the FHA reduces the riskiness of the loan to the lender, a consequence that encourages both more lending and lending at interest rates lower than otherwise would have been charged. Insurance also makes the mortgages marketable to secondary facilities (e.g., Government National Mortgage Association, Federal National Mortgage Association), which in turn increases their attractiveness to loan originators. FHA traditionally has insured market-rate housing projects designed for elderly occupancy and also nursing homes and intermediate care facilities. Legislation enacted in 1983 also permits FHA to insure congregate housing facilities, board and care facilities, and "life care centers," which offer services beyond those provided in congregate facilities. (On the

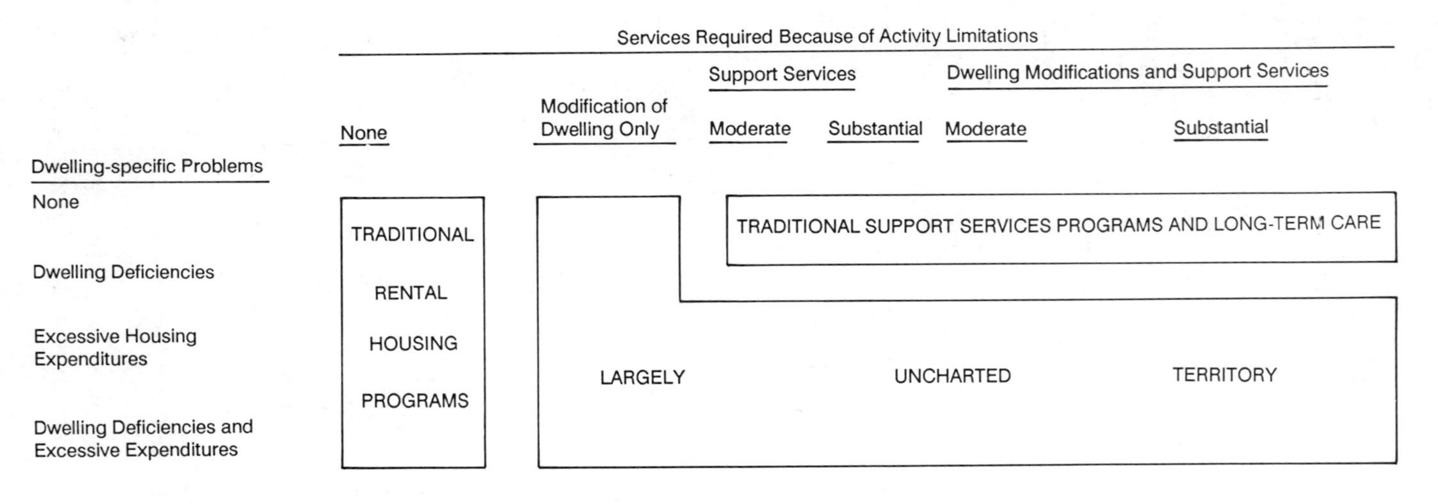

FIGURE 1 Traditional federal policies for housing-related needs of the elderly.

other hand, rather surprisingly, FHA has not yet been willing to perform its traditional innovative role by insuring home equity conversion mortgages.)

In the second program area, the federal government has been most active among the lower income elderly in addressing traditional dwelling-specific housing needs, mainly through a variety of subsidy programs that are largely directed toward renter households. Although most of the rental subsidy programs have long required that occupants be lower income persons, in 1981 the income targeting of such assistance was considerably tightened. As a result, assistance is now quite sharply limited to households with income levels that are no higher than 50 percent of an area's median family income, adjusted for family size. (For more on the changes enacted in 1981, see Struyk et al., 1983.) Help is provided through a wide range of programmatic vehicles including those under which the development of housing projects have been sponsored, such as public housing, the Section 202 program, and Section 8, New Construction. Aid has also been provided to households through rental assistance programs, most notably Section 8, Existing, and the new housing voucher program.

Federal housing programs per se have been directed toward renters; yet elderly homeowners have received substantial one-time aid in repairing and rehabilitating their homes through locally operated programs funded under the federal community development block program (CDBP). Rough calculations suggest that, in the early 1980s, this form of aid was equivalent in expenditures to about 15 percent of the housing assistance payments to the elderly participating in the rental program. CDBP has also been the funding source for many of the "house matching" programs and other innovative local efforts. In addition, elderly homeowners have been substantial beneficiaries of weatherization and fuel payment assistance programs (Struyk, 1984a, pp. 59–62).

The figures in Table 3 provide an accounting of the number of households currently eligible to receive housing assistance and the number that are actually receiving such payments.[8] The figures exclude those households receiving the kind of one-time help described in the preceding paragraph. The federal emphasis on renters is amply evident in these figures. Currently, some 4.9 million households participate in these programs, all but .6 mil-

TABLE 3 Estimates of Households (in millions) Currently Eligible for and Receiving Federal Housing Assistance and Expected Participation in an Open-Enrollment Housing Voucher Program

	Elder-headed Households		Nonelder-headed Households		
Participation	Owners	Renters	Owners	Renters	Total
Eligible to receive housing assistance (1981)[a]	5.0	3.0	5.0	8.8	21.8
Currently receiving assistance (1985)	—	2.0	0.6[b]	2.3	4.9
Eligible but not receiving assistance	5.0	1.0	4.4	5.5	16.9
Likely to participate in voucher entitlement program[c]	1.6	0.5	0.8	2.1	5.0

[a]Estimates of those eligible are from Irby (1984); estimates of current participants are based on estimates by Burke (1984) for 1981 with the elderly–nonelderly split applied to figures in the HUD 1986 budget (HUD, 1982, p. H-25). The same elderly–nonelderly split as for HUD programs is applied to aggregate figures for the Farmer's Home Administration Section 515 program (exclusive of Section 515/Section 00); figures on FMHA programs are from Drews (1982, p. 8).
[b]This figure includes HUD programs plus Farmer's Home Administration Section 502; no assistance to the elderly has been assumed in these programs because it was impossible to locate data on the actual elderly–nonelderly split.
[c]Participation rates are from the housing allowance supply experiment; see Kingsley and Schlegal (1982), Table 5.1.

lion of which are renters. Based on participation rates from the experimental housing allowance program, we estimate that an additional 2.6 million renters would participate if they had the opportunity to do so. The figures illustrate that, compared with the nonelderly, the elderly have been very well served—indeed, overserved—by the federal programs. Among income eligible renters, two-thirds of the elderly participate, but only about one-quarter of the nonelderly participate.

The final area of federal activity is that combining assistance for housing with assistance for supportive services. These arrangements come in three forms; what they have in common is that they all involve subsidized housing projects.[9] The first type consists solely of projects that have been specially designed for use by the physically impaired. Even if no additional services are provided, such living environments may be instrumental in helping their occupants remain in the community, although there is no "hard" evidence on this point. To the knowledge of this author, there is no accurate count of the number of such specially designed units in the subsidized inventory; a reasonable guess might be 400,000. There is also no information on the number of these units that are, in fact, occupied by persons who take advantage of their special features; the absence of any requirements that such units be occupied by the impaired suggests that their use by those needing such environments could be improved.

The second type of program provides supportive services for those living in assisted housing, whether it has been specially designed or not. In this case the supportive services are not specifically part of the overall housing package; rather, local agencies—housing, social services, and health—identify the elderly who need these services and try to arrange to provide them. Yet the housing projects play an important role. Because they are occupied exclusively by the elderly, they are attractive to those who provide supportive and limited health services because they facilitate the identification of those requiring services and increase the efficiency with which the services are delivered. There is no systematic information on the extent to which arrangements of this kind have been made. However, the data that have been gathered on the services available at a large sample of elderly-only public housing and Section 202 projects[10] as part of the evaluation of the demonstration congregate housing services program would suggest that such arrangements are fairly common. The problem with them, of course, is the uncertainty about continued funding for these services and the pattern of managers of housing projects accepting the services that are available as opposed to being able to provide those that are most needed.

Finally, there is the small congregate housing services program (CHSP), which thus far has existed rather precariously as a demonstration program, although continued congressional support seems likely. CHSP operates in 60 public housing and Section 202 projects, with about 1,800 persons receiving supportive services under the program (Nachison, 1985, p. 34). Participation is limited to those genuinely needing the services. The service bundle consists of a mandatory component of twice-a-day meals and options under which services are tailored to the needs of the individual. Possibly the most distinguishing characteristic of the program is that the funding for both housing assistance and supportive services comes from HUD, thus solving the often difficult problem of patching together funding for supportive services at the local level. (CHSP is discussed further in a later section.)

Overall, the earlier characterization of federal policy as being concentrated on dwelling-specific problems seems fair. Most service provision in federal projects comes through local initiatives.

A POLICY FRAMEWORK

In previous sections, we have seen that dwelling-specific and dwelling-use problems often occur independently. Nevertheless, in a substantial minority of cases, they occur together. It also seems probable that as dwelling-use problems become more acute, the incidence of dwelling-specific problems will increase rapidly. Activity limitations on the part of a family member (and the energy required of others in the household to provide informal care) means that dwelling upkeep is likely to be diminished. In addition, "drawing down" assets to pay medical bills or to support formal care expenses will lower incomes, possibly to the point at which housing expenditures become "excessive." We have also seen that current housing assistance deals only minimally with the nexus of housing and dwelling-use problems.

The challenge is to design a programmatic response that is flexible enough to deal with the variety of need mixes and ability-to-pay circumstances that will be encountered. If the response is properly designed—that is, if better alternatives to institutional long- and short-term care are developed—such programs may well permit savings in the total public resources going to the elderly. In a number of instances, for example, in-home services have been found to defer institutionalization and to reduce the number and length of visits to acute-care hospitals (see, e.g., Miller and Walter, 1983).

Three principles should guide the design of the general federal policy response. First, cost-effectiveness is essential. The criterion here is that the new approach should be no more costly and at least as effective as present programs. In this calculation, costs include assisting additional households beyond those to whom the assistance is actually directed; that is, serving those who otherwise would have received informal assistance is viewed as a cost. One issue in particular is the substitution of formal for informal supportive services. Also, achieving cost-effectiveness may well require a degree of coordination among services that is far beyond what is now occurring, especially between housing and support services that are currently administered independently in most cases. A further dimension worth exploring is that financial costs can be lowered by the elderly making in-kind assistance contributions to others in some types of residential arrangements.

Second, to the maximum extent feasible, the programs should be constructed to permit a range of choice to the elderly in terms of the solution adopted to meet each individual's needs: whether a recipient remains a homeowner or shifts to rental quarters; whether he or she uses community-based versus institutionally based services. Of course, the recipient may have to pay a larger share of the cost of more expensive solutions, but the choice should still be present.

Third, the options should be structured so as to foster timely adjustments in the "housing bundle" selected. As noted earlier, the housing needs of the elderly can be highly dynamic. Solutions that are offered in response to those needs ought to encourage timely changes in the elderly person's basic housing situation—for example, from living alone in a single-family home to living in an apartment in a congregate housing project. Because of the understandable resistance of the elderly to multiple moves, however, in-place changes through dwelling modifications and room use solutions must also be an integral part of the adjustment process.

The key idea behind the framework set forth here is that it is essential to tailor solutions to fit each of a range of housing-related needs. As needs change, alternative solutions should be available. To achieve this matching requires that one differentiate both among types of housing needs and among recipient populations. The various types of housing-associated needs were discussed at length earlier. Three household attributes seem to be most important: (1) economic resources (and hence the ability to pay for services); (2) mode of tenure (owner-occupancy versus renting), and (3) type of structure—single versus multiunit structures. The latter strongly affects the efficiency with which many support services can be provided, and tenure affects the range of options available for coping with dwelling deficiencies and excessive housing expenditures.

Figure 2 summarizes some of the public interventions that might be appropriate for households in differing circumstances.

Extent of Activity Limitation Requiring Nonfamily Assistance—Dwelling-use Problem				
Dwelling-specific Problem			Requires Support Services	
None	None	Requires Dwelling Modification Only	Moderate	Extensive
Low income	A.	B. (1) Grants for modifications; for renters, assistance finding specially equipped subsidized rental units	C. (1) Local service provision, some federally supported	D. (1) Congregate services voucher; Medicaid waiver for homeowners
Moderate income		(2) Loans for modifications; renters, as above	(2) Local service provision on copayment basis	(2) Same as above
Middle income		(3) Assistance in finding reputable contractors; housing referrals for renters	(3) Referral services	(3) Private congregate services referral
Dwelling Deficiencies				
Low income	E. (1) Homeowners: subsidized dwelling repair and maintenance program Renters: housing allowance, relocation assistance	F.	G.	H. (1) Same as D(1)

Moderate income	(2) Homeowners: loans; RAMs Renters: relocation assistance, housing referral	Same as B above, combined with elements of E	Same as C above, combined with E	(2) Congregate services vouchers; homeowners: D(2) with loans, RAMs for repairs
Middle income	(1) Homeowners and renters: various kinds of referral assistance			(3) Same as D(3)

Excessive Housing Expenditures

Low income	I. (1) Homeowners: weatherization grants (if appropriate) or housing allowance Renters: housing allowance or non-specialized housing projects	J. Same as B above, combined with elements of I	K. (1) Congregate housing voucher for renters Homeowners: local service provision plus I(1)	L. (1) Congregate services voucher for renters; homeowners: Medicaid waiver plus housing allowance combined with counseling
Moderate income	(2) Homeowners and renters: counseling on options; possibly housing allowance in highest cost areas		(2) C(2) and I(2) combined; in some cases, congregate vouchers where this is more cost-effective than a combination of other approaches	(2) Same as above

FIGURE 2 Possible types of public intervention to improve the housing situation of the elderly.

The key here is explicit differentiation among types of needs and types of households requiring services. The role of government (which is listed in each box in the matrix) is also defined quite differently, depending on the household's ability to pay for services. (Note that "congregate services" is shorthand for a variety of supportive community housing environments.) For example, for households needing extensive support services, a voucher for a congregate housing program (described later) is appropriate; but only referral services to market-rate programs are necessary for middle-income households. Similarly, for those homeowners needing dwelling modifications only, grants make sense for those in the low-income groups, while referrals to contractors and possibly reverse annuity mortgages are the best form of government assistance to the more well-to-do.

In cases in which the household has both dwelling-specific and dwelling-use problems, greater coordination is essential. For renters, such needs will frequently be addressed most efficiently through a congregate services program, either subsidized or at market rates. For homeowners, the solution varies with their ability to pay and their desire to remain in their home. For lower income homeowners, in-home services provided through Medicaid (in states that have applied for this waiver) and housing assistance provided through a housing allowance may be economically feasible.

The leadership in the provision of a number of the services listed in the figure devolves on the local government, although federal support may be instrumental. The superiority of local organizations and solutions seems likely for most referral services, for grants for housing rehabilitation and modifications to owner-occupied dwellings, and for the provision of modest amounts of support services. At the same time, however, it is important to ensure that those nominally eligible for such assistance actually fall within an active service area. Spotty coverage—both between and within jurisdictions—has been an unfortunate hallmark of local initiatives for the elderly.

SELECTED INTERVENTIONS

Since the late 1970s, discussion of housing policies for the elderly have been dominated by reports of innovative activities being undertaken first at the local level and then at the state level. Most of these initiatives grew out of the perceived absence of available alternatives to deal with the frail elderly in a community context. Among the alternatives that have been launched or at least seriously proposed as local programs have been accessory apartments, granny flats, house sharing implemented through "matching" programs, small group homes, congregate housing, revamped board-and-care facilities, and home equity conversion mortgages (also known as reverse annuity mortgages). It is probably fair to say that the perspective in starting such programs locally has been a version of "try it and see if it works." The federal government has been largely an observer of these initiatives and a passive observer at that. Consequently, we have a poorly documented record of the effectiveness of many of these local programs, while at the same time, there is a groundswell of sentiment for these programs to be replicated, often through federal legislation and appropriations. In general, however, the record is far too weak to justify proceeding on anything but a more rigorously organized demonstration basis.

Given the scope of this paper, it is simply not possible to give even cursory treatment to so many programs. Instead, three have been selected for comment based on their meeting at least one of two criteria: (1) the appearance of the potential to play a substantial role in the evolving long-term care system and (2) the ability to illustrate the range of possibilities in public housing interventions for the elderly.

Those alternatives that have been selected for discussion are congregate housing, the implementation of modifications to the dwelling to offset some of the effects of physical impairment, and small group homes. Each program is described, what is known about the program's effectiveness in reducing institutionalization is inventoried, and what appear to be the next steps in developing the approach are outlined. In particular, the following question is considered: Should the federal government now sponsor more demonstrations and evaluations, or should it begin to encourage such approaches by making them eligible for voucher recipients, by providing direct support or mortgage insurance, or through other means?

Congregate Housing

We may define a congregate housing facility as a rental housing complex in which households have separate units that include kitchens and bathrooms; the complex includes public spaces that can be used for social functions and for serving meals to residents on a regular basis (at least one meal per day). Housekeeping, chore performance, and personal services are available to the residents who need such assistance; the residents are frail, elderly persons who are capable of living quite independent lives but need limited assistance. The congregate facilities would be carefully targeted to this particular segment of the frail elderly who would otherwise probably be institutionalized. As defined here, congregate housing would be an integral part of the long-term care system.

Congregate housing is seen as a vehicle of great potential for the elderly and as a cost-effective alternative to institutionalization; that is, it is viewed as a way to permit persons who would otherwise be in institutions to remain in a more stimulating and less expensive community setting. If such an approach can be proven to be cost effective, federal assistance for residences (in lieu of Medicare payments for institutional care) would certainly make sense.[11] Early evidence on the cost of congregate housing versus long-term care facilities certainly looks promising.[12]

Several states already have operating programs that incorporate at least some of the elements listed above, although they appear to differ significantly among themselves in regard to structure and the services they provide. These programs in general are expanding rapidly, and other states are seriously considering similar programs (see Nenno et al., 1985, p. 13; and Anthony, 1984).

The only information on the effectiveness of the congregate approach comes from CHSP, the recently concluded HUD demonstration project that served a population somewhat different from that just described. The key question behind the demonstration was the effects on institutionalization of providing supportive services to households living in HUD-assisted elderly projects.

In the CHSP setup, participants were limited to about 20 percent of the residents of a project, with assistance concentrated on those most vulnerable to institutionalization. (The limitation was imposed to maintain an atmosphere of independent living.) A professional assessment committee was formed at each project to screen applicants regarding their need for the services that would be provided.

Twice-a-day meal service was seen as the core of the supportive services. Additional nonmedical services such as housekeeping/chore, personal assistance, transportation, escort, and social services could also be provided to fill gaps in a project's service delivery system.

Although 48 projects participated in CHSP, the part of the evaluation dealing with its impact on institutionalization drew on 17 projects. Each of these projects was "matched" with a control project of the same type (public housing or Section 202) in the same area. Baseline data (i.e., prior to CHSP implementation) on samples of residents were obtained at the experimental and control projects; data were also obtained at two later times—on average, at 14 months and 26 months after the baseline samples.

The results regarding institutionalization can be briefly summarized: at the end of the period, there was no significant difference in the rate at which participants and controls were permanently placed in institutions. On the other hand, there was a difference in the rate at which members of the two groups were temporarily institutionalized over the period: 15 percent of the experimentals versus 23 percent of the controls (Sherwood et al., 1985, Table IV.2). On the basis of these findings, it would certainly be difficult to argue for the enactment of a major congregate housing program.

Still, there were several problems with the program that was demonstrated and with the evaluation that need to be considered in reaching a balanced judgment about congregate housing. Four points in particular are important:

1. The population served by the program was not restricted to those that were vulnerable to institutionalization, according to the definition used in the evaluation; also, the share of participants who were vulnerable varied considerably from project to project.
2. CHSP was structured around the provision of twice-a-day meals, a service that many of the participants neither needed nor especially wanted. Hence, a great many of the services provided would not have been expected to affect institutionalization rates.
3. Many of the control projects were fairly rich service environments themselves. Thus, the comparison was not between a

case of no services available to residents and CHSP but rather between some services (which varied sharply among projects) and more and possibly better tailored services.

4. The observation period may have been too short, given the kind of program and control projects employed in the demonstration. Even with all of the problems just listed, some significant effects may have been evident over another year or two. (Alternatively, if a short observation period was to be used, there should have been better measures of health status in addition to the relatively crude institutionalization rate measure.)

My own conclusion after reviewing the CHSP experience is that we do not know nearly enough to proceed with a larger congregate services program at this time. On the other hand, we have learned a great deal from the demonstration, and HUD should launch another demonstration as soon as possible, a demonstration designed to overcome the problems of the initial one. In particular, the service bundle should be adjusted away from meals, and the control population should be drawn from clearly service-poor environments, even if this means having to draw on those of the elderly who are not living in subsidized or even elders-only housing projects. An additional such demonstration will permit the design and testing of a program that may well be ready for use as a key element in the long-term care system.

Dwelling Modifications

The alteration of the features of a dwelling to make it easier for a person with a physical impairment to use is a logical response to the onset of activity limitations. Some have thought that the installation of appropriate modifications to dwellings occupied by elderly homeowning households that have an impaired member, through public programs if necessary, could be cost effective in terms of helping sustain the person in the community. The modifications could be directly effective by permitting the person to do more for himself around the unit; they could be indirectly effective by relieving those providing help to the impaired person of some of the burden of assistance. The case for the cost-effectiveness of these modifications is bolstered by their modest one-time charge, compared with the costs of continuing service provision. Yet, while such cost-effectiveness may indeed be the case, as we shall see, there is really no evidence currently available to support this contention.

It may be worthwhile to note that modifications are only one of a series of adjustments that households can and do make to their housing without relocating. Three other adjustments include changing the use of rooms (often in response to the activity limitations of a household member); taking in a roomer or boarder to generate additional income or for the companionship and help they might provide; and changing (typically, lowering) the amount of repairs and improvements to the dwelling because of changes in the ability to make such repairs.

The figures in Table 4 show the rate at which a sample of households made these adjustments over a 2-year period. The sample consists of households in selected neighborhoods from seven large central cities that did not relocate over a 5-year observation period. Only a very small percentage of households took in a roomer or boarder or changed the use of rooms within their homes over this period. A rather surprisingly high 10 percent of elder-headed and 5 percent of nonelder-headed households undertook modifications to their homes to facilitate their use by a physically impaired family member. Taken together,

TABLE 4 Incidence of Housing Adjustments (percentage) by Age of Household Head for Selected Households in Seven Large Central Cities

Adjustment	Elder-headed Households	Nonelder-headed Households
Roomer or boarder present in last 2 years	3	1
At last one room use change in last 2 years	5	6
Dwelling modified to assist impaired person during last 2 years	10	5
Dwelling repairs and improvements over last 2 years:		
Repairs in both years	69	80
Moderate-sized repair in at least 1 year[a]	77	83
Major repair in at least 1 year[b]	19	22
Only small or no repairs in both years	20	14
No repairs	5	3

[a]Moderate repairs are those costing between $100 and $1,000, inclusive.
[b]Major repairs or improvements are those costing over $1,000.

SOURCE: Struyk and Katsura (1985), Table 1.2.

these figures indicate that about 8 percent of elder-headed and 6 percent of nonelder-headed households make one of these three types of housing adjustment each year. These rates can be put into perspective by noting that about 3.3 percent of elderly homeowners and 13 percent of nonelderly homeowners adjust their housing circumstances by changing residence each year. As a result, the rates of in-place adjustments for the elderly are at least double those achieved by relocating.[13]

A better idea of the national incidence of dwelling modifications is available from data gathered by a special supplement to the 1978 annual housing survey (AHS). These figures, which are shown in Table 5, indicate that only about 10 percent of elderly households with at least one member with self-reported health or mobility problems had made a modification to their unit at the time of the survey. These rates appear to be considerably

TABLE 5 Dwellings Occupied by Elder-headed Households with at Least One Member with Health or Mobility Problems

Modification	Number of Dwellings (in thousands)	Percentage of Dwellings
Extra handrails or grab bars	548	6.6
Sink, faucet, or cabinet adjustments	103	1.2
Wall socket or light switch adaptations	103	1.2
Elevators or lift chairs	69	0.8
Specially equipped telephone	69	0.8
Ramps	60	0.7
Extra-wide doors or hallways	60	0.7
Door handles instead of knobs	26	0.3
Bathroom designed for wheelchair use	26	0.3
Flashing lights	26	0.3
Raised lettering or braille	9	0.1
Push bars on doors	9	0.1
Other features	163	1.9
Total number of dwellings with at least one modification	886	10.3
Total number of dwellings	8,600[a]	

[a]Figures do not add to total because not all dwellings have modifications and some report more than one modification.

SOURCE: Struyk and Zais (1982), Table 2.

lower than those cited earlier for the seven-city sample; because the AHS data are from a national representative sample of dwellings, the lower rates presumably are more generally valid.

The available research strongly suggests that the receipt of assistance from inside or outside the home, including such services as meals programs, significantly reduces the likelihood that a household will undertake a dwelling modification. Such changes do not seem to be very sensitive to the household's economic position. The likelihood does increase, however, when the person with activity limitations or the person who must use assistance (e.g., a cane or wheelchair) in getting around is the spouse in a husband–wife household (Struyk and Katsura, 1985).

Although this information is helpful in understanding why households make unit modifications, it tells us nothing about the effectiveness of such changes in delaying institutionalization. Some research on this topic using the 1982 long-term care and annual housing survey data sets is just now getting under way. Until more information on effectiveness is forthcoming, it is very difficult to argue for any type of broad-based public intervention to provide dwelling modifications.

All of the information generated to date, however, points to the fact that a decision to make such changes to a dwelling is complex, and it is critically dependent on the types of supportive services available to the impaired person. Under these conditions, the provision of modifications may make little difference over a wide range of cases and, hence, may not be cost effective. It is to be hoped that the work now beginning will help to isolate those instances in which such modifications will be the most effective strategy for delaying institutionalization.

Group Homes

The terms "house sharing" or "group home" usually refer to a single structure in which a number of unrelated people live. Many group homes are single-family homes that have been converted to provide private rooms as well as common space for residents. In these small group home arrangements, outside health or social services can be provided to individuals who need them, although they are seldom provided to all persons in the structure.

Arrangements of this type have been organized by individuals (sometimes an elderly person who wants to share his or her home in a particularly expansive way) and by local agencies. Our attention is on those that have been developed by local agencies. The central premise of such arrangements is that the occupants help each other and together take care of common tasks such as meal preparation. The occupants thereby substitute their own labor for that of others, which could lower considerably the cost of living in a relatively "service-rich" environment. (See Morgan, in this volume, for a more detailed discussion of the possibilities for mutual support without cash transactions.)

There is little systematic information about small group homes, largely because the development of these homes has been so dominantly one of local initiative. One survey in 1982 of 21 shared residences found the "typical" resident to be a woman in her early seventies who had resided in the group household for at least a year. The majority of residents had at least weekly contact with their families. As might be imagined, monthly charges varied widely as did the service package provided by the residence. All resident households used community services such as a senior center or visiting nurse. According to a study by the Shared Housing Resource Center reported in Gold (1985, pp. 49–50), two-thirds of the organizations expected the residents to participate at least minimally in housekeeping chores. Another survey of such living arrangements (van Dyke and Breslow of the Jewish Council for Aging of Greater Washington, reported in National Policy Center on Housing and Living Arrangements for Older Americans, 1983, pp. 26–27) found that residents tended to be somewhat old and in declining health; the shared living arrangement was clearly viewed by occupants as the only real alternative to a nursing home. Perhaps the most significant aspect of these arrangements is their diversity, as recently documented in 15 case studies by Streib et al. (1984, chap. 6).

With so little material of even a descriptive nature about shared living, the absence of any real evaluation on the impact of such arrangements on institutionalization is not surprising. In this case, three distinct types of issues should be addressed in any demonstrations and accompanying evaluations that might be mounted.[14] First, the effectiveness of such arrangements in forestalling institutionalization should be documented. Second, the potential for shared housing to allow the elderly to assist each other actively, thereby extending their own period of productive activity and lowering the cost of this alternative compared with others, should also be studied. Third, it will be important to understand the types of people who do well in this environment. The limited information we do have is clear about the fact that such arrangements do not work for everyone; it would be helpful to have more accurate profiles of those who seem especially suited to shared housing.

The Impact of Such Arrangements

What would be the effect of the widespread adoption of the kind of living arrangements just described, assuming that they were found to be effective in delaying the institutionalization of the frail elderly? To begin with, it seems quite evident that the life satisfaction of those who would have been placed in institutions otherwise will be significantly improved. Although the value of such improvements is difficult to quantify, it is nevertheless clearly important.

The possible savings to society in the resources that must be used could be substantial. Let us assume that 20 percent fewer persons would be institutionalized in the future because of the existence of congregate and other housing arrangements. We will also use Heumann's (1985) estimate that equivalent services for those needing less than nursing home care can be provided in a congregate setting for about one-third less cost than in the long-term care facilities. Together, these figures imply a reduction in long-term care costs of about 7 percent. The overall resource savings would presumably be greater because the incidence of couples continuing to live together would rise, thereby cutting down the need for two separate living arrangements (one of which would have been in an institution).[15] Such effects might raise the savings from these alternatives to the equivalent of 8 or 9 percent of long-term care costs.

This is clearly the upper limit of such savings, however, because we have tacitly assumed that only those persons that would have been institutionalized would be served in congregate facilities. From Heumann's study (1985, Table 10), we know that the services portion of the congregate package constitutes about half of the total cost. If we assume that a household would have been paying for the shelter component in any event (or would have received a subsidy to help pay for it), then for a system of congregate facilities and long-term care facilities to operate with the same resources as the present arrangement would require that no more than half of the households in congregate facilities be without a member who would otherwise have been in an institution. Of course, if the households would have purchased some of the supportive services in other environments, then a higher share of congregate housing occupants could be those who would have been in community housing. If congregate "slots" were targeted in such a way that one-third of the occupant households were living in such facilities "inappropriately," then the savings figures cited above would be cut in half.[16]

The foregoing suggests two things. First, the savings potential is large—in the billions of dollars—from the use of congregate and other arrangements that provide appropriate levels of supportive services as a substitute for those provided in long-term care facilities. Second, the realization of such savings depends critically on the effectiveness of such arrangements in preventing institutionalization and on the degree to which services can be targeted toward those genuinely at risk of being institutionalized.

CONCLUSIONS

This paper has argued that the central issue in federal housing policies for the elderly is the development of public assistance that will help them make necessary housing transitions in such a way as to allow community-based housing to be an active and integral element in the overall long-term care system. Current housing policy for the elderly only gives passing attention to this issue. Consequently, the programs now in operation are poorly designed to address broad housing needs.

There is no shortage of suggested alternatives for using housing-oriented programs to assist the elderly to remain in the community rather than being institutionalized. Indeed, local governments and some states are moving forward on a number of options. There has, however, been little evaluation of the effectiveness of these interventions in reducing institutionalization and little assessment of the extent to which they substitute formal for informal care.

It seems clear that the first step must be for federal policy to be reoriented toward the nexus of dwelling specific and dwelling-use problems, as they have been defined in this essay. We are not, however, in a position to argue for any particular programmatic package to implement this policy. Rather, the next phase must be one of intense experimentation and evaluation. The role of the Department of Housing and Urban Development in carrying out the essential evaluations will be paramount. If we proceed with alacrity, it may be possible to be in a position by 1990 to make forceful recommendations for the adoption of operational programs in this area.

APPENDIX

Definitions

Dwelling Deficiency

See Table A-1. Specifics of the definition were dictated by the data available in the annual housing survey. This definition is the same as that employed by HUD.

Excessive Housing Expenditures

Here we follow HUD's lead so that our results will be consistent with other tabulations. Excessive burden is defined separately for renters and homeowners. For renters, a gross rent (the contract rent plus utilities paid by the tenant) above 30 percent of gross household income is considered excessive. For owner-occupants, out-of-pocket expenditures for housing (excluding expenditures for maintenance and improvements) above 40 percent of family income is considered excessive. The higher standard for homeowners is based on the tax advantages accruing to homeowners and on the capital gains-producing investment embodied in their housing expenditures. (See Feins and White, 1979, for more discussion on this point.)

Need for Supportive Services

Two definitions are used, based on data in the 1979 National Health Interview Survey. The "generous" definition, developed

TABLE A-1 Deficiencies that Cause a Housing Unit to be Judged Physically Inadequate (using the HUD/Simonson Definition), Based on Annual Housing Survey Items and a Revised Definition (1981)

Type of Deficiency	Description
Plumbing	1. *Lacks or shares some or all plumbing facilities.* The unit must have hot and cold piped water, a flush toilet, and a bathtub or shower—all inside the structure and for the exclusive use of the unit.
	2. *Lacks adequate provision for sewage disposal.* The unit must be connected with a public sewer, septic tank, cesspool, or chemical toilet. (Units with this deficiency are almost invariably defined as having a plumbing deficiency as well.)
Kitchen	3. *Lacks or shares some or all kitchen facilities.* The unit must have an installed sink with piped water, a range or cookstove, and a mechanical refrigerator—all inside the structure and for the exclusive use of the unit.
Physical structure	4. *Has three or more of five structural problems:* leaking roof; open cracks or holes in interior walls or ceiling; holes in the interior floors; either peeling paint or broken plaster over 1 square foot of an interior wall; evidence of mice or rats in the last 90 days.
Common areas	5. *Has three or more of four common area problems:* no light fixtures (or no working light fixtures) in common hallway; loose, broken, or missing stairs; broken or missing stair railings; no elevator in building (for units two or more floors from main building entrance in buildings four or more stories high).
Heating	6. *Has unvented room heaters that burn oil or gas.* If the unit is heated mainly by room heaters burning gas, oil, or kerosene, the heaters must have a flue or vent.
Electrical	7. *Lacks electricity.*
	8. *Has three out of three signs of electrical inadequacy:* One or more rooms without a working wall outlet; fuses blown or circuit breakers tripped three or more times during the last 90 days; exposed wiring in house.

SOURCE: Simonson (1981), pp. 84–85.

by Soldo (1983) includes any person with at least one of the following characteristics:

- needed or received help with at least one of the seven activities of daily living (ADL);
- needed or received help with at least one of the four instrumental activities of daily living (IADL);
- was not able to perform one or more of the ADL functions;
- stayed in bed all or most of the time; or
- needed help with urinary or bowel devices.

The "stringent" definition includes only those persons in the above group who receive formal home care services.

NOTES

1. The annual housing survey is the primary source of national housing data. For analyses of the neighborhood data included in the survey, see Bielby (1979) and Marans (1979).
2. Since 1979 we know, in general, from annual housing survey data that the share of households with "excessive" housing expenditures has increased, whereas the share living in dwellings with deficiencies has decreased slightly.
3. Less detailed estimates with 1981 data by Irby (1984) and using somewhat different definitions for deficiencies show about 1.2 million elderly households in deficient units and 2.55 million households with excessive expenditures.
4. This procedure seems to be reasonable, given that Newman (1985), using a similar definition of impairment, found about 13 percent of elderly households had at least one member with such a condition.
5. Together with the information on the determinants for the receipt of support services, the higher rate also implies that the services received do not have much effect on dwelling conditions.
6. In doing this calculation, the rate was applied only to those elder-headed households that were not participating in a housing program, the general assumption being that, if they were part of a housing program, they would not have excessive expenditures for housing.
7. Services provided under the Older Americans Act are not means tested. Those funded by the social services block grant program have varying income limits that are set by the states; almost universally, however, these limits are less stringent than those in the housing programs.
8. These figures correspond generally to those prepared by the Congressional Budget Office; see Levine (1985, p. 11).
9. Of course, one could approach the issue from the other direction, that is, starting with households that are receiving supportive services and then examining their housing circumstances. The housing-oriented approach has been chosen here because it is more in keeping with the overall perspective of the paper.
10. The Section 202 program is one in which specially designed housing is developed by nonprofit sponsors for occupancy by elderly households and households with a handicapped member. Federal subsidies are provided in the form of direct loans that carry interest rates below the market level and, in recent years, through rental

assistance payments, available under the Section 8 program, for all occupants who are eligible to receive them.

11. For a discussion of a congregate housing voucher program for low-income households, see Struyk (1984b).

12. Heumann (1985) in the first careful analysis calculates that, for equivalent services, congregate facilities are about one-third less expensive overall than long-term care facilities.

13. Repairs and improvements are associated with the types of adjustments we have just reviewed and with longer term strategies of housing upkeep and investment. A central hypothesis considered here is that there is a cohort of elderly homeowners who, because of economic or health circumstances, decide implicitly to draw on the equity in their homes through a program of lower maintenance. Similarly, we are interested in which households persistently are investing in their homes. The last two rows of figures in Table 4 show that 20 percent of the elderly in the sample undertook little or no repair activity over 2 years and that they were somewhat more likely to do this than their nonelderly counterparts; the differences between the two groups are not large, however. Similarly, the elderly as a group are undertaking repairs, and improvements—even large improvements—to their homes at quite high rates. Still, they undertake fewer such repairs and investments, and each year they spend less, than their more youthful counterparts. The overall pattern is one in which properties are indeed largely being maintained, and disinvesting households are a definite minority and comparable in size with the proportion of such households in the nonelderly population.

14. The implied call for a demonstration may seem odd, given the existence of ongoing projects. It might be that one could evaluate the present programs, but as a group, they may be so heterogeneous as to preclude anything but a series of case studies. Although case studies may be an essential first step in designing a demonstration with an evaluation, they probably could not serve as the basis for an evaluation by themselves.

15. For a discussion and projections of future long-term care costs to the federal government, see Palmer and Torrey (1984).

16. It is assumed that supportive services constitute half of all congregate costs and that congregate costs are about 67 percent of long-term care costs. It follows that services in congregate facilities are equivalent to 33 percent of long-term care costs.

REFERENCES

Anthony, A. S. 1984. "Prepared Statement." In *Sheltering America's Aged: Options for Housing and Services,* U.S. Special Committee on Aging. Senate Hearing 98-875. Washington, D.C.: Government Printing Office.

Bielby, W. T. 1979. *Evaluating Measures of Neighborhood Quality in the Annual Housing Survey.* Washington, D.C.: Government Printing Office.

Burke, P. 1984. *Trends in Subsidized Housing, 1974–81.* Washington, D.C: U.S. Department of Housing and Urban Development, Division of Housing and Demographic Analysis.

Drews, R. 1982. *Rural Housing Programs: Long Term Costs and Their Treatment in the Federal Budget.* Washington, D.C.: Congressional Budget Office.

Gold, M. 1985. *The Older American's Guide to Housing and Living Arrangements.* Washington, D.C.: Institute for Consumer Policy Research.

Heumann, L. 1985. *A Cost Comparison of Congregate Housing and Long-Term Care*

Facilities in the Mid-West. Urbana: University of Illinois, Housing Research and Development Program.

Irby, I. 1984. *Housing Problems in 1981: A Synopsis.* Washington, D.C.: U.S. Department of Housing and Urban Development, Housing and Demographic Analysis Division.

Kingsley, G. T., and P. M. Schlegel. 1982. *Housing Allowances and Administrative Efficiency.* N-1741-HUD. Santa Monica, Calif.: The Rand Corporation.

Levine, M. 1985. Statement Before the Subcommittee on Housing and Consumer Interests, Select Committee on Aging, U.S. House of Representatives, March 7. Washington, D.C.: Congressional Budget Office.

Marans, R. W. 1979. *The Determinants of Neighborhood Quality: An Analysis of the 1976 Annual Housing Survey.* Washington, D.C.: Government Printing Office.

Miller, L. S., and L. Walter. 1983. "The Comparative Evaluation of the Multipurpose Senior Services Project—1981." Berkeley: The University of California.

Nachison, J. S. 1985. "Who Pays? The Congregate Housing Question." *Generations* Spring:34–35.

National Policy Center on Housing and Living Arrangements for Older Americans. 1983. *Alternative Housing and Living Arrangements for Independent Living.* Ann Arbor: University of Michigan.

Nenno, M. K., J. S. Nachison, and E. Anderson. 1985. "Support Services for Frail Elderly or Handicapped Persons Living in Government-Assisted Housing." Washington, D.C.: National Association of Housing and Urban Development Officials.

Newman, S. 1985. "Housing and Long-term Care: The Suitability of the Elderly's Housing to the Provision of In-Home Services."

Palmer, J., and B. B. Torrey. 1984. "Health Care Financing and Pension Programs." In *Federal Budget Policy in the 1980s,* G. Mills and J. Palmer, eds. Washington, D.C.: The Urban Institute Press.

Sherwood, S., J. N. Morris, C. C. Sherwood, S. Morris, E. Bernstein, and E. Gorstein. 1985. *Final Report of the Evaluation of Congregate Housing Services Program.* Boston: Hebrew Rehabilitation Center for the Aging.

Soldo, B. 1983. "A National Perspective on the Home Care Population." Working Paper in Demography CPR 83-4. Washington, D.C.: Georgetown University, Center for Population Research.

Streib, G., W. E. Folts, and M. A. Hilker. 1984. *Old Homes—New Families: Shared Living for the Elderly.* New York: Columbia University Press.

Struyk, R. 1982. "The Demand for Specially Adapted Housing by Elderly-Headed Households." Project Report 3014-1. Washington, D.C.: The Urban Institute.

Struyk, R. 1984a. "Home Energy Costs and the Housing of the Poor and the Elderly." In *Energy Costs, Urban Development and Housing,* A. Downs and K. Bradbury, eds. Washington, D.C.: Brookings Institution.

Struyk, R. 1984b. "Housing-Related Needs of the Elderly Americans and Possible Federal Responses." In *Sheltering America's Aged: Options for Housing and Services,* U.S. Senate Special Committee on Aging. Senate Hearing 98-875. Washington, D.C.: Government Printing Office.

Struyk, R. 1985. "Housing-Related Needs of the Elderly and Possible Federal Responses." *Journal of Housing for the Elderly* 2(4):3–26.

Struyk, R., and H. Katsura. 1985. *Aging at Home: How the Elderly Adjust Their Housing Without Moving.* Urban Institute Report 3166-03. Washington, D.C.: The Urban Institute.

Struyk, R., and B. Soldo. 1980. *Improving the Elderly's Housing.* Cambridge, Mass: Ballinger.

Struyk, R., and M. Turner. 1984. "Changes in the Housing Situation of the Elderly." *Journal of Housing for the Elderly* 2(1):3–20.

Struyk R., and J. Zais. 1982. "Providing Special Dwelling Features for the Elderly with Health and Mobility Problems." Washington, D.C.: The Urban Institute.

U.S. Department of Housing and Urban Development. 1985. *FY 1986 Budget.* Washington, D.C.: U.S. Department of Housing and Urban Development.

Weissert, W., and W. Scanlon. 1983. "Determinants of Institutionalization of the Aged." Working Paper no. 1466-21 (rev.). Washington, D.C.: The Urban Institute.

The Role of Transportation in the Social Integration of the Aged

Martin Wachs

Mobility, the ability to travel from place to place, is a basic determinant of the quality of life in old age, yet it is often overlooked in discussions of the social and built environment. Perhaps this oversight occurs because mobility does not give us satisfaction in its own right. Few people drive on freeways or ride buses because they value these experiences; we value instead excellent health care, housing, and recreational activities. Mobility is valued, in turn, as a link to other elements of the built and social environments. Thus, transportation may be the means by which our environment conspires to isolate the elderly or one of the keys to an active and healthy old age.

Just a century ago, the city was primarily a "walking city." Most people walked between home and work, to do their shopping, to schools and churches. Within a very short period of time—in fact, within the memory of many still living—the city has been transformed by transportation and communications technology. First, streetcars enabled people to live and work in separate quarters of the city. Later, trucks and telephones freed businesses of their dependency on downtown locations. By 1930 the auto had become the primary means of transportation for

Martin Wachs is a professor in the Graduate School of Architecture and Urban Planning, University of California, Los Angeles.

most families, and the location and scale of shopping centers, social activities, and human services have evolved to reflect nearly universal access by means of the automobile. Low-density residential areas, decentralized health care, diversified regional shopping centers, and suburban office centers work quite well for those who drive without difficulty. Yet these same structures provide a harsh environment for people whose lives differ significantly from the norm of the suburban, auto-oriented household. The very poor, ethnic minorities, disabled people, and many of our elderly are isolated in a world that assumes that the two-car, two-worker, two-child, two-story household in suburbia is typical and caters only to it (Schaefer and Sclar, 1975).

Because travel in our society is largely derived from the production and consumption of other goods and services and is rarely an end in itself, we must be careful when interpreting statistics about travel patterns. We can be pretty certain that a household having less wealth and income than another is likely to have a lesser degree of well-being, but it does not follow that a household that travels less than another has a lower degree of mobility. A person's mobility should be judged by the extent to which his or her need to travel is being met and not by how much he or she travels in comparison with others. Surprisingly, the fact that many old people travel less than many younger people is often interpreted as a lack of mobility when it should be obvious that relief from the traditional morning and evening commute is for most people a blessing rather than a deprivation. The critical question is not how much elderly people travel but whether or not mobility limitations restrict their freedom of choice and, hence, the quality of their lives. The following paragraphs summarize some of the major differences between the travel patterns of the elderly and other population groups, and interpret these differences in an effort to gain greater understanding of the mobility patterns and needs of the elderly. Later sections of the paper review national policies for improving the mobility of the elderly in an effort to suggest some directions for possible improvement, especially with respect to the integration of transportation requirements in the planning of housing for the elderly.

INTERPRETING TRAVEL BY THE ELDERLY AND DETERMINING NEEDS

The 1977 Nationwide Personal Transportation Study (NPTS) of more than 20,000 households shows that travel patterns change dramatically during a person's life cycle. For example, childless couples in their twenties on average make about four trips per day totaling approximately 36 miles of travel. Travel peaks among families with children and whose heads are in their late thirties. Such families on average make a dozen trips per day and travel nearly a hundred miles daily. Households of very old people typically make the smallest number of trips per day and travel the fewest miles. Couples in their eighties, for example, average about one trip per day for a total of about 3 miles of travel (Zimmerman, 1981). Such figures, as indicated above, do not necessarily indicate relative deprivation in mobility among the aged and may reveal more about changes in activity patterns than about mobility and aging.

At every stage in the life cycle, household travel patterns are correlated with a few key variables. Travel is always statistically associated with the number of automobiles owned by a household and in turn, this variable is most often highly dependent on household size and income. In statistical terms, then, we often find that households consisting of elderly people travel less than households consisting of younger people in large part because they are smaller households and they have fewer workers, fewer automobiles, and less disposable income. It is hard to prove that aging directly affects one's propensity to travel but easier to identify with elderly households certain economic and demographic characteristics that are associated with reduced travel.

One-third of all trips and about 40 percent of all vehicle mileage are associated with earning a living—the trips made to and from work and the trips made while on the job. Because old people are less likely to be working, these trips are eliminated from their travel patterns. Similarly, social and recreational travel exhibits a marked decline with age. Married couples in their seventies make fewer than half as many social and recreational trips as married couples in their thirties. The one component of travel that seems invariant with age is "family business," which includes trips for shopping, medical care, and banking. The NPTS showed, for example, that single people in their seventies who lived alone made about the same number of trips for these purposes as single people in their twenties who lived alone (Zimmerman, 1981). These data may illustrate that declines in aggregate travel by elderly people are mostly associated with retirement from work and changes in social and recreational preferences. The trips that the elderly consider to be most essential seem to continue to be made. Mobility may well be a severe problem for many elderly people, but the dimensions of the problem cannot be grasped fully by the aggregate analysis of travel patterns alone.

COMMON STEREOTYPES OF THE ELDERLY AND THEIR MOBILITY NEEDS

The mobility problems of the elderly are complex and in some cases severe, but the conventional wisdom regarding such problems is dominated by stereotypes that are for the most part untrue. The elderly are frequently portrayed as "transit dependent," people who have "given up" their cars as they reach retirement age, in part because of declining vision and reflexes and increasing fears about the dangers of driving. The reality is that most Americans of all ages make the vast majority of their trips in automobiles. In the aggregate, we make 84 percent of our trips in cars; we make 9 percent of our trips walking and use public transit for only about 3 percent of our trips (Klinger et al., 1982). The elderly do not appear to be substantially less reliant on automobiles than are younger people. In my own research on travel patterns in Los Angeles, for example, I found that 89 percent of all vehicle trips made by people over the age of 65 were made in automobiles, although the elderly were more likely than younger groups to be passengers and somewhat less likely to be drivers. Only 7 percent of the trips by older people in Los Angeles were made on public transit. Although this is still twice the proportion that characterizes younger groups, it is still a small percentage of all the trips made by the elderly (Wachs, 1979, p. 50).

The physical changes that accompany aging do eventually rob people of the ability to drive an automobile safely and comfortably, but these changes occur gradually over many years. The vast majority of drivers are able to continue operating cars well into their seventies, and many keep driving into their eighties. There are few physiological or medical reasons to associate transit dependency with retirement status, but many public policymakers often make this association. Perhaps because elderly people do not travel for work-related purposes and this type of travel is for most Americans the most common type, reductions in the volume of travel during the early years of retirement are mistaken for reductions in the ability to travel, especially by automobile.

The stereotype of a transit-dependent elderly population may also in large part be drawn from the fact that more than 90 percent of all people in their thirties, forties, and fifties are licensed to drive and less than half of the population over the age of 70 is so licensed. I believe, however, that we are misinterpreting this difference if we attribute it to the process of aging. Many of today's elderly people never learned to drive, having grown up before automobile driving was as universal as it is today. The fact that this pattern is culturally determined and not an inherent function of the aging process is illustrated by the difference between the rates of elderly men and elderly women who are licensed to drive. Only 33 percent of women over the age of 70 are licensed to drive, but nearly 70 percent of men in this age group are presently licensed to drive (Asin, 1980). In the early years of the automobile, it was far less common for women to learn to drive, and most of the elderly women who do not drive have never done so. Because women outnumber men quite substantially in the older age groups, women who never drove dominate the nondriving component of the elderly. By comparison, among people in their thirties, forties, and fifties, there are almost no differences in the proportions of men and women who possess driver's licenses (Asin, 1980). More than 90 percent of men and women in these age groups have licenses. Thus, we would conclude that as the present elderly are replaced by the next generation, a much larger percentage of the total elderly population will consist of people having driver's licenses and that the biggest difference will be among women.

Looking at vehicle ownership as another indicator of relative mobility, a pattern similar to that for driver's licenses may be seen. Although the elderly appear to be relatively less mobile than younger people, as a group, they are hardly transit dependent. About two-thirds of American households headed by people over the age of 65 own at least one automobile, and about one-third own no automobiles (Motor Vehicle Manufacturers Association, 1984, p. 43). The rate of carlessness is more than twice as high for those over the age of 65 as it is for those in their fifties, but it is difficult to classify a group as transit dependent when two-thirds of its members own vehicles. In addition, I believe that many of these households (the one-third who own no cars) never owned autos and that they will be replaced in the coming decades by older people who enter the retirement years possessing automobiles.

Because many of today's elderly live in denser central-city neighborhoods and do not drive, and a greater proportion of the younger population lives in the suburbs and does drive, it is often said that elderly people give up their suburban communities and relocate to central-city areas after retirement when the decline in their mobility forces them to live closer to essential services. This may be true for some older people, but as a generalization, the picture is more in error than it is accurate. A simple examination of census data indicates that differences with age between suburban low-density living and inner-city high-density living have little to do with the process of aging. Rather, the observed pattern is explained more accurately by major economic and cultural differences among population cohorts. Census data on tenure of residence show that most of today's transit-dependent inner-city elderly have lived at their present addresses for decades. They are largely people who grew older at their central-city locations, and they include many who never drove and never lived in the suburbs. The suburbs are largely inhabited by different cohorts of people, many of whom are beginning to reach retirement age and most of whom have been driving for decades. Rather than concluding that these people will become less mobile and move to inner-city neighborhoods served by transit, it appears more likely that they will continue to live at low densities and continue to drive throughout their sixties and seventies and into their eighties.

I believe that the population will continue to suburbanize during the coming decades, resulting in more and more elderly suburbanites. This process will occur, despite frequent predictions of the revival of the inner city, because of the basic economic relationship between housing and mobility. During the past 20 years, "typical" American family budgets for low-, middle-, and upper-income households have devoted more than 20 percent of total expenditures to housing and about 6 to 8 percent of total expenditures to transportation. During the same years, trends in the consumer price index reveal that the price of housing has multiplied by a factor of four while transportation prices have roughly doubled. Despite the well-known effects of the energy crises on the prices of gasoline, then, the reality is that housing is both a larger item of household expenditure than is travel, and it is becoming relatively more expensive over time. Because the cost of housing generally declines as distance increases from the center of the city, it remains economically rational for most American households to trade increases in the cost of transportation for decreases in the unit cost of housing by moving farther from downtown in order to get more housing for their housing budget. As developers recognize this trend, they put up smaller and denser housing units in the suburbs, and each year the population continues to move farther from the city centers.

By focusing attention on the stereotype of the elderly as a relatively carless, nondriving, transit-dependent group in a relatively car-owning and -driving world, we often fail to take note of the fact that old people are an incredibly diverse group with life-styles and behavior patterns that are as varied as those of any age group. By focusing on the richness of this diversity instead of the simplistic stereotype, we may arrive at a completely different understanding of the mobility patterns and needs of old people. Let me illustrate this by focusing on the mobility patterns of the elderly in the inner city versus the elderly of the suburbs.

MOBILITY PROBLEMS OF THE INNER-CITY ELDERLY

The elderly of our inner cities include many people who are transit dependent and accustomed to the high density of activities and neighborhood services that characterized urban neighborhoods of the early decades of this century. Many of these people grew older with their communities and never experienced the total automobile orientation that characterizes later generations more accustomed to suburban low-density living. Many of the inner-city elderly are widows whose husbands did drive. These women experienced a severe blow to their mobility when their husbands died, separating them from their access to automobiles as well as from their lifetime partners. Also included among the inner-city population are most of our ethnic minority elderly, including those who grew older with their communities and some who arrived rather late in life as part of multigenerational households that migrated to the barrios and ghettos of larger cities.

Many of the urban elderly are mobility dependent. Having never driven, and being economically limited to using taxis only for rare emergency trips, these people must rely on the public transit system and on relatives or friends who drive. By depending to some extent on others to drive them, elderly people in this situation suffer substantial reductions in their freedom of choice. Spontaneity is an important ingredient of mobility, consisting, as it does, of the ability to decide at a moment's notice that a trip to a doctor, park, or theater would be appropriate. Depending on a child or a friend to provide transportation to such activities usually means accommodating to their availability and perhaps deferring a trip when a lift is not available. This dependency becomes part of the psychological sense of dependency widely associated with aging. It explains why, in a number of attitudinal studies, elderly respondents have reported that accepting rides from others was more convenient and less physically demanding than using public transit, but it also made the respondents feel that it put them under an obligation that they would not repay, or saddled them with feelings of indebtedness (Carp, 1972a, 1972b).

Although public transit may allow for greater spontaneity than dependence on friends or relatives who drive, it is fraught with additional problems for many old people. First, and most obviously, a person who uses public transportation is limited to choosing destinations that are served by such transit and to traveling at hours of the day when service is conveniently available. These constraints do limit one's choices, as I found in a study that I did a number of years ago. When I calculated, for example, how many hospitals and clinics a person could reach from the center of a low-income, inner-city community by bus versus by automobile, relying on published bus schedules and actual driving times at the noon hour on a typical weekday, I found that a person could reach 40 hospitals and clinics within 15 minutes of driving time but only 2 within a similar travel period using public transit. If the acceptable access time was lengthened to 30 minutes, the citizen of this neighborhood could reach 143 hospitals and clinics with a car but only 14 by transit service. The point is not that an individual needs to use a large number of facilities in the course of his or her daily activities but rather that the automobile provides much greater freedom of choice than transit. The transit-dependent elderly person must either choose from a smaller number of available hospitals (or parks, theaters, and educational facilities) or invest a much larger amount of time in traveling than automobile users spend on such efforts (Wachs and Kumagai, 1973).

A second problem with public transit is that it may involve substantial physical barriers that are difficult or impossible for some elderly people to surmount. Because buses and rail systems operate on fixed routes that generally are not designed around the travel patterns of particular citizens, many elderly people must walk long distances, exposed to cold, heat, or rain, involving hills, stairs, and broad, busy streets to cross. The vast majority of people who are classified as elderly by virtue of being age 65 or older can easily negotiate the urban landscape, but we have a special interest in those who cannot. As life expectancy lengthens and more and more inner-city elderly people are in their eighties, the physical barriers involved in transit travel become extremely significant factors. A national survey conducted for the U.S. Department of Transportation's Urban Mass Transportation Administration (1978) found that 7.4 million persons living in the urban areas of the United States were physically limited in their ability to use public transportation. Although this number included many people who were young, some 47 percent were over the age of 65, and 67 percent were over the age of 55. About one-fifth of these people were physically unable to use public transit at all; an additional 30 percent did use transit but only with considerable physical difficulty or discomfort.

Elderly people who depend on public transit face another barrier to mobility that is perhaps the most distressing of all and that has only recently been studied. It appears that transit patrons are frequently victimized by criminals who prey on people walking to and from bus and train stops, waiting at transit stops, and riding on transit vehicles. Many elderly people report that they are fearful of using public transit, especially after dark, and their fears appear to be well founded. I recently conducted a survey of more than a thousand households in a central portion of Los Angeles that is well served by transit and densely populated by people of a variety of income levels and ethnic groups (Levine and Wachs, 1985). The area, like many inner-city communities, contains a large number of households headed by elderly people. The results of the survey were astounding. Adding up the crimes respondents reported had occurred walking to and from bus stops, waiting at bus stops, and riding on buses, my coworkers and I discovered that incidence rates among our sample were 30 times the crime victimization rates reported by the local transit police. The gap between the reported crime rates and the responses to our survey were attributable to poor reporting of crimes by the victims and by the police failing to categorize crimes as being related to transit travel. The findings showed that 17 percent of those who used the bus regularly had been victims of a crime during the previous 3 years. Among the respondents to the survey who were over the age of 65, 20 percent had been victimized in that time period; among the respondents under the age of 30, only 8 percent had been so victimized. It is clear that the elderly are victims of crime while traveling on public transit to a far greater extent than other groups. Their greater vulnerability occurs in part because the elderly make up a disproportionate share of transit users, being relatively transit dependent, but it also happens because the elderly are singled out as easier targets by criminals. Most of the crimes committed against all age groups were purse snatchings and pickpocketings; as a rule, they did not involve injuries, but substantial numbers of victims reported being pushed, shoved, punched, and threatened with weapons.

To sum up, the inner-city elderly, who include a relatively small proportion of car owners and drivers, have a mobility problem related to their dependency on public transit or on others to drive them. This dependency reduces their mobility because it reduces individual control over decision making and spontaneity in travel. Depending on public transit means accepting a limited selection of possible destinations, negotiating physical barriers that for some may be substantial, and exposing oneself to the risks of victimization by criminals.

MOBILITY PROBLEMS OF THE SUBURBAN ELDERLY

The majority of people reaching retirement age today are not the inner-city, transit-dependent elderly. They are suburban, and most typify what Bernice Neugarten describes as the "young old." They are classified as elderly by their chronological age but are active and healthy, the kind of people likely to take advantage of senior citizen discounts at theaters and sporting events. They are, for the most part, mobile because most of them both own and drive automobiles. Each year, there are more and more of these active, mobile elderly, including larger and larger numbers of people who adopted low-density, suburban life-styles decades ago and who continue to live in the suburbs well into their retirement years. Most have no difficulty thriving in environments that lack public transportation and in which the doctor and supermarket may be located many miles from their residences. My studies of the elderly of Los Angeles County indicated that about half of the elderly there are already to be found in such environments, that they are roughly twice as likely to have driver's licenses than the central-city elderly, and that they make two to three times as many vehicle trips per household per day as the inner-city elderly (Wachs, 1979, chapters 3 and 5). In rough terms, by the turn of the next century, the number of suburban low-density, auto-oriented elderly will more than double, and the number of transit-dependent inner-city elderly will decrease in absolute numbers and decrease even more dramatically as a proportion of the total elderly population.

The mobility problems of this group will arise later in life, as increasing numbers of them survive into their late seventies, eighties, and nineties. When failing vision and increasing frailty ultimately make it impossible for them to drive, these people can become in relative terms, and rather suddenly, more isolated and dependent on others than the inner-city elderly who may never have driven cars. Because their life-styles were more dependent on their ability to drive and, consequently, they chose to reside in environments having lower densities of services in close proximity to residences, a greater void is left in their lives when they can no longer drive. Because of these low densities, medical care and shopping is even harder to reach than it is in the inner city, and for the same reason it is far more costly for public agencies to operate transit in such areas. Many who are deprived relatively late in life of their mobility are forced to relocate, move in with their children or other relatives, or move into congregate living facilities. The trauma of such moves is accentuated because they come relatively late in life and because they are forced on an individual by a lack of mobility rather than being the result of preference. The fact that this population enjoys mobility the longest of any of the elderly does not make the ultimate adjustment to its loss easier, and it is interesting to note that each year a larger and larger number of us will face just such an adjustment.

NATIONAL POLICY ON THE MOBILITY NEEDS OF THE ELDERLY

For 20 or more years, meeting the mobility needs of the elderly has been an explicit element of national transportation policy. Yet despite this commitment, there is no clear consensus on the most efficient ways to use public resources to accomplish our goals. There is also widespread disappointment that the hundreds of millions of dollars that have already been spent have resulted in little tangible progress. The subject has become highly politicized, and it is difficult to take a position on the issue without appearing to "take sides."

In 1968 Congress adopted the Architectural Barriers Act,[1] which was intended to ensure reasonable access to public buildings by physically handicapped people. Passage of the law was the first result of a series of political actions that included numerous lawsuits, legislation, and regulations affecting the transit industry. In San Francisco, for example, a bitter fight took place over the question of wheelchair access to BART stations and cars, and in 1970 Congress amended the basic Urban Mass Transportation Act of 1964 to declare that "it is national policy that elderly and handicapped persons have the same right as other persons to utilize mass transportation facilities and services; that special efforts have to be made in the planning and design of mass transportation facilities and services so that the availability to elderly and handicpped persons of mass transportation which they can effectively utilize will be assured."[2] Yet the broad national policy stated here did not specify how agencies and transportation authorities were to meet the needs of the elderly, and that omission has been the source of a bitter debate that remains unresolved despite numerous revisions of federal regulations and thousands of hearings, court cases, and scholarly analyses.

One source of difficulty has been the lumping together of "elderly and handicapped" in this policy statement, as though these citizens by definition had identical mobility needs. The majority of the elderly are not handicapped, and the majority of the handicapped are not elderly. Labeling the two as one group has several negative effects. First, it stigmatizes the elderly who deserve and demand to be considered a group with unique characteristics and who vigorously assert that aging is not a handicap but a normal part of living. The label also focuses the attention of transportation planners and managers on the physical requirements of the handicapped and associates the removal of physical barriers to travel with the attainment of all of the mobility needs of the elderly. Efforts to remove physical barriers to travel certainly deserve applause, but proper consideration of the needs of the elderly can hardly be limited to the removal of physical barriers. Nevertheless, although lumping together the "elderly and handicapped" has harmful effects, it must also be observed that it has probably resulted in more attention for the transportation needs of older people than would otherwise be the case. It is much easier to capture policymakers' attention when speaking for disabled veterans, the blind, and the deaf instead of competing with these groups for attention.

The tension over labeling the elderly as synonymous with the handicapped is part of the background for what we might call "the great debate" in the field of mobility for these groups. This debate, which has been raging for decades and is far from resolution, is between the proponents of "mainstreaming" or total accessibility on the one hand and those advocating the provision of separate specialized services for the elderly on the other. The proponents of total accessibility or mainstreaming argue that the law requires all transit facilities and equipment to be totally accessible to the elderly and handicapped and that emphasis should be placed on the removal of all architectural barriers and the equipping of all buses with wheelchair lifts. Others argue that changing the entire public transit infrastructure to accommodate wheelchairs will cost billions and that it will provide inferior service for the elderly and handicapped in comparison to separate door-to-door services, which are available exclusively to these groups (Fielding, 1982). The cost of mainstreaming has been vigorously debated, but it is certainly high. Transit agencies have purchased wheelchair lifts for thousands of buses at an extra cost per vehicle that is reported to be in the range of $12,000 and that involves annual maintenance costs ranging from $500 to $4,000. The lifts reduce the seating capacity of buses, and their use slows travel for all passengers on the vehicle.

Furthermore, the use of these buses by the handicapped has been low. One transit company, for example, which has about 120 lift-equipped buses, reported that the lifts are actually deployed to serve one to four handicapped riders per day throughout its entire system; the nation's largest all-bus transit system in Los Angeles carries 51 daily wheelchair users although approximately 1,900 of its total fleet of 2,600 buses are equipped with wheelchair lifts (Southern California Rapid Transit District, 1984, p. 24). The lifts have been unreliable, and handicapped riders have been embarrassed by the delays they cause other passengers when wheelchair lifts are operated. In addition, surveys of the handicapped have shown that wheelchair occupants usually find it difficult to get from their homes to bus stops, certainly hindering their use of fixed-route "mainstream" service in comparison with separate fleets providing door-to-door service (Wachs, 1979). The Congressional Budget Office (1979) estimated that it would take 30 years and over $7 billion to achieve full wheelchair access to the nation's transit systems. The American Public Transit Association reported that the average capital and operating cost per trip by handicapped people among five transit agencies was over $700, primarily because of the low rates at which the facilities were actually utilized.

For nearly 20 years, a variety of draft regulations, adopted regulations, lawsuits, amendments to legislation, and public debates have come in rapid succession. They demonstrate the clear differences between the transit industry's perspective, which emphasizes the cost-effectiveness of separate door-to-door systems, and the activist's perspective, which emphasizes mainstreaming and full accessibility as a basic human right (Rosenbloom, 1982).

In 1983 proposals to amend the requirements for providing service to the elderly and handicapped were again made, although they still await adoption because of continuing controversy. The proposed regulations would require transit operators to provide separate paratransit services for the elderly and handicapped or to offer a combination of wheelchair lifts and paratransit. Whichever option were to be chosen by the operator, the transit agency would not be required to spend more than 7.1 percent of its federal financial assistance, nor more than 3 percent of the agency's annual operating budget, on expenditures to meet the needs of the elderly and handicapped. These limits would constitute an uneasy compromise between activist and management perspectives. Because of the heated political climate in which decision making on this issue has taken place, it has taken more than 20 years of debate, legislation, and litigation, and billions in public spending, to arrive at this accommodation. In the end, however, the compromise would appear to ensure rather little in the way of mobility to the elderly.

A second element of transportation policy for the elderly and the handicapped has been the requirement that these groups be offered lower fares than the general public on existing public transit systems. Under current regulations, to be eligible for federal transit operating assistance under Section 5 of the Urban Mass Transportation Act (as amended), the operator must provide elderly riders with fare reductions (they must not pay more than half the regular fares during nonpeak hours). In fact, many transit companies charge lower fares than required by the regulation, and many extend the fare reduction to the rush hour as well as to nonrush-hour periods. The emphasis on fare reductions, like the removal of physical barriers, is of great importance to a segment of the elderly—in this case, the elderly whose use of transit is limited by small disposable income. Yet reduced fares do little to improve transportation service for those who receive infrequent, sparse, or nonexistent transit service. Indeed, the requirement that they receive lower fares for serving elderly passengers might even discourage transit companies in some cases from making special efforts to improve those services that are tailored to meeting the needs of the elderly. Public transit service in the United States covers less than half of its operating costs from the fares its passengers pay, the majority of the costs being borne by subsidies. If a transit company must charge its elderly riders only half the normal fare and receives no special subsidy for carrying a larger number of elderly passengers, it faces the prospect of increasing deficits if it spends money for improvements that will bring additional elderly riders. Although reduced fares for the elderly seem a benefit, they actually result in larger economic losses as more passengers are served, and they clearly discourage transit managers from being creative in trying to serve larger markets of elderly patrons.

Another area in which a national commitment has been made to the provision of transportation services for the elderly is the financial support of specialized paratransit services operated by social services agencies, volunteer organizations, and municipalities across the nation. Using funds available through the Older Americans Act, the Social Security Act, the Housing and Community Development Act, and hundreds of state and local statutes, senior citizen centers, health care facilities, veterans programs, and many other groups operate their own door-to-door transportation services. A variety of researchers have shown that we are spending perhaps a billion dollars per year on such services, most employing vans and drivers in fleets of a few vehicles. Studies have consistently shown that there is a great deal of duplication and inefficiency in what has come to be called the "social services" transportation sector. The small scale of operations, low patronage rates, inexperienced staff, and reluctance to rely on larger public agencies for transportation services have made it difficult to overcome the high costs of such services by forcing "coordination" as a condition for receiving subsidies. A number of studies have shown that efforts to force mergers or consolidations of specialized transit operations have been met with institutional resistance, and, ultimately, the costs of consolidation and cooperation have been so high that they tend to eliminate all of the benefits anticipated from these policies. In the social services sector, the cost of providing a ride to a senior center or health care facility is often on the order of $20 or more; in newer, smaller, and inexperienced systems, it is often closer to $100. Yet the rides are often provided free or for a token fare of 50 cents or a dollar.

The reality, then, is that most Americans over the age of 65 provide their own transportation through private automobiles. For most, such provision is not a problem, and it is consistent with their life-styles prior to old age. For those who are unable to drive, however, the choices remain limited, and there is little prospect for dramatic improvement. Some can rely on traditional fixed-route public transit, but they are then limited in their travels to visiting those destinations that are served by transit. Reduced fares and the removal of architectural barriers are increasing the proportion of the elderly population that is able to use public transit, but the increase is small in relation to the cost. In addition, those who rely on public transit to fulfill their travel requirements run a high risk of becoming the victims of crimes. Social services agencies frequently provide specialized door-to-door transportation services for their clients, and these services do overcome the physical barriers and safety problem of many public transit users. Yet the costs are enormous, and when the services are considered in combination, it is clear that they are least able to meet the needs of the growing number of isolated elderly people in suburbia—the former drivers who live in low-density areas reached by few public transit routes and few social services transportation agencies.

RESEARCH DIRECTIONS IN HOUSING/ MOBILITY TRADE-OFFS

An active and satisfying old age requires the opportunity to engage in a variety of activities at reasonable costs in terms of effort, time, and money. Older people are diverse in their lifestyles, needs, and preferences, and it is therefore difficult to prescribe an appropriate type and level of mobility. We must be equally understanding of and attentive to the needs for social integration of active and mobile recent retirees and of housebound disabled people, even though the two groups may have very different needs. Funding arrangements and legal requirements must be more flexible than they have been to date. The diversity of mobility needs among the elderly indicate that by prescribing narrowly defined programs we are limiting the opportunities of those whose needs are not addressed under those programs.

In general, elderly people meet most of their travel needs by private means: walking, driving, and being driven by friends and relatives. Because each year an increasing proportion of elderly people own and operate automobiles, cars are likely to remain the major source of mobility in coming decades. As a result, more research is needed on the aging driver to provide a better understanding of the physiological, sensory, and attitudinal aspects of driving in old age. We could, perhaps, do a better job of designing automobiles, highways, and traffic control systems to reflect the fact that the proportion of drivers who are old is increasing more rapidly than the proportion of the population that is old. Motor vehicle accidents are the leading cause of accidental deaths for people over the age of 65, as they are for younger people, and they account for half the accidental deaths among people over the age of 75. Older people are physically vulnerable and are more likely than younger people to be killed when involved in a car crash. Although people over 65 account for 7 percent of those involved in accidents, they account for 12 percent of those killed. And in fatal accidents in which one driver is over the age of 65, it is reported that the older driver is 3.5 times more likely than the younger driver to be killed (Koltnow, 1985, p. 21). Automobile manufacturers, for example, do surprisingly little research on product design for elderly drivers, offer few options specifically tailored to old people, and devote a surprisingly small proportion of their budgets to market research targeted to an older market.

In a society in which the automobile is nearly universal, we know relatively little of the psychological and behavioral effects of the declining ability to drive in advanced old age or the effects of declining driving skills on housing and locational decisions. These are both fruitful areas for research in the coming years. The Transportation Research Board is planning a 2-year study to review research on and experience with older drivers and pedestrians and to recommend actions that should be taken on the basis of future population characteristics. This research could be an extremely important undertaking.

Traditional public transit, which usually involves fixed-route, scheduled bus and rail service, meets another share of the mobility needs of the elderly, especially in the inner cities. Efforts are proceeding slowly but surely to remove architectural barriers to public transit, but for many, these services are difficult to get to, frightening to use, and limiting to the extent that they cannot serve every destination. To date, research has focused on the physical mobility of the elderly to use transit vehicles; much more is to be learned regarding the elderly user's attitudes toward transit service improvements. I believe, for example, that a well-founded fear of crime is one of the greatest barriers to transit use by older people and that greater attention to security might be one of the most important directions for public policymakers attempting to better tailor transportation for the elderly. More market research is needed on the social and psychological barriers as well as the physical barriers to the use of conventional public transit by older people.

Although they provide fewer trips for elderly people than autos or transit vehicles, specialized paratransit services provide critical door-to-door services for those having more severe mobility limitations. To date, however, these services have been limited in their geographic coverage and limited to certain types of trips and clients and to those making advanced reservations. In addition, in many cases, such services have been duplicative, expensive, and inefficient. Efforts to coordinate and consolidate services of this type have had limited success. The most promising area for improvement is in what economists call "user-side" or "demand-side" subsidies. Under these subsidy plans, clients are provided, at low or moderate cost, with vouchers or coupons they can use to purchase taxi rides, bus rides, or specialized escorted van rides within a fairly large jurisdiction and without limits as to trip purpose. The service operators are reimbursed for the services actually provided. Although a subsidy is involved and there is some potential for fraud, this type of mechanism has a potential for flexibility and efficiency that is matched by few current social service agency transportation services.

To some extent, retirement communities and congregate living facilities provide collective transportation services for their residents that take the place of private automobiles and substitute for door-to-door paratransit services. Transportation provided in this manner becomes part of the infrastructure of housing services. In some instances, regular shuttle services are provided to nearby transit stations or shopping centers; in other cases, regularly scheduled recreational outings are provided; and at least one large San Francisco housing development has compact autos available for rent to its residents at short notice on an hourly or daily basis. We know relatively little about the economics of such transportation services or about the size of the community at which it becomes economically feasible to incorporate transportation services with housing. Case study research and systematic comparisons of such services with traditional transit options would reveal a great deal about the potentials and the limits of integrating mobility into the residential environment.

Today, for those who are most severely limited in mobility, we try to bring the services to the client instead of providing the client with mobility. Meals-on-wheels, home health care, and friendly visitor services all take the place of trips for those having the least mobility and the greatest need. These services are, of course, quite costly to provide, but they are critical to a small but important segment of the elderly. From my observation, what such programs often need most is a stable funding base. So many in-home services are of such small scale and short duration that the bulk of staff time is devoted to proposal writing and fundraising rather than the delivery of services.

Housing and mobility are clearly interdependent elements of our social environment. If one chooses a low-density suburban living environment, far from friends, relatives, and services, it may entail high mobility costs for the individual and society, especially in old age. High-density inner-city environments may impose high housing costs and less aesthetically pleasing environments on their residents, but it may cost individuals and society much less to provide access to services at such locations. Although we recognize these principles, we know less than we would like to know about the economic, social, and cultural trade-offs between housing and mobility. Therefore, any investigation of the interrelationships between housing and mobility in old age must include attitudinal and social dimensions as well as physical and economic ones.

NOTES

1. Public Law, 90-480, "Public Buildings: Accessibility to the Handicapped" (1968), 82 Stat. 718.
2. Public Law 91-453, "Urban Mass Transportation Act" (1970), 84 Stat. 962.

REFERENCES

Asin, R. H. 1980. *Characteristics of 1977 Licensed Drivers and Their Travel.* Report No. 1, Nationwide Personal Transportation Study. Washington, D.C.: U.S. Department of Transportation, Federal Highway Administration, Highway Statistics Division.

Carp, F. 1972a. "Retired People as Automobile Passengers." *The Gerontologist* 12(1, Part 1).

Carp, F. 1972b. "The Mobility of Older Slum Dwellers." *The Gerontologist* 12 (1, Part 1).

Congressional Budget Office. 1979. *Urban Transportation for Handicapped Persons: Alternative Federal Approaches.* Washington, D.C.

Fielding, G. 1982. "Transportation for the Handicapped: The Politics of Full Accessibility." *Transportation Quarterly* 36 (2, April):269–282.

Klinger, D. J., et al. 1982. *Household Travel.* Report No. 9, Nationwide Personal Transportation Study. Washington, D.C.: U.S. Department of Transportation, Federal Highway Administration, Highway Statistics Division.

Koltnow, P. G. 1985. "Improving Safety and Mobility for Older People." *TR News* 120(September/October):20–23.

Levine, N., and M. Wachs. 1985. *Factors Affecting the Incidence of Bus Crime in Los Angeles.* Report No. CA-06-0195, Washington, D.C.: U.S. Department of Transportation, Urban Mass Transportation Administration, Office of Technical Assistance, University Research and Training Program.

Motor Vehicle Manufacturers Association. 1984. *Motor Vehicle Facts and Figures '84.* Detroit, Mich.

Rosenbloom, S. 1982. "Federal Policies to Increase the Mobility of the Elderly and Handicapped." *Journal of the American Planning Association* 48(3, Summer):335–350.

Schaeffer, K. H., and E. Sclar. 1975. *Access for All: Transportation and Urban Growth.* Harmondsworth, England: Penguin Books.

Southern California Rapid Transit District. 1984. *Fare and Service Policies for the 1985 Fiscal Year.* Staff Report and Discussion Paper. October 11.

U.S. Department of Transportation, Urban Mass Transportation Administration. 1978. *Technical Report of the National Survey of Transportation Handicapped People.* Prepared by Grey Advertising. Washington, D.C.: U.S. Department of Transportation.

Wachs, M. 1979. *Transportation for the Elderly: Changing Lifestyles, Changing Needs.* Berkeley: University of California Press.

Wachs, M., and T. G. Kumagai. 1973. "Physical Accessibility as a Social Indicator." *Socio-Economic Planning Sciences* 7(5):437–456.

Zimmerman, C. 1981. *A Life Cycle of Travel by the American Family.* Report No. 7, Nationwide Personal Transportation Study, Washington, D.C.: U.S. Department of Transportation, Federal Highway Administration, Highway Statistics Division.

Cross-National Perspectives on Environments for the Aged

Sven Thiberg

As a foreign "reporter" in the area of environments for the aged, I have, with some difficulty, defined my task in this paper as one of providing a cross-national perspective by discussing phenomena that I consider to be characteristic of the Swedish situation regarding "the aging society." I have chosen to begin my paper with a brief summary of what I consider to be the extrascientific or social goals of Swedish aging policy within the social and built environment sectors and the research policy goals or tasks that follow from them. I base this summary on extensive material from reports by government commissions, research reports, and political documents. It would be going too far to maintain that there is consensus concerning the points I raise. Yet I consider that they reflect broad opinions and to a large extent can be stated to form a basis for practical action within the sectors concerned.

The advantage of my model is that it can be used as a structure for analyses both of actual conditions and changing trends and of research and research needs. In this context, I see one important research task being the evaluation of social goals: checking to ensure that government policy and programs have been set up to comply with what citizens see as necessary and

Sven Thiberg is with the Royal Institute of Technology, Stockholm, Sweden.

that society is able to meet their desires to a reasonable extent. In addition, researchers must clarify a number of quantitative and qualitative assumptions regarding aging and the society in which we grow old. The social and built environment constitutes a kind of intermediate link in this broad spectrum of phenomena, whose breadth does not exactly simplify our task or render the limitations of our subject field particularly self-evident.

In attempting a cross-national overview, the differences between the American and the Swedish views of society must be addressed early on. The American society is characterized by a greater pluralism. It is expected that different alternatives will emerge spontaneously and that the market mechanisms will function in such a way that satisfactory solutions successively crystallize. Swedish society is more homogeneous, and the welfare of all is a prominent societal goal to be attained through universal measures. National and local governments, therefore, also undertake the responsibility for development and change.

The great material and social gaps that exist in the United States among population groups would be unacceptable in Sweden. It is difficult to say exactly what sacrifices Swedish citizens make to achieve the material standard offered by our system of security based on taxes, pensions, allowances, and financing measures. The differences in the U.S. and Swedish social systems are particularly distinct when it comes to the elderly, who in neither country can any longer base their social and economic security on their own work or on relatives but are dependent on different types of welfare. How these welfare systems are constructed, who they cover, and who stands outside them are fundamental factors that also affect the design of the social and built environment.

IS THERE A GLOBAL PATTERN?

The changes in the age pyramid in all industrialized countries are characterized by a falling birth rate and growing longevity. Urbanization and industrialization often level out cultural and societal differences and lead to increasingly uniform life patterns.

An element in these life patterns is the separation of the generations as their economic dependence on one another diminishes. Improved health and a growing material standard enable the elderly to live an independent life. Only the very oldest are dependent on intensive care.

This trend has reached varying proportions and differs in its dramatic qualities in different countries. Sweden is an extreme case in terms of the economic independence of elderly persons and public responsibility for their care. Other countries base their policy toward the aging largely on assistance from relatives and on the elderly living together.

Yet to provide an answer to the question, "Is there a global pattern?", one must make assessments ranging over three fields. First, one must describe the present situation of the elderly. Depending on the resources and economy of different societies, the availability of data on this issue varies enormously. As is true of the United States and most industrialized countries, Sweden possesses abundant data about the demographic structure of the elderly population as well as about medical, social, and material conditions. The production of data in the developing countries is limited, and it is difficult to make statistically satisfactory comparisons. Yet the data suffice to confirm the great differences in living conditions in general terms *between* different countries and *within* different countries.

Second, one must describe the goals that exist for the lives of elderly persons in society across nations, a question that becomes immediately more difficult and of greater interest. Cultural differences appear that cannot be explained by simply coupling them to the degree of development in a country or to its material standard of living. A good example of this phenomenon involves Japan and Sweden. The differences between these two countries in material standard of living, education, and system of production are far less than the differences in cultural views and social valuations of the forms of life of the elderly. It is not merely that 7 percent of the elderly in Sweden and 60 percent in Japan live with relatives. The declared social goals of the two nations differ just as much. In Sweden, the national policy is that an independent life is desirable and that it can only be attained if older people live in their own homes; in Japan, the state advocates that the elderly shall live with their relatives. Great efforts are made in Sweden to support old people living on their own; in Japan, no reason is seen to develop such support because it is considered to conflict with the desirable social pattern.

Third, one must describe the factual changes in the respective countries and find explanations for them. Thus, although the Japanese policy toward the elderly may show the contrary (i.e., no change) or at all events a great inertia in the pattern of change, everything indicates that a growing degree of industrialization leads to increased mobility, the splitting up of households, and less stable families. In the long run, the trends have the effect of separating the young and the old even more than they are at present, and in general, cultural ties do not appear to be strong enough to prevent this development. This split, in turn, has necessitated changes in the financial maintenance systems of many nations and has given the elderly an economy that is even more independent of the young.

In the Western nations, we have become accustomed to speak of generation gaps. That such divisions exist is manifest. But it is not correct for that reason to draw the conclusion that economic independence creates such gaps. Recent Swedish studies show the contrary: that economic independence for both parties can lead to relations on equal conditions and with mutual social exchange.

THE SWEDISH EXPERIENCE

In 1984 a Swedish government commission summarized the housing conditions of the nation's elderly as follows.

The great majority (90 percent) of the Swedish population over 65 years of age live a normal life in ordinary housing. Of those citizens older than 75, 80 percent live in their own flat or house. Even in the group aged 85 and older, more than half live in an ordinary dwelling. Of the old-age pensioners, 2–3 percent live in a service block, pensioners' home, or the like; 7 percent live in institutions, 4 percent of which are old-age homes.

Nearly 90 percent of the elderly who live in ordinary housing have fully modern flats. Despite a rapid improvement in standards during the 1970s, however, the pensioners' housing standard is still inferior to that of the remainder of the population. Nearly half (43 percent) of the nonmodern housing stock is occupied by old-age pensioners. Every tenth pensioner lives in a nonmodern flat, every fifth pensioner in sparsely populated areas. Of the households of elderly persons—there are 428,999 in Sweden—43 percent are in small houses and have a lower average standard of equipment than those in blocks of flats. Many of the semimodern and nonmodern flats are pensioners' dwellings and pensioners' homes.

Some 135,000 elderly persons (29 percent) who live alone live in one room and a kitchen; that is, they lack a separate bedroom. Of households of two or more persons some 23,000 are in flats of at most one room and a kitchen, which for Sweden, constitutes a very low space standard. Many of these households are pensioners' dwellings or pensioners' homes.

According to the 1975 pensioners study, 40 percent of old-age pensioners who were not living in hospitals, nursing homes, and old-age homes were living on their own; broken down by sex, 20 percent of elderly men and 50 percent of elderly women were living on their own. The differences between the sexes may be explained by differences in length of life, differences in the ages of husband and wife at marriage, and differences in sex roles having to do with the availability of other people and the ability to look after a household by oneself.

More elderly people in Sweden now live on their own, both in absolute and relative terms. Today 47 percent (around 470,000) of all pensioner households consist of people living on their own. It is more common to find elderly persons living in blocks of flats than in small houses. There is also an increase in the number of people living on their own with age: 28 percent in the group aged 65–69 years compared with 56 percent in the group 85 years and older. According to a Swedish Control Bureau of Statistics forecast, the number of single persons aged 80 and older will increase by 40 percent by the turn of the century, at which point the total single population aged 80 and older will be 275,000.

Special Forms of Housing for the Elderly

In Sweden, pensioners' flats in ordinary blocks of flats, pensioners' homes, and service flats are examples of special solutions for the elderly within the framework of ordinary housing. Pensioners' flats in ordinary blocks are usually one- or two-roomers dispersed within a residential area. In 1975 there were about 22,000 such flats altogether, almost half of which were in the three metropolitan regions. The flats have varying standards: some are poor and not easily accessible, but there are also new and reconstructed flats with good accessibility. New production is on a small scale. There are also some 6,000 temporary pensioner flats, mostly in sparsely populated areas.

In 1975 there were about 41,000 pensioners' flats in approximately 2,500 pensioners' homes, most of them built before 1965; 80 percent were of the one-room-plus-kitchen/kitchenette type. Their standard varied greatly. Today, many of these homes are now closed down; some are being converted into service blocks.

In the early 1970s the local councils began to build service blocks for pensioners as a complement to ordinary housing and old-age homes. In 1982 there were just over 500 service blocks with about 26,800 service flats—ordinary flats but with access to a dining room, community and hobby rooms, social services, and medical care. The services offered by the service blocks vary according to the needs of the residents and to the block's proximity to the general services (e.g., post office, bank, social insurance office, library, cafeteria, and the like) available to all inhabitants in the area. Several local councils have also combined service blocks with local nursing homes/health centers to share premises and staff and to provide care and services to the service block residents.

The experience gained from the service blocks that have been built has led to a cutback in the plans for their extensions and to a reduction of the number of flats in them. During the period 1983–1987 the local councils planned nearly 400 building projects with some 10,600 service flats. In the planned service blocks, about 40 flats is the most common construction goal but several of the local councils do not plan to incorporate more than 10 to 15 flats in order to avoid segregation. One-third of the projects are for reconstruction and additions to old-age homes.

The Swedish Institutional Elderly Population

Sweden is among the countries that have a large number of places in institutions in relation to the number of elderly. Nearly three-quarters of the total cost for care of the elderly goes to institutional care, with slightly more than one-quarter going to service and care in the home. Of the 7 percent of the elderly who live in institutions, a little more than half are in old-age homes. In 1982 there were about 1,100 old-age homes with some 56,500 places. The size of the homes varies from 10 to more than 100 places. About half of the homes came into use after 1960. The average age of the residents is high—about 83 years.

In Sweden, the old-age homes are seen as a residential form for elderly persons who cannot look after themselves because their dwellings are uninhabitable or because they have a need for social assistance, or both. Staff are available around the clock. The pensioners have their own rooms, often with a toilet (72 percent) but seldom with a shower (12 percent); they also have access to a common dining room/sitting room. The standard of the oldest homes is low compared with ordinary housing. The average size of rooms is 12 square meters. Of about 500 two-story old-age homes, in 1975 about 200 had no lift. In 350 homes a wheelchair user could not pass in or out through the outer door.

The queues that had existed for places in the old-age homes are beginning to disappear; now, there are even vacant places. In fact, the number of places is falling by about 1,000 a year as the houses are being closed down or converted into service blocks with day centers, whose services—catering and pedicure—are available also to other pensioners in the neighborhood. Practically no old-age homes are being built in Sweden today.

Institutions for the Chronically Sick

Nearly 48,000 patients, 80 percent of whom are 75 years and older, are looked after in somatic long-term therapy. The hospitalization periods are long; according to the Association of County Councils' patient survey in 1983, every fourth patient had been hospitalized for more than 3 years.

According to the 1974 policy program of the Swedish National Board of Health and Welfare, the main function of long-term therapy is to provide for the long-term needs of treatment, activation, care, and nursing in as homelike a form as possible. Yet care is hardly a matter of homelike form in these institutions. The medical services have had a decisive influence on their organization and form. The standard of accommodation is very low. In 1975, according to the board, about 20 percent of the patients were in single rooms, 20 percent were in double rooms, 4 percent were in rooms with three beds, 40 percent were in rooms with four beds, and nearly 8 percent were in rooms with five or more beds. About half of the rooms had only a washbasin; about 6 percent of the rooms had a toilet, washbasin, and bath/shower. In about 4 percent of the rooms, there were no sanitary fixtures at all. About 2,800 patients had their own pictures, and around 1,000 had their own furniture. About 3,000 had radio, TV, and/or a tape recorder.

Of the patients currently in long-term therapy, 20 percent could be discharged—that is, according to a patient survey, they are judged to be no longer in need of treatment. That they have not been discharged may be due to several reasons: (1) they have no home to return to, (2) the housing conditions to which they could return are poor, (3) primary care and home help service is inadequate, and (4) they have no relatives who can help with care and nursing.

A study by the Swedish National Board of Health and Welfare within the framework of the development of a policy program for future health and medical services (HS 90) reveals the interaction between housing conditions and hospitalization: the utilization of hospitals, the number of stays in hospitals, and the mean duration of hospitalization are correlated to the size of dwelling. The mean duration of care was longer for those who lived in small flats. The numbers of patients discharged increased with the size of their flat. Elderly persons living on their own consistently have longer stays in hospital and fewer discharges than people living together.

It is often chance circumstances that decide whether an elderly person is institutionalized. Investigations show that transferences of the elderly are sometimes made to an unnecessarily high level of care. Many people who should have been able to move to nursing homes or service blocks are today placed in long-term care. Others are forced to move to a nursing home from a casualty department while waiting for a place in a service block.

Studies show that there is great economic scope for an increased assignment of resources to care in the home. At Sundsvall, where arrangements in the home have been sought for those waiting to enter institutions and service flats, the consequences after 3 years have been a certain surplus of places in institutions. There have been similar experiences at other places in the country.

Psychiatric Institutions

In October 1982, according to the National Board of Health and Welfare's patient survey, there were some 10,000 persons above 65 years of age in psychiatric care at institutions, the standard of accommodation at which is quite low. A trend toward less institutional forms of care, decentralization of resources to small units in people's local environment, and increased coordination with the social services is one of the fundamental principles for Swedish psychiatric care in the 1980s. Deinstitutionalization is thus a goal, and in the board's opinion, a substantial number of the persons now in psychiatric institutions could be discharged in the next few years, most to a normal dwelling with the support of the home help service and decentralized medical care.

THE SWEDISH WAY OF CHANGE

The official description of the progression of Swedish old-age policy development may be summed up as from the family, through the institution, to independent life.

Historical studies have shown that the so-called extended family has not been as commonplace nor as harmonious as nostalgia maintains. On the contrary, old people in an agricultural society had a difficult time. They were dependent on the young, and in a weak economy, they were set aside—shut out—and their rights were restricted. In reality, there was a "contract-out" system, a formal contract between children and parents. The contract stipulated the rights of the parents when they surrendered their property to the next generation. In rich farming families, those rights might consist of a dwelling of their own and free necessities. If the family was poor, the rights and freedom of the old people were limited. In an agricultural society, it was common that poor or childless old people were "farmed out" in the community to pay their way according to their ability by work.

The poorhouse was the predecessor of the Swedish old-age home, which in due course became the standard solution of the housing problems of the elderly. The building of old-age homes began in 1944. No old-age homes are now being built, however, and the existing ones are being converted into new residential forms as the phasing-out of institutions continues. The nation's housing policy for the elderly is directed toward independent living—in practice, remaining in one's dwelling on entry into the age of retirement. The question of institutionalization now crops up only when there is great need for continuous care. How great such care needs to be to necessitate institutionalization is a matter of dispute. Many experiments are now being conducted to evaluate home care as an alternative to institutionalization. Various intermediate forms that offer alternatives to home care have also been developed—for example, having one's own kitchen but also access to a dining room for collective meals.

In conjunction with the current major reconstruction of the housing stock in Sweden—chiefly those dwellings built from the turn of the century up to the 1940s—the question arises of the forms of dwellings for the elderly. This housing, which is situated in the central and semicentral parts of the larger towns, is occupied chiefly by elderly persons. Reconstruction and modernization, therefore, are directed toward the improvement of the quality of housing (chiefly in regard to accessibility and sanitary facilities) without forcing the occupants to move because of the work of reconstruction or increasing housing costs. The term "cautious reconstruction" has been coined and stands for the cautious handling of both the environment and the residents. In fact, cautiousness is often taken so far that consideration is paid to an individual's personal needs and desires, which has placed new requirements on organization and building methods that are in sharp contrast to the highly industrialized mass production technique the Swedish building industry developed during the so-called "million-flats program" during 1965–1975.

In parallel with the change of methods for the conversion of the physical environment, a change is also taking place in Sweden in the methods of the care and service organization. This change is at least as radical as those that occur in the physical domain. There are two forms of organization that meet and are on the way to becoming integrated with one another. Home care is a practical service consisting of cleaning, shopping, cooking, walks, and social intercourse that the local council offers old people in accordance with an estimate of need made by the social authorities.

Home nursing is provided by county council nursing personnel stationed in the so-called primary medical service. This form of care has always been offered but on a restricted scale. Earlier, when the need for care grew, the pensioner was quickly moved to an institution, usually an old-age home, but later to establishments for the chronically sick. Now, with old-age homes and institutions for the chronically sick being phased out, "heavy" care is increasingly assigned to local nursing homes. The chief tendency now, however, is to increase nursing service in the home and thus postpone or render unnecessary the move to an institution. It is also becoming increasingly common that, after temporary care in an institution for the chronically sick, perhaps following a transitional rehabilitation period, old people return to their normal accommodations with service and nursing in the home.

In sum, the number of persons in Swedish institutions is being drastically reduced, and a rapidly growing proportion of old people live on in their homes until the end. Rehabilitation for a return to normal living becomes increasingly common at ever higher ages. In short, in Sweden, independent living in normal housing is now common practice.

SCRUTINIZING THE GOALS

Presented below is the structure of "societal prerequisites" and "aims of research" mentioned earlier in this paper, which are to be used as a model for the analysis of the social and built environment for the aged. The societal prerequisites can be divided into four main areas: (1) fundamental attitudes, (2) aims of housing policy, (3) aims in the provision of housing, and (4) aims of the medical and nursing services.

The aims of research can be divided into three main areas: (1) research tasks, (2) the development of methods, and (3) the dissemination of knowledge.

Societal Prerequisites

Fundamental attitudes should include the following:

• The elderly are individuals with the same rights to independence, privacy, participation in community life, and security as persons of other ages.

• The provisions of dwellings for the elderly shall in all essential respects be based on a housing market common to all; and

• The housing market shall give the elderly a choice between different forms of dwellings and tenure to the same extent as other age categories.

The *aim of housing policy* can be stated as follows:

• The task of housing policy is, on the foundation of solidarity, to guarantee an abundant supply of forms of housing for all ages and types of households.
• Forms of housing shall be made economically and technically available through government financing and a governmental distribution policy.
• The elderly shall have their choice of dwelling according to need and desire and shall not be referred to special forms of residence as long as adequate care can be given to them in their own homes.

The *aim of housing provision* involves these factors:

• The existing housing stock shall be systematically converted to full accessibility by such methods and such financing as to make it easier for the elderly to remain in their homes. The modernization shall also comprise the external environment, service establishments, and communications.
• New housing efforts shall be directed toward strategic additions to the existing stock. It is especially important to provide for new forms of living environments that are difficult to realize in existing housing and to guarantee a good housing standard for the older small households.
• Both reconstruction and new construction shall be carried out with consideration given to the necessity of medical care for the elderly occurring to an increasing extent in their homes. Administration, maintenance, and care of the residential environment shall be of good quality and shall take place in close contact with the residents in order to increase well-being and security and reduce the risk of accidents.

The *aim of care services* subsumes these areas:

• Medical and health services, social services (home help), and local council consumer advisory services must be directed toward the provision of support and care in the home and the residential area. This focus will make it easier for the elderly to remain in their homes, and the need for institutional care will be reduced and directed toward the very oldest.

• The care of the chronically ill must be humanized by decentralization, conversion into small units, and increased openness and flexibility. Coordination between the governing bodies and within the administration shall bridge the gap between noninstitutional and institutional care. The institutions shall function as central points for noninstitutional care.

• All forms of care shall have as their goal to give security and facilitate daily life and, at the same time, release the elderly person's own resources for independence. Voluntary efforts play an important role in this context.

• Informal care—for example, by relatives—shall be voluntary on the part of both giver and recipient and does not absolve society of its responsibility. Care by relatives shall be given the support and relief that are the precondition for quality services.

• Staff development shall be directed to support for the changed view of care, to strengthening the capability of nursing staff, and to improving their working conditions and security of employment.

Aim of Research

The following research tasks should be pursued:

• Increased attention shall be devoted to societal changes in the long and short term that have a significance for the elderly person's life and conditions. Of special interest is the study of economic, social, and cultural changes in society; knowledge of their origin and structural effect is basic to the development of long-term strategies.

• Studies must be made of the environmental factors of importance for the elderly person's living conditions, of methods for affecting them, and of ways to develop good alternatives.

• Decision processes should be developed that allow the elderly a greater influence over their environment and that better serve their interests.

• The critical examination and evaluation of unusual solutions and experiments can be conducive to development and renewal.

Methods development should include the following:

- Creative but critical use of today's unused data in files and survey studies, and the linked processing of data bases with respect for the privacy of the persons studied, are needed.
- Methods for case studies should be developed as complements to surveys on an aggregated level. Of special interest are different degrees of action in the research and mobilization of the elderly in studies of their own conditions. Combinations of hard and soft data are important.
- The experience of those directly engaged in nursing and service delivery should be collected in categories that will make use of everyday field occurrences in the development of care methods and buildings.
- Scientific methods and results should be examined as a basis for the development of research capability and for relevance of the results as a basis for decisions; comparative studies are a step in the development of methods.

The dissemination of knowledge should proceed in a number of ways:

- Two-way communication is needed between the researchers and the surrounding world.
- The development of new channels for dissemination of results (e.g., through associations, trade union organizations, etc.) is needed.
- New media for communication, such as video and educational material, should be tried.

CONCLUSION

Even if it has not been stated outright, in both the United States and in Sweden, the question of an aging society is regarded as a problem. It is assumed that significant social adjustments are required to solve this problem. The discussion surrounding this issue has been primarily concerned with which adjustments are required, how they can be implemented, which sacrifices are demanded, and what results can be expected. This is apparently so self-evident that no one has found it necessary to mention the basic issue. Yet, in order to formulate the initial problem, one can start from the postulate that the aging of society would be no problem if the aging of the individual were not problematic.

It is possible to identify four frames of reference of problem areas under which many different questions about the aging of society and alternative solutions to the problems it seems to bring can be subsumed:

- Economics—The aging individual is economically dependent on resources that have either been acquired earlier in life or that others must offer.
- Social life—The aging individual slides out of the social networks offered by working life, family, and friends, and moves toward a growing state of isolation.
- Cultural context—The aging individual risks becoming estranged from the surrounding, rapidly changing society.
- Functional independence—The aging individual requires more practical support, care, medical treatment, and a greater adaptation of the environment to his capacities than do other age groups.

Both in Sweden and in the United States a large number of factors that fall within these frames of reference have been discussed. I find many similarities in the two countries in descriptions of the current situation and suggestions for action. Nevertheless, some important differences can be pointed out. One such difference is that the Swedish system of state welfare has been created with the objective of giving every elderly person, irrespective of his or her previous position in working life, an adequate economic base from which to maintain independence. To that end, we have a comprehensive pension system, complemented by individual-oriented support and subsidies, that is intended to make the common society also accessible to the elderly.

Another difference is that Swedish policies view the elderly as wishing to remain in their previous neighborhoods as long as possible. This is an area in which we offer flexible, versatile, and relatively generous individual support. In the long term, the individual's ability to remain in his or her former environment is facilitated by methodically constructing housing, neighborhood services, and communications to be easily accessible to all. Economically and socially, development has been rapid, which can be seen from the changing patterns of consumption among the elderly and in the processes of deinstitutionalization and increasing mobility.

On these two points, my North American colleagues have been less clear. Consequently, I hazard to assume that, in the United States, policy and thus perhaps also the work of research and development tend to focus on solving the problems of the elderly in isolation from other parts of society and other age categories.

The two other frames of reference of this "problematization" are, relatively speaking, "emptier" in Swedish debate and research. As a formerly homogeneous society, we are unfamiliar with both social and cultural tensions and differences. Only in recent years has the inflow of foreign life-styles and cultural patterns become so widespread that we can talk of a multicultural society. In addition, economic stratification is again increasing. The dearth of longitudinal studies has made it very difficult to determine what is happening at the individual level over time, as well as between generations and within society as a whole.

Perhaps it is this lack of historical insight that has led us to treat the social and cultural implications of aging so clumsily in Sweden. On this point, the North American contributions to the study of this issue have been of particular interest to me. The question can be formulated: Do the opportunities for physical integration, which the Swedish system offers, also lead to social and cultural integration between generations and individuals?

Our experience tells us that relations between relatives and work colleagues of the elderly are of such importance that it is difficult to compensate for their lack at advanced ages. For the elderly, to remain where they have always lived is the only available alternative, so as to maintain neighborly contacts built up in previous years. Beyond this point, we do not seem to know very much about what is actually happening other than that the generation that is elderly now is very much in favor of remaining in their accustomed housing.

If I have correctly interpreted the North American studies, the attitude in this country is somewhat different. There is no hesitation about creating new environments for old people; indeed, they are expected to demonstrate a great capacity for adaptation and be capable of building up new networks together with other elderly people. Yet, considering the differences between various strata of the U.S. population, about which there has been relatively little discussion, it seems reasonable to assume that the very large range in the standard of living of the poorest and the middle classes in the United States ought to also be reflected in attitudes and not only in the conditions offered to the elderly.

With these comments I approach what is my main impression of this conference: that we who work with the question of housing for the elderly, both in Sweden and in the United States, have a backward-looking perspective rather than a cross-cultural one. There is something of a weakness in not being able to imagine the view of aging in an aging society that coming generations will hold.

During the last few decades the health and economy of elderly people in Sweden have dramatically improved, but neither working life nor social and cultural patterns have adapted to these realities. Will this lead to a deepening of the generation gap? Can these social tensions lead to increased competition for social resources, compared to earlier generations, who "sacrificed" themselves for their children's well-being?

Will the divisions found in our societies between different economic and social strata increase with age? Can society compensate those who do not succeed in building up resources for their old age during their working life? And finally, what is the actual role of the growing number of elderly in the developments that lie ahead?

Technology and the New Environment for the Elderly

Robert L. Kane

Everyone from futurists to laymen can recognize the growth of technology. We are already capable of doing more than we can afford to do and often more than we dare. With capability come consequences and choices. Some choices reflect concerns about direct costs—are we willing to pay the bill? Other choices raise issues involving more subtle, indirect costs—if we change a manufacturing process, will a generation be unemployed? Ours is a society accustomed to seeing a problem as a challenge. We climb mountains because they are there; will we use technology for the same reason?

We now suffer as a society from technophilia. The level of our passion for technological answers has led us to respond almost instinctively with a technological solution to each problem posed. For a population frequently beset with functional incapacity, as are the elderly, there is no difficulty compiling a list of technological needs. Deficits in vision call for better lighting. Loss of memory motivates automatic prompts. Instability suggests new architecture and better design.

One question to be considered is who should supply and finance the new technology. The commercial response to our aging society is already apparent. Toothpaste ads have shifted from

Robert Kane is dean of the School of Public Health, University of Minnesota.

preventing cavities to avoiding plaque. Breakfast cereals promote fiber. In an entrepreneurial system, those things that can find a market are likely to appear. But many of the expensive technologies are charged to the public purse. The rules for personal consumption and public policy are different.

How could we choose to forgo technology when it can accomplish so much? A pair of refractive lenses can allow the myope to get around. A lens implant can restore active life to the cataract sufferer. A radial keratotomy means freedom from glasses. Should we pursue the first two and not the last? Is there a rule for deciding how much technology is appropriate?

Examples of technology to improve the environment of the elderly abound. We have mentioned eyeglasses. What about hearing aids? Certainly, more people could profit from them than currently use them, but part of the problem is that too many people profit already. Should society bear the cost of a relatively inexpensive mechanism to facilitate communication? At present Medicare pays for open-heart surgery but not for hearing aids. Why not? For one thing, hearing aids are not very expensive. But Medicare does not cover automobile purchases, either. Surgery is performed by relatively few persons in generally supervised surroundings; hearing aids are widely available. We are tempted to respond impatiently that open-heart surgery saves lives and reduces symptoms, but does a hearing aid not make a major difference in functioning?

The recent hearings surrounding cardiac pacemakers illustrate the power and the problem of medical technology. For the patient with complete heart block, a pacemaker may represent the difference between living and dying. Yet the system can be easily abused. Technology is both potent and lucrative. Once a procedure or a technology is covered by a third party, there is a strong incentive to use it actively. Manufacturers and physicians, and even patients, may collude to promote its use. When the level of persuasion reaches bonus payments and inducement gifts, we cannot help but note that we have gone too far. Yet how do we decide to curb our zeal at an earlier stage?

We have entered an era of artificial parts. Kidney transplants are commonplace; hearts still get attention. But we are well along in eyes, ears, and other brain functions as well. We can maintain people on respirators for years. Perhaps a better example is something less exotic, a treatment for the most prevalent condition of aging—arthritis. It is now possible to replace joints with artificial ones. Some orthopodists argue that aggressive replacement surgery can restore fine motor function and ambulation. Encouraged by the experience with hip replacements in the elderly, enthusiasts were silastic about treating osteoarthritis.

If we shudder at the prospect of extensive and expensive therapies, we are likely to be more enthusiastic about preventive technologies with their widely accepted 16:1 value ratio over cures. Age is not a barrier to preventive activities, although many of the most effective actions are better begun earlier in adulthood. Certainly, efforts aimed at screening—especially those that require only increased attention to frequently overlooked problems like depression—are appropriate. But so, too, are programs aimed at reducing risks such as smoking, providing nutritional therapy for osteoporosis, or immunizations against influenza pneumonia (Kane et al., 1985).

It is difficult to stop progress. Knowledge, especially technical knowledge, seems to increase logarithmically. Engineering problems are solved with increasing speed as equipment is packaged into even smaller units. The progress of social science has not been as rapid. We talk a great deal about costs and benefits and cost-effectiveness, but we avoid facing the critical assumptions that underpin these analyses. How do we measure the value of functioning? It used to be simple. We relied on measures of social productivity—earning capacity. Under such a system a rich man is worth more than a poor one; an unemployed person has no value. This kind of human capital approach has obvious limitations, especially for the elderly (Avorn, 1984). Yet the techniques proposed to replace it are difficult to use and generally unsatisfactory (Kane and Kane, 1982). Nonetheless, we cannot escape the question of values. If we are to compare the relative benefits of technologies, we must confront the value questions.

Koshland (1985) has remarked on society's inability to think in quantitative terms. He is concerned with our society's failure to appreciate the importance of the scientific approach to problem analysis. How much more difficult is the task of developing a sensitivity to the large numbers. We simply do not think well in quantitative terms. We are a risk-aware society. We go to great lengths to avoid major catastrophes but ignore the daily small-scale disasters. In fact, in 1984 there were only 69 accidents in this country that killed five or more people. Yet we design our public transportation to avoid crashes and deaths. We insist on strict and often redundant life safety codes for the institutions that house our elderly, even when these requirements may interfere with the quality of life for the residents. When quantification is used as the basis for measuring values, the results are often confusing. Tversky and Kahneman (1981) have documented the problems of getting consistent responses to even simple value dilemmas; nonetheless, it is possible to explore differences among different groups about value-laden issues concerning care of the elderly (Kane et al., forthcoming).

The forecasts for technological change are not confined to the health area. One does not need scientific studies to recognize the growth of computers in all phases of our lives. Personal computers are developing almost as rapidly as did the ballpoint pen. It is easy to anticipate that we will be linked in various kinds of networks to exchange information and accomplish daily tasks. This form of technology can have major benefits for segments of the elderly population by creating a new environment in which social isolation can be reduced. For example, it permits a new form of automated home care with telemetric monitoring. Older individuals confined to the house can now participate in various kinds of interactive exchanges with service providers without incurring the high costs necessary for home visits.

At the same time, the introduction of new information-processing approaches raises the specter of intellectual obsolescence. Stereotypically, older workers are seen as having greater difficulty in accommodating to new situations. Anecdotally, one hears about the aversion of older persons to computers and similar machines. They are reported to be less willing to use automated tellers at banks, for example. The recent (1985) report by the Office of Technology Assessment (OTA) challenges this view. It notes several instances in which older individuals have begun to work effectively and enthusiastically with computers. The potential for using such computers for self-care and health education, as well as for direct communication on the monitoring of physiological and psychological functioning, strongly argues for a more aggressive effort to encourage older people to become comfortable in the computer world. Our own recent experience in conducting pilot tests using computers to screen for cognitive dysfunction confirms the OTA conclusions. We found that older subjects were enthusiastic and adapted well to computerized testing. The challenge is to develop comfortable mechanisms to bridge the man–machine interface.

It is also important to recognize that the elderly do not arise de novo. They come as part of a life-cycle transition. The elderly of tomorrow will have been far more exposed to computers during their earlier lives than is the case with the current generation of older persons. The discomfort with the introduction of new social technologies is not so much an effect of age as it is the effect of novelty across all age groups.

This same theme of changing technologies influences the work place. The introduction of increased mechanization can have at least two principal effects. It may alter the nature of the job in such a way that older workers have increasing difficulties in adapting to newer tasks and find themselves uncomfortable because the skills previously in high demand have now been replaced by automated devices. Automation will often have a more profound effect in reducing the need for manpower. As the number of available jobs decreases, older people are seen as a blockage in the pipeline to upward mobility. Increasing pressures develop for early retirement. Because older workers tend to have accumulated more seniority and have higher rates of pay, employers are often eager to move them out as quickly as possible in order to make room for younger, cheaper workers.

The push to early retirement has created a whole new technology: the technology of leisure. With the increase in life expectancy and the tendency toward early retirement, we are now looking at periods of 15 to 25 years of unemployed time. For many this is a period with relatively good incomes but inadequate stimulation to make the time meaningful. Some have expressed a fear that retirement may lead to increased morbidity, but this view is not universally shared. At present the evidence to support either position is scanty at best.

IMPLICATIONS OF TECHNOLOGY FORECASTS

The growth of technology has expanded our definition of the art of the possible. More than ever before, we are in a position to provide more services to more people. Looked at individually, many of these services promise significant benefits. For example, a recent study of total knee replacement for advanced joint disease among chronic arthritis patients suggests that the surgical procedure improves psychological well-being by reducing or eliminating knee pain. Investigators argue that these quality-of-life improvements may be enough to offset the annual cost of the procedure. Positive outcomes are expressed in terms of reductions in anxiety, depression, fatigue, and psychosomatic complaints as well as an improvement in family relationships and participation in social activities—an impressive array of benefits (Christianson, 1985).

Although we may find fault with studies that rely simply on before-and-after measures, the problem is less with the methodology of the research than with the implications of the findings. Are we now to embark on a series of similar ventures in which most of the several hundred joints in the body are tested for their replaceability? We have the capacity to maintain respirator-dependent individuals for long periods of time. Many of these individuals can function productively with such maintenance. Are we going to ration such care and on what grounds?

Prior to 1972 we used just such a rationing approach with the treatment of end-stage renal disease. Under those circumstances, the elderly were generally excluded from access to such treatment, although they were the only group covered under Medicare at the time. With the passage of the 1972 amendments to the Social Security Act, however, coverage was expanded to all age groups. Ironically, the elderly, the only group whose benefits did not change, suddenly were offered ready access to treatment that had previously been denied. The difference was the expansion in the supply of treatment facilities for end-stage renal disease. Looking back, many social commentators have identified the decision to cover this disease as a policy mistake. The Medicare program now faces similar decisions about covering other categories of intervention, especially other forms of organ transplantation.

The study by Aaron and Schwartz (1984) of health care rationing in the United Kingdom raises the specter of similar approaches in this country. Until now the United States has operated on a different ethic. Given our inherent entrepreneurial nature, Americans have been quick to promote any intervention that appears to respond to a need or attract a market.

A first line of defense may lie in challenging the efficacy of any given intervention. Yet many of these therapies will indeed prove to be efficacious. The real issue will revolve around the relative efficacy of one strategy over another. More and more we are hearing concerns that our society cannot afford all the things it wants to do. As our capacity for providing more care increases, the pressure to make difficult choices will increase as well.

In some instances, this choice is being expressed as a competition between different age groups. For example, a magazine article criticized expenditures on the elderly at the expense of children (Preston, 1984). These accusations of intergenerational inequity open a Pandora's box of questions about the obligations of one generation for another.

Part of the issue involves the question of whose resources are at stake. We are seeing people enter the retirement years at increasing levels of affluence supported by private as well as public funds. In the main, we have generally argued that decisions made about the disposition of private funds were the responsibility of the individual, whereas those involving public funds used a different set of criteria. As private outlays influence the rate of demand for public support, however, this distinction may be rapidly evaporating.

The question then becomes one of how we will ration rather than whether we will ration. Up to now, much of the power in the area of health care has been placed in the hands of care providers, particularly physicians. The push toward capitated systems of health care and the active involvement of employers in seeking to control the costs of care have created a new environment with new players but no evidence of new rules. In the past, we have argued that prepaid health care systems provided consumer protection by permitting the consumer to leave whenever he was dissatisfied. However, closer inspection suggests that this consumer protection is illusory. A consumer frustrated at not receiving expensive care to which he feels entitled may exercise his departure option, but the prepaid system is happy to see him go as a liability. Thus, decision making must find a way to encompass the value systems of both the consumer and the provider-payer. To accomplish this end, we need a better articulation of the relative value preferences of all of the groups concerned.

For the elderly worker the growth of technology represents a danger of obsolescence based on the rapid turnover of knowledge. Old skills are no longer valued and may prove to be impediments if they are held too tightly. The introduction of machinery for manual performance and computations places a great emphasis on the speed of performance, one area in which age has been shown to be associated with deterioration in function. These factors, coupled with a major expansion of the work force created by the maturing of the baby boom generation, produce a condition of worker excess that produces additional pressures for early retirement. The challenge to society is thus to cope with a generation of retired, productive individuals.

A number of suggestions have been offered as to how we might respond to this situation. We have been encouraged to think of the "third age" as an opportunity to develop new career patterns. Some have suggested that the natural life history of an individual should include a shift to a second and even a third career as a source of regeneration. None of these suggestions has dealt with the question of an excess labor force, however, nor with the competition presented by younger workers for a berth in the second career slot.

Another suggestion has been to advocate volunteerism. A variety of options have been presented. In some cases the volunteerism is purely altruistic, or at least it has as its major reward the satisfaction that comes from doing something meaningful. In other circumstances, volunteer work produces credits that can be cashed in for services when the volunteer himself becomes dependent. Volunteerism is enormously popular with the current administration, which is dedicated to reducing public expenditures on social services, but it carries with it a potential stigma in a society in which we are used to paying for things we value. Much of the experience with volunteers in general suggests that they are expensive to maintain and difficult to direct toward the really unpleasant jobs. There is a fine line to be walked between volunteering and coercion. Especially for those dependent on public pensions or other forms of public support, the incentives to volunteer may become stronger than the internal motivation.

GENERAL ISSUES

Gerontologists have pointed out the need to differentiate between age groups and cohorts. As we begin to look toward the future and its implications for the aged, we must be careful to distinguish which group of the aged we are addressing. It is dangerous to extrapolate from our current experiences with the elderly toward those who will be elderly in one or two decades.

These future elderly may age with a number of different characteristics. Physiologically, they may be quite different from those who have gone before them. For example, they have been exposed to a higher level of socioeconomic status and better medical care than ever before. Although some have argued that advances in medical care will reduce mortality at the expense of morbidity by allowing the less fit to survive, others have suggested that, indeed, those surviving into old age may bring to it much healthier bodies.

Not only are the bodies of the elderly likely to be different; so, too, are their psyches. The last several decades have witnessed a society very much steeped in consumerism. If old age is associated with dependency, how much greater will be the dependency of those who are bred to depend on external agencies for services at much younger ages? In some parts of the United States today, it is fashionable to have a manager for one's finances, one's diet, one's exercise, and even one's personal life. What can we expect such a well-managed individual to be like when he becomes old and dependent?

We have already seen the emergence of the major market forces in response to the increasing amount of leisure time available to people during their working years. What can we expect of technology for leisure time amidst a group of individuals with few other commitments? Information technology may become focused on re-education—not for careers but for the pleasure of learning and the entertainment value derived therefrom. Machines may become companions, adapting themselves to the needs and demands of their users, providing a bridge to the outside world that compensates for various disabilities. The same machines may serve as prods and reminders to encourage individuals to pursue invigorating activities that maintain function and maximize health.

As we move into an era of increasing electronic communication, we may see ourselves giving up much of our traditional patterns of social contact. It is difficult to estimate the effect of this kind of electronic social isolation on the elderly. Anecdotal evidence suggests that programs such as the call-in radio shows provide an important vehicle by which older, housebound individuals stay in contact with society. A more sophisticated linkage by telephone or electronic media that goes beyond electronic mail to put people into visual communication may overcome much of the social isolation that has plagued the disabled elderly until now. The ability to interact with machines as well as with other people may provide the elderly with a much more patient, reinforcing set of social partners than they have experienced before.

One of the choices we make as a society is the degree to which we can and will steer the development and direction of technology. Looking back over the last several decades, we have seen several good examples of specific, goal-directed technology in programs like the space program. To some extent the by-products of the technological investment have spun off into some civilian applications. Certainly, the development of the computer industry and the microchip are direct by-products of that activity. That program was undertaken in a spirit of competition. Somehow success in space was equated with maintaining the preeminence of our culture. Although it is not easy to see how one can readily develop an analogous argument, it is tempting to speculate on how we might mobilize our society in quest of a better life for the elderly as a test of our national spirit. If such activity and commitment could be viewed as evidence of the power of society, we might find ourselves embarking on a program that would benefit us and our children.

REFERENCES

Aaron, H. J., and W. B. Schwartz. 1984. *The Painful Prescription: Rationing Hospital Care.* Washington, D.C.: Brookings Institution.

Avorn, J. 1984. Benefit and cost analysis in geriatric care. *New England Journal of Medicine* 310:1295–1301.

Christianson, C. L., et al. 1985. *Total Knee Replacement Study.* PB85-236909/A5. McLean, Va.: National Technical Information Service.

Kane, R. L., R. M. Bell, and S. Z. Riegla. Forthcoming. Value Preferences for Nursing Home Outcomes. *Gerontologist.*

Kane, R. L., and R. A. Kane. 1982. *Values and Long-term Care.* Lexington, Mass.: D.C. Heath.

Kane, R. L., R. A. Kane, and S. B. Arnold. 1985. "Prevention and the Elderly: Risk Factors." *Health Services Research* 19 (Part 2):945–1006.

Koshland, D. E., Jr. 1985. "Scientific Literacy." *Science* 230:391.

Office of Technology Assessment. 1985. *Technology and Aging in America.* Washington, D.C.: U.S. Congress.
Preston, S. H. 1984. "Children and the Elderly in the U.S." *Scientific American* 251:44–49.
Tversky, A., and D. Kahneman. 1981. "The Training of Decisions and the Psychology of Choice." *Science* 211:453–458.

Design Problems in Enhancing Productivity and Independence in Housing for the Elderly

Victor Regnier

Design research addressing the behavioral aspects of built environments is a relatively new area of investigation. The professional organizations and journals that deal with this body of scholarship are less than 20 years old and continue to sort out the fundamental relationships that exist between the designer and the behavioral based environmental design researcher. In the last few years, several books (Moore et al., 1985; Sommer and Sommer, 1981; Zeisel, 1981) have been written that inform designers in a careful and thorough way how to interpret research findings and how to use the methodology of social science inquiry in the design and programming process to ensure that the final product is responsive to the social and behavioral needs of users.

BEHAVIORAL RESEARCH AND ENVIRONMENTAL DESIGN

For the last 16 years, organizations like the Environmental Design Research Association (EDRA) have attempted to develop a dialogue between architectural designers and social science

Victor Regnier is associate professor of architecture and gerontology, University of Southern California.

researchers. This organization has been committed to sharing research methods and techniques that clarify the relationship between a designed environment and the human response to that environment.

EDRA has experienced some difficulty in its efforts to serve both designers and researchers. The design-oriented members of the organization are generally concerned with communicating findings and with the ultimate application of behavioral research to the design of the environment. Social science researchers, on the other hand, are concerned with increasing the sophistication of research methods and modifying traditional social science models to better understand the relationship between the physical environment and human behavior. Social science researchers tend to be more interested in the development of theory-based research that contributes to a better understanding of predictive models of human behavior. Designers are interested in the evaluation of the environment and in identifying the design details, physical design parameters, and design concept modifications that lead to a more successful and satisfying design product.

An Application Gap Between Designers and Researchers

There is a lack of overlap between the interests and work of environmental designers and that of social science researchers. The gap has widened as a result of the tendency of environmental design researchers and social scientists to define the goals of their research or design activities in such a way as to preclude the interest and influence of one another's work. The result is that designers retreat further from the application of theory-based methodologies and social science researchers become less concerned about how to "apply" their findings.

Design research in gerontology and other aspects of life-span development has played a fundamental role in the development of design research methodologies and the creation of new knowledge. The activities of the Gerontological Society's Aging and Environments Committee occurred at a strategic time in the development of the field of design research inquiry. This project, which brought together social scientists and designers with interests in aging (Byerts et al., 1979; Lawton et al., 1982), provided a tremendous boost to the development of research in this field. Many environmental design researchers who had not been interested in gerontology immediately recognized the information needs of designers who hoped to create settings that supported a clientele who were considered "at risk." Social science researchers saw the opportunity to develop new social and behavior theories of environment that capitalized on the psychosocial changes in later adult development.

In 1981 Zeisel wrote a book entitled *Inquiry by Design,* which provided methods and suggestions for how designers and researchers could work together in improving theory and offering better applications of evaluation research to the design process. The book carefully inspected the iterative process used by designers to develop acceptable design solutions and suggested where and how behavioral issues and social science input could be linked to the holistic process of design decision making that is sensitive to behavioral concerns.

Research Should Inform Design

Zeisel conceived of the design process (Figure 1) as a linked spiral influenced by two types of input: image information and test information. Image information is used to refine aesthetic and visual expression in the design product; test information that comes from standards, environmental (natural forces) research, and behaviorally based research allows the designer to evaluate the design's functional attributes objectively. The designer typically arrives at a solution by using image information to create a drawing of the proposed environment. Test information is used to judge the quality and soundness of that design idea. The final design solution is the product of hundreds of these iterations, which vary in scale and application. One iteration could be as broad as testing the overall design concept; the next could fine-tune details related to a kitchen cabinet design (Figure 2).

Design behavior research, in addition to being used as test information in the design process, is also used at the programming stage. An architectural program is a written document that serves as the communication between the architect and the client. It specifies design intentions, behavioral objectives, equipment, and furnishings. It is developed early in the design,

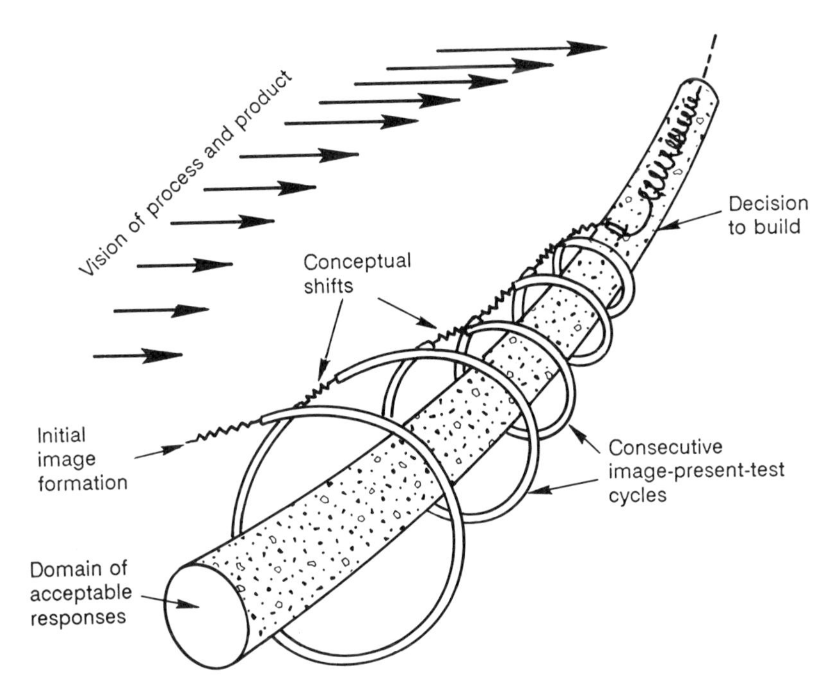

FIGURE 1 The design development spiral. SOURCE: Zeisel (1981).

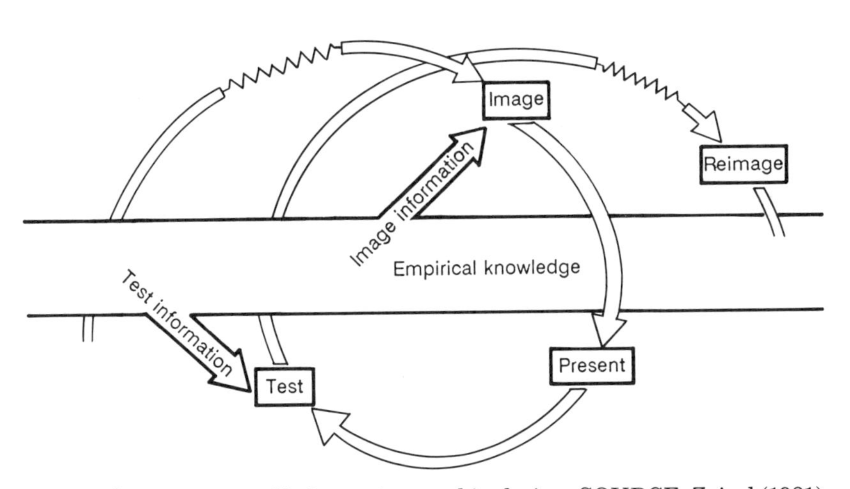

FIGURE 2 Two types of information used in design. SOURCE: Zeisel (1981).

often before drawings are completed. The program contains information that places parameters around the design problem. Behavioral research is frequently used to arrive at principles and concepts that are articulated through the program.

The program from a fully developed design can also provide working hypotheses for design research. Postoccupancy evaluation is the term for the design evaluation process commonly used to test design intentions and behavioral assumptions articulated in architectural program. New knowledge, which results from the evaluation of an occupied building, is used to aid design decision making and to correct behavioral assumptions in future programming documents. When postoccupancy evaluation is carried out, design intentions and hypotheses developed during the design process can be tested as research questions, thus measuring the appropriateness and accuracy of design assumptions.

Captain Eldridge Congregate Housing

One example of how postoccupancy evaluation can be structured and made more explicit and meaningful to designers is through annotated plans that state environment behavior hypotheses (Zeisel, 1981). The Captain Eldridge Congregate House in Hyannis, Massachusetts, illustrates 11 design-based research questions. The designers and the researcher developed these design hypotheses and linked them to the appropriate area on a plan of the first floor. This project is a sheltered housing environment that accommodates 20 older people. Many of these design hypotheses are based on the results of previous research that has been used to develop the design solution. For example, the design of the stair landing and the rail detail near the elevator lobby have been constructed to allow residents to "preview" the lower floor lounge before entering that setting. One design hypothesis suggests that "building residents will use the opportunity to preview spaces before making a commitment to enter them." This behaviorally based design issue can be tested after the building has been constructed and occupied.

The design–behavior hypotheses illustrated in the Captain Eldridge Congregate House range from statements dealing with the mix of unit types and sizes to assumptions that the environment will mediate social interaction. Developing intention statements as a by-product of the design process allows important ideas to be made explicit for later testing.

PROBLEMS ASSOCIATED WITH RESEARCH TRANSLATION

The most effective means of recording and testing the behavioral outcomes of design are through the development of a complete behaviorally based program and the postoccupancy evaluation of the design objectives established for the project. When program development and evaluation take place, behavioral intentions are made explicit and the intended social purpose of the building can be judged as successful or unsuccessful.

Unfortunately, the architectural profession often treats programming as an added predesign service and considers postoccupancy evaluation to lie outside the normal range of services needed to design a building. This philosophy often results in structures that are designed without either of these two elements. In the future, programming services may become more common as architects recognize how an architectural program can (1) stimulate effective communication between client and architect, (2) minimize misunderstandings that may often lead to litigation, and (3) lead to more confidence in the architect, repeat work, and a greater likelihood of being referred to other clients for future work.

Postoccupancy evaluation (POE) research will become more common as academic institutions and independent research organizations pursue design evaluation. Yet it is unlikely that the amount, pace, and precision of future POE research in the near future will be great enough to satisfy the overwhelming needs of design decision makers.

Greater Professional Recognition for Research

Another problem that leads to a lack of interest in the behavioral impact of design is the lack of attention it receives from the architectural profession and the most prestigious architectural journals. The architectural design journals (*Progressive Architecture, Architectural Record,* and *Architecture*) typically display "current" work and are most interested in the expressive, artful design solution that explores new design styles and rarely addresses the social and behavioral aspects of design explicitly. This disregard for how architecture affects people is also reflected in the way architectural criticism is conducted. In some cases, architects may even pursue solutions that are antithetical to the needs of specific clients in search of a new philosophy of expression. Although functionalism is considered by some to be an important attribute of a "good" architectural design, in the eyes of critics it is definitely a necessary but not sufficient condition for judging the design creativity and overall quality of a final architectural product.

The 1980s have seen radical changes in the acceptance of design philosophies as "post-modernism" and a wave of expressive and highly decorative building forms replace the more staid and disciplined philosophies of the "international school." Architectural journals that had little of philosophical interest to report in the 1970s now find themselves leading the effort to communicate the stylistic interpretations of this new wave of design ideas. The behavioral design movement has suffered as attention has shifted to art expression in design while ignoring the effects of design on users.

Design Journals Ignore Behavioral Impacts of Design

New design ideas use design metaphors, search for historical precedents, and generally involve more ornamentation and decoration. The design professions and design journals have encouraged the pursuit of new directions at the expense of any careful understanding of how these new design ideas affect people. In fact, only one U.S. architectural journal has a specific policy of reviewing buildings that are completed and occupied before they are "published." Interest in pursuing the newest ideas at the expense of understanding how buildings work for occupants and users has encouraged a type of irresponsible architectural style that pursues stylistic expression at the expense of a more thorough and deeper understanding of the building and its qualities.

On the other hand, behaviorally based journals dealing with design themes, such as the *Journal of Architectural and Planning Research,* rarely pursue design in the context of research. The reporting of the results of postoccupancy evaluations is frequently undertaken with little understanding or concern about the overall quality of the design work being evaluated. Furthermore, the lack of a critical tradition in design research makes the architects whose buildings are being evaluated very uncomfortable with the process of "objective" evaluation.

Designs that do not work for occupants or that are outright behavioral failures ironically can be design award winners. One need go no further than Pruitt-Igoe, the infamous St. Louis public housing development, to uncover a project that received widespread professional recognition and several design awards upon completion. In less than 10 years, it was recognized as a behavioral design failure, and plans for demolition were approved.

DESIGN ISSUES AND CONCEPTS

The following six design-related issues and concepts are important themes that frequently appear in the environmental design research literature:

- physiological issues,
- sensory aspects of design,
- social interaction and social exchange,
- way-finding,
- neighborhood concerns, and
- management and design.

The following discusses how each theme has been defined in research efforts and the implications for design application.

Physiological Issues

One of the most critical yet overlooked aspects of the physical environment is the matching of equipment, furnishings, and design details to the special physiological needs of the older person. The most obvious and embarrassing design errors are those that reflect an ignorance of basic physiological requirements. Windows that are impossible for the arthritic hand to manipulate; kitchen storage that requires back-breaking bending or a reaching device to access; doorknobs that are difficult to turn; controls that are impossible to read; and furniture that is difficult to enter or exit are a few of the most frequently cited design mistakes (Koncelik, 1979).

Better Communication of Research Findings

The results of numerous postoccupancy evaluations and the growing experience and sensitivity of manufacturers to the "graying" profile of the American consumer have had some influence on product development. Yet it is still relatively easy to find new elderly housing projects without lever door handles or congregate housing projects that specify bathtubs with poorly located grab bars. Problems in this area frequently do not require more research but rather better communication of research findings and good practice habits to design decision makers.

Older consumers who have been sensitized to these issues now frequently insist that safety features and "considerate" design solutions be employed. Some solutions, however, appear so institutional as to make them clearly unacceptable (Steinfeld, 1979) because of the associations they have with disability or nursing home environments.

Barrier-free Design and Adaptable Housing

Steinfeld conducted extensive analyses that involved research in human factors as well as empirical tests of various design solutions for the physically disabled. The findings from his research were used to revise the new American National Standards Institute (ANSI) (1980) handicapped design standard.

In analyzing the existing research in the area of disability, Steinfeld discovered a complete lack of empirical data regarding the use of bathrooms and limited data regarding the use of kitchens and small circulation spaces such as elevators. He also found the literature on the use of ramps to be conflicting.

One of the most promising new ideas that arose from the research project was the notion of "adaptable" housing. Steinfeld identified three major areas of the dwelling unit that have significant effects on the adaptability of the unit; kitchen design, bathroom design, and circulation/clearance. His primary thesis was that housing designed from the outset using accessibility criteria and including tolerances and clearances for wheelchair users will not add significantly to building costs and later can be easily adjusted for various disabled or handicapped users.

Among the requirements for an adaptable kitchen are: adjustable features such as sink and work areas that can be lowered and raised; wall cabinets mounted 48 inches above the floor; wall-mounted, self-cleaning ovens; pantry storage; and double-door refrigerators with 50 percent of the freezer space lower than 54 inches.

The simple idea that housing may be adapted to the particular needs of the occupant resolves the question of what type of "special hardware" should be specified in housing for the elderly. Steinfeld's adaptable housing prototype develops a flexible foundation that can be changed as the resident's increasing disabilities warrant greater support.

Much work needs to be done in understanding how inexpensive adjustments to single-family housing can enhance safety and independence. Because approximately 70 percent of those over age 65 live in independent, single-family, owner-occupied dwellings, solutions that retrofit these environments to support the older person's independence can have great influence.

Sensory Aspects of Design

Changes associated with normal aging frequently affect the acuity, accuracy, and general functioning of sensory organs. Taste, touch, sight, and hearing can all experience normal incremental losses as an organism ages. In some cases, these losses or partial losses can profoundly affect the way in which the environment is perceived or used. Sensory losses must be fully understood so that design practices can compensate and not exacerbate these problems.

The most common and design-sensitive sensory loss is that of sight. Low light levels and poor figure-to-ground contrast in designs, labels, and graphics can make it difficult to read important messages and cues (Pastalan, 1979). One of the strategies available for dealing with problems of visual loss is to create a high level of diffused light on critical surfaces where light is needed (Hiatt, 1980).

The Treatment of Light Is a Major Issue

The addition of more light can cause major problems by introducing glare. To mitigate glare, single light sources and high contrasts in light levels should be avoided. Design solutions should strive to use indirect light sources because they minimize glare. Food preparation counters in the kitchen, the toilet and bathtub, and corridor spaces in which older person can trip and fall are a few of the critical settings in which careful attention to lighting can increase safety.

Hearing loss can also be a critical sensory issue. Increasing the absorption of unwanted sound in spaces in which conversations take place and minimizing reverberation and background noise are common environmental strategies that are used to respond to hearing problems.

The Empathic Approach to Age-related Vision and Hearing Changes

The "empathic model," which simulates the environment as it is experienced by older persons with normal sensory losses (Pastalan, 1979), can be a useful training and research device. The model consists of a pair of glasses with specially coated lenses to simulate normal, age-related vision losses and an audio baffling device that reduces the volume and filters out high-frequency sounds. When outfitted with this equipment, a younger researcher can simulate the conditions under which an older person may perceive the physical environment. The empathic model has been used as a postoccupancy evaluation device outfitting the researcher with a way of noting the perceptual problems an older person might have in negotiating an environment.

Normal age-related changes in vision involve a decrease in visual acuity and a decrease in the ability to refocus on objects at different distances. Older people also find it difficult to see well under low light conditions, to discern certain color intensities (color differences between green and blue are often confused), and to judge distances.

Progressive hearing loss normally leads to an inability to hear high-frequency sound and a reduction in the ability to hear all sounds in general. Background noises, particularly low-frequency sound, interferes with the older person's ability to hear normal conversations. The empathic model allows the design researcher to literally place himself in the perspective of the older user. Problems such as glare, color differences, and contrast problems are vividly perceived. Additionally, design solutions that take into consideration normal aging sensory losses can be tested with this device.

Redundant Cueing Relies on Several Sensory Messages

Because sensory loss varies by individual, it is important for designers to use compensation devices fully. Redundant cueing is a concept that involves a combination of light, sound, and surface texture; it is used to alert the older person of an upcoming event or problems. Redundant cueing is particularly helpful with older people who may be suffering a severe loss of one or more senses. One of the most common examples of redundant cueing is the simultaneous use of a lighted button and a synchronized tone in an elevator (Figure 3) to alert the rider when the appropriate floor has been reached. Also becoming popular are street signals coupled with a two-tone sonic alarm to alert the blind when to safely cross the street.

FIGURE 3 Redundant cues in an elevator. SOURCE: Koncelik (1976).

Social Interaction and Social Exchange

One of the primary purposes behind the development of age-segregated housing for the elderly has been the desire to increase opportunities for social interaction and friendship formation. Implicit in this topic is the assumption that the environment can increase one's control over social activity levels, which, in turn, can combat depression and lead to a higher level of life satisfaction. Yet there is a general lack of experimental or quasi-experimental research that has carefully tested this assumption.

Much of the research in this area has come from postoccupancy evaluations that, through behavior observation and tenant interviews, have sought to identify environmental features and physical configurations that support or encourage socializing (Carp, 1966; Howell, 1980; Lawton, 1975; Regnier, 1985a). Spaces intended to promote social interaction, such as community rooms, entry areas, and lounges, are closely scrutinized in these evaluations. Patterns of spatial use from behavioral mapping research are combined with attitudinal data from tenants and management to resolve evaluation questions related to use.

The Use of Shared Spaces

Howell has focused a major part of her research on the performance of public housing designed for the elderly. In-depth case studies of shared spaces using postoccupancy evaluation techniques are documented in her book, *Designing for Aging: Patterns of Use* (1980). Howell's study is limited to high-rise public housing facilities located in New England and occupied by older persons who moved into the buildings in the 1970s.

Shared spaces are defined as all areas within the building other than apartment units and areas for machinery and maintenance equipment. They include all spaces used by residents for social purposes. Such spaces range from laundry rooms to multipurpose/recreational rooms to hallways and elevator lobbies.

In housing facilities for the elderly, shared spaces become behavioral settings for activities such as social exchange and the formation of new friendships. Howell discovered that several important space relationship factors led to differential shared space use. Figure 4 illustrates three typical relationships between shared space in a housing project and the primary path.

(The primary path is the circulation route that links the front door with the elevator.)

The Branch Provides More Choices and Control

In Howell's research, the "branch arrangement" was considered an optimum social/behavioral solution. The "corridor," which is symbolic of an open-plan solution, was thought to create uncomfortable confrontations between older people who are entering or leaving the building and those using social spaces. The "cul-de-sac" arrangement had the opposite effect. Because of the isolation of shared spaces, typically at the end of a double-loaded corridor, few residents felt they could drop in casually and interact with others. The decentralized cul-de-sac arrangement required the resident to make a special commitment to enter the shared space, thus discouraging impromptu social exchange. The implication for this research is that designers may inadvertently create "friendly" or "isolated" buildings, depending on how they arrange spaces for groups to share and how they treat the visual connections between popular circulation routes and shared spaces.

The design variables that were thought to have the greatest impact on social behavior in the study included length of the primary path (front door to elevator); location, differentiation, and size of the social spaces; and visual connections between shared spaces and corridors.

Designing housing for the elderly to promote friendship foundation and sociability is a goal that all designers should embrace. An emphasis on promoting socializing, however, should be coupled with an understanding of privacy and the need to control, manage, and sometimes avoid social interaction. More research is needed to understand how furniture, partial partitions and screens, amenities and activities, and the ecological composition of the resident population mediate the social successfulness of housing for the elderly.

Way-finding

One design feature that affects a person's self-confidence, as well as his or her level of anxiety when using a new building, is the degree to which one can orient and move from one area of a building to another without getting lost. The disorientation that

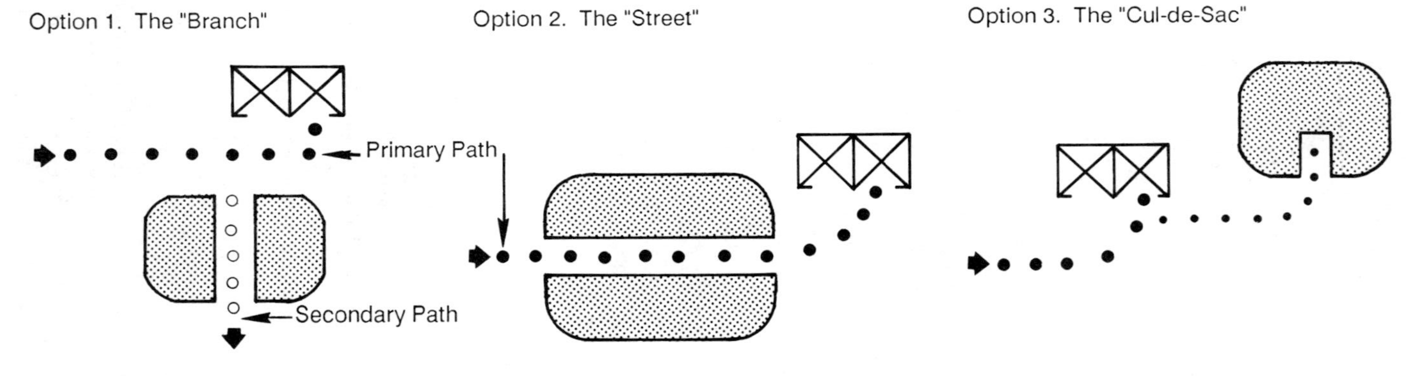

FIGURE 4 Positive and negative relationships between the primary path and shared spaces.
SOURCE: Regnier and Byerts (1983); adapted from Howell (1980).

results from not knowing where you are is both disturbing and frustrating. The ability to find one's way in the environment is so fundamental a concept that it may even account for misdiagnosed confusion in some older people. Complex and poorly organized buildings that provide very few orienting cues can easily confuse the user.

Architectural Features Can Assist in Way-finding

Weisman (1981) has identified four classes of environmental variables that can affect orientation and way-finding. Each of these concepts can be used to design or retrofit environments, and they are commonly accepted ways to create more legible and comprehensible buildings.

- Signs—The strategic use of information through the use of graphic displays like a sign can provide directional information and identification at critical times in the user's experience of an environment.
- Perceptual access—Orientation and way-finding may also be enhanced by providing a view to a familiar exterior landmark or a view through the building to an important unifying element such as a central atrium.
- Architectural differentiation—Treating each section or region within a building with different wall coverings or floor materials can also facilitate recognition and recall, as well as contributing to effective way-finding.
- Planned configuration—The layout or shape of the floor plan can influence the ease with which one can build a mental map to navigate within that building.

Relocation Trauma Is Related to Way-finding Research

The importance of design cues in aiding navigation within a novel environment makes this line of research intriguing to those interested in relocation. For example, some theorists contend that having a difficult time orienting oneself to a new environment may contribute significantly to the relocation trauma many nursing home patients experience when they are transferred from one setting to another (Weisman, 1981).

Future research in this area should attempt more effectively to link cognitive processes with the types of environmental cues that aid orientation and navigation. Such linkage will further outfit designers with ideas, images, and design techniques to simplify complex environments. In addition to its importance in cases of relocation, being able to find one's way in the environment is particularly salient to older people living in long-term care facilities who suffer cognitive losses that reduce their spatial ability.

Neighborhood Concerns

Urban planners have long recognized the dependency that younger people have on the neighborhood. A number of publications including the classic U.S. Public Health Service document *Planning the Neighborhood* (1947) have stressed the importance of safety and convenience. Concepts such as the "neighborhood-centered school," separation of vehicle and pedestrian circulation systems, and small, nearby shopping facilities were developed in part to ensure the safety of younger people.

This same level of attention has not been paid to the social, functional, and security concerns of an older population that is equally dependent on the convenience of a local neighborhood setting. Senior citizen centers, demand–response transportation systems, and crime prevention strategies are services and features that are best delivered at the neighborhood level. Urban designers and planners whose job it is to alter the physical environment rarely do so with the best interests of older people in mind.

Housing and Neighborhood Problems Are Often Interrelated

Struyk (1977a, 1977b) in initial analyses from the annual housing survey has reported the higher rate of difficult older people seem to have with neighborhood conditions as opposed to housing conditions. In their book *Improving the Elderly's Housing,* Struyk and Soldo (1980) view housing satisfaction as dependent on three issues: (1) structural conditions of the dwelling unit, (2) residential location, and (3) personal needs and preferences.

They argue that elder-occupied housing stock in neighborhoods built prior to 1940, with high concentrations of older people (14 percent or more), plays a unique role in the process of urban deterioration. Examining the characteristics of these marginal neighborhoods, they discovered that "older residents in aging neighborhoods are likely to be owner occupants in neighborhoods dominated by rental property" (Struyk and Soldo, 1980). Therefore, programs for repair or renovation assistance to older owner–occupants may be the key to preserving the quality of housing and may be sufficient to stop or slow down the process of general neighborhood decline.

Importance of Access to Neighborhood Resources

The 1974–1977 Annual Housing Survey census tapes analyzed by Lawton (1980) revealed a relatively high percentage of older people who classified public transportation, shopping, and medical resources as inadequate. Of the individuals surveyed, 32.8 percent, 15.8 percent, and 12.1 percent, respectively, found these three services to be of "inadequate" quality. Although these percentages seem small, compared with concerns regarding housing conditions they appear extremely high. This level of concern about the inadequacy of neighborhood services is particularly significant when one considers the tendency of older people to express satisfaction with whatever urban services and housing conditions are made available to them. One might hypothesize that older people could more comfortably criticize the neighborhood than something as tangible and personal as their own housing unit. The fact still remains, however, that nearly a third considered transportation services in their neighborhood to be inadequate.

Lawton (1977) created Figure 5 to represent the consensus of findings from seven authors who conducted research regarding the use of neighborhood services. The figure represents three superimposed polar diagrams that rate and compare (1) the frequency, (2) the physical distance, and (3) the proportion of older people using 13 important community resources.

Lawton concludes that four resources (i.e., physicians, clubs, children, and relatives) represent destinations to which distance was often a problem. The physical distance from the older person's home to these resources was relatively great, even though the frequency of use varied. The most critical resources were

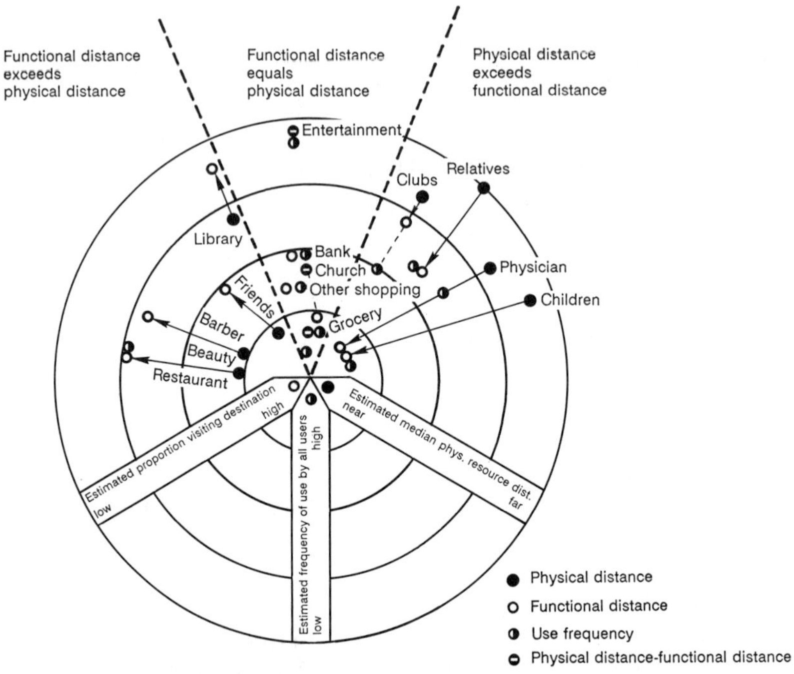

FIGURE 5 Schematic representation of differences between physical resource distance, functional resource distance (indexed by the proportion of all older people who visit a destination once a year or more), and frequency of use. SOURCE: Lawton (1977).

relatives and physicians. In these two destinations, the frequency of use was high, and thus distance seemed to pose a problem more often.

Five resources located near the center of the diagram (i.e., entertainment, bank, church, other shopping, and grocery shopping) have distances well matched to their frequency of use. For these five, distance is not considered to be a major problem. For example, the grocery store, although used frequently by many older people, is usually located nearby. Entertainment facilities, although located some distance from the older person's home, are used less frequently by older people.

The four resources located on the left edge of the diagram (restaurant, beauty, friends, and library) are more conveniently located than might be considered necessary. The ubiquitous location of these four destinations provides some modicum of choice. The frequency of use and proportion of older people using these four destinations seem not to be impeded by location or distance.

Principles, Goals, and Objectives for Interventions

The choices available for program and policy interventions to reinforce, renovate, rehabilitate and otherwise improve the neighborhood for older people are numerous. Regnier (1982) suggests that each planned intervention should be measured against the following four performance criteria:

- *Accessibility*—Does the intervention contribute to making the neighborhood more accessible or convenient?
- *Communication*—Does the intervention contribute to developing a more substantive dialogue between older people and other community residents?
- *Coordination*—Does the intervention bring together into an active coalition various community groups and institutions to promote meaningful positive change?
- *Housing improvement*—Does the intervention contribute to improving the housing situation of older residents in such a way as to have secondary and tertiary effects on the neighborhood?

Management and Design

In the field, the success of elderly housing is often considered to depend on three factors: (1) the quality of the neighborhood (service access and safety), (2) the sensitivity of the design to the needs of older residents, and (3) the competency of management and the effectiveness of management policies (Regnier, 1982). Managers and administrators are frequently faced with a job that requires technical understanding of building equipment; accounting skills for rent collection; a sociable, outgoing presence to stimulate group activities; and counseling skills for solving personal problems or tenant conflicts.

Much of the work in the area of management has focused on how management policies have encouraged or discouraged the use of various activities, spaces, and settings. Management can influence the overall success of a building design by interpreting spaces as opportunities to facilitate resident activities or discourage activity by establishing rules and policies that forbid certain behaviors, activities, or uses (Lawton, 1975).

Managers Often Unaware of Design Intentions

The instructions provided to administrators about how to manage a complex housing environment are usually minimal. Environmental programmers frequently quip about the detailed owner's manuals provided for relatively simple appliances that describe in detail how to "trouble shoot" and problem solve when the equipment dysfunctions. Yet rarely are managers of complex environments provided with any guidance whatsoever about how activities can be accommodated on the grounds or within rooms that have been set aside for social purposes.

There is a need to understand how spaces are used and how they could be improved for social purposes. Dialogue with management or a design/management guide book (developed from the architectural program) can detail how spaces are intended to function. Management should be aware of how various spaces have been designed to accommodate programs and desired activities. Dialogue between management and the architectural programmer normally defines how spaces are intended to function, a process that can lead to more careful design attention.

The Therapeutic Environment

Lawton (1975, 1979) has written extensively on the practical aspects of management and the theoretical aspects of person and environment fit. His book, *Planning and Managing Housing for the Elderly,* provides some of the most practical information available for developing a clear understanding of management's role and influence on tenant satisfaction. Among Lawton's major contributions is the ecological model of person/environment fit, in which he expanded the early theoretical work of Murray (1938) and Lewin (1951) to create a theoretical model that illustrates the transactional relationship between the person and the environment. The fit between the environment and the resources of the individual has been explored in institutional arrangements by Kahana (1982) and Moos (1976). Their efforts have been directed toward classifying the many dimensions of environmental press. The relationship between these theoretical explorations of environmental support and design has been tenuous, although Moos and Lemke (1979) have developed a physical and architectural features (PAF) checklist that is useful to design decisionmakers.

CASE STUDIES

One of the best ways to understand how design preferences and management response can be combined is to look at several projects in which new ideas have been tested. The following three case studies are of different-sized residential settings for older residents.

The Villa Marin, San Rafael, California

The Villa Marin is a new, 220-unit continuing care retirement community located in Marin County, California. It is unusual from a management, administrative, and design perspective. The concept involves an onsite nursing home and a personal care unit that are administered through a condominium-style financing program. Residents own their own units and pay a monthly charge for maintenance and for health care service. The condominium-style arrangement allows residents an equity investment in the project, while at the same time they receive the benefits associated with a traditional continuing care retirement community.

The Villa Marin has pursued a number of interesting ideas. From an administrative and managerial perspective, the project offers the following features:

- It is managed by a condominium governance system that allows residents to make and direct policies regarding the provision of health service, maintenance, and upkeep.
- Meal services are "unbundled." Residents are required to take only one meal a day in a large communal dining room. Other meals can be purchased on an à-la-carte basis, prepared in the full kitchen of each unit, or taken in one of several neighborhood restaurants.
- Residents are required to join a health care organization that has negotiated a capitated fee agreement with the Villa Marin management. This feature allows management to control

health care costs while providing residents with high-quality health care.

With regard to physical characteristics, the Villa Marin offers the following features:

• Units are large, and each is designed to include a full kitchen. In the majority of units, two bathrooms are provided. Sixty-five percent of the units are 2-bedroom units that average 1,200 square feet. When two bathrooms are designated in one unit, one bathroom has a shower and the other a tub to provide choice and ensure safety.
• The common services located on the first floor include not only the traditional sedentary activities, such as a library, card room, arts and crafts area, and auditorium; they also include an indoor swimming pool, a spa, and an exercise room. The emphasis on exercise, health, and nutrition and the central location of these amenities in the building encourage residents to pursue an active life-style.
• The architectural treatment emphasizes residential style, eliminating any implications of institutionalization. The nursing home and personal care units are located below the first floor and are recessed into the downslope of the hillside. Each personal care or nursing unit has an attractive view of the surrounding foothills. This treatment carefully conceals this institutional element; in conventional projects, it is often handled as a separate building that lends an institutional character to the campus. The entrance to the nursing unit is convenient and centrally located for residents who choose to visit friends and relatives.

The Villa Marin is one of many new continuing care-type communities being developed for higher income older residents who wish to have the social, health, and recreational supports of congregate housing and a less institutional service network with larger residential units.

Congregate Housing, Beverly Hills, California

A new congregate facility designed for a higher income population and located in the city of Beverly Hills, California, is currently in the planning stage. This project has also pursued a number of social, behavioral, and administrative goals in its planning and design. The building has been designed through a participatory process that involved 20 older community members in design decision making. Focus group discussions, reviews of model units/designs, community service preferences, and expert opinions were used to arrive at a housing design and a management-governance document for residents (Regnier, 1985b). Some of the administrative and physical features that this project pursues include the following:

- Residents have the choice of taking meals in six different ways in this project. They can dine in a large communal dining area or a private dining room. They can take a snack at the bar/delicatessen or have an informal breakfast of rolls and coffee in an area that overlooks a garden area in the morning. They can prepare a meal in their own room or have a meal delivered there. Maximizing choice and providing opportunities for taking meals is an integral part of the project's concept.
- A resident-centered management and administrative governance system will place the responsibility for building evaluation in the hands of an elected resident committee. The committee will be structured to evaluate the operations, management, and environment each year and will be provided with technical assistance to do so. Space is set aside for a resident council meeting room with copying equipment, a typewriter, and a personal computer for resident use only.
- An emphasis on exercise and physical therapy (swimming pool, spa, exercise room) will encourage residents to maintain a regular exercise regimen. Office space for visiting doctors (massage, therapist), and individual health assessments will also be available.
- A "main street" pedestrian area near the center of the building with skylights and plantings will provide a convenient and central area for social interaction. Various activities will be clustered around this open space (lounge, library, post office, convenience store, beauty/barber, bar/deli, auditorium).

The Beverly Hills congregate residence is a rather exclusive congregate housing facility oriented toward high-income residents. It follows the trend of numerous self-contained congregate facilities that vary in size from 100 to 150 units and that are being developed throughout the country. These settings are designed to support residents who desire the social interaction, food service, and health security services provided by such a facility. This particular project pursues the idea of maximizing choice and creating settings for informal social interaction.

Captain Eldridge Congregate House, Hyannis, Massachusetts

Small congregate housing developments designed for between 15 and 25 residents are also being constructed in various parts of the United States. These settings are similar in nature to the sheltered housing arrangements that have been popular for many years in England and northern Europe. The Captain Eldridge Congregate House, Hyannis, Massachusetts, is a state-financed housing development. It is a remodeled, nineteenth-century sea captain's single-family house that has been expanded to accommodate 20 older residents. The project used a design process that capitalized on the experiences of administrators and project directors of several similar, earlier projects. Some of the administrative and physical features that this project pursues include the following:

- The management office is a small, unobtrusive alcove located adjacent to the front entry. The full-time manager is nearby for assistance and counseling, but the office does not overpower the residential quality of the housing environment.
- Small-scale, noncommercial food preparation equipment was used in order to minimize the fixed costs associated with the production of food. Two dining rooms, one a small informal kitchen nook and a second larger communal dining space, are provided. Residents also have a small kitchen in each unit.
- A dramatic atrium design was used to create a focus for the interior of the project. The space not only provides better visual integration between the first and second floors, but it also serves to naturally ventilate the space during the spring and fall.
- Unit entries are designed with sitting spaces, double-hung windows, Dutch doors, and exterior lights, all of which are used to control the relationship between the unit entry and the common corridor that links the units together.

Small congregate houses are becoming a more popular solution to the problem of creating residentially scaled communities in which individuals can provide informal support to one another while receiving the care, attention, and assistance they may need in order to live independently.

DESIGN COMMUNICATION

There are a number of different ways in which information about the behavioral aspects of design can be communicated to design decision makers. Before environmental design research can be considered truly useful, it must find its way to the drawing board. Some of the following approaches represent avenues for effectively communicating research findings to design professionals, while at the same time emphasizing behaviorally based design decision making.

Design Communication Through Training

The most effective ways to influence architects, landscape architects, and interior designers to think about the needs of the elderly is through the educational system. Schools of architecture frequently consider themselves to be on the cutting edge of design methodology development. Many schools have faculty members with interest and expertise in behavioral evaluation who teach seminar and design studio classes. Exposing students to applicable techniques, such as behaviorally based programming and postoccupancy evaluation, can be quite useful.

In design studio projects, developing a literature review that includes behavioral data can influence the way students think about how their designs affect people. The interdisciplinary aspects of design evaluation can be facilitated in an academic institution that provides opportunities for sharing knowledge between disciplines.

Professional Seminars

Professional seminars that provide practicing architects with advice about the current state of the art in behaviorally based research can be effective. Providing information focused on a problem that is considered to be important and relevant is an effective way to intervene.

Journals and Books

Publishing projects that have been evaluated or that are particularly good examples of thoughtful, behaviorally based design can be instructive to architects searching for examples of buildings that work well. Often, a project that pursues a behaviorally based design idea in a careful and thoughtful way can provide evidence of both a design methodology as well as an illustration of an excellent design idea.

Development and Recognition of Exemplary Projects

An architect who designs housing may find visiting examples of excellent projects both useful and constructive. Rarely are projects judged by any objective criteria; therefore, "walking through" a project may provide the visiting architect with as much misinformation as it does valuable insights. Exemplary projects should be identified and evaluated.

Competition and Design Awards

Frequently, design competitions are used as a vehicle for exploring new design ideas or for applying those ideas to a specific context. Normally, designs are judged only by site design and aesthetic criteria. Competitions that stress excellent behavioral solutions to complex problems can be a way of assembling ideas to stimulate careful thinking on the part of designers. The publication *Low Rise Housing for Older People* (Zeisel et al., 1977) is an example of a design competition that was used to produce a handbook on the development of low-rise housing.

Making Future Market Preferences Explicit

Examining past housing products can provide only a partial viewpoint of what new cohorts of older people will expect and prefer in retirement housing. The careful scrutiny of market preference research and cohort-based analysis of preferences will provide architectural programmers with a sense of what new activities, amenities, and management–governance should be explored.

Support for Postoccupancy Evaluation

More support and recognition for postoccupancy evaluation research will lead to a better research base from which programming input and tested behavioral design ideas can be developed. The lack of tradition and support for postoccupancy evaluation must be changed if designers are to learn from past mistakes and avoid future problems.

Problems with Information Transfer and Experimentation

One of the most troublesome difficulties in design-based evaluation is the communication of information to design decision makers. Training architectural students to understand and use behaviorally based research in the design process is one way to deal with information transfer problems. Another way is to encourage collaboration with consultants whose expertise focuses on the behavioral aspects of design. Nonetheless, there are many impediments that keep designers and sponsors from developing buildings that are sensitive to the needs of older residents.

Regulatory Requirements

Health and safety requirements frequently discourage architects from pursuing more humane and less institutional solutions, a pattern that is more pervasive in nursing home design than for other building types. The regulations that protect health and safety are frequently so restrictive that they discourage any innovative ideas. In addition, such regulations may be inappropriate and can be applied unevenly in differing communities.

A lack of understanding regarding the social and behavioral qualities associated with residential-type solutions often keep the environment from appearing more humane. For example, some occupancy codes and nursing home policies are written in such a way as to discourage an individual from bringing furniture and equipment from his or her former home. This provision eliminates the visual and perceptual continuance of a life-long association with important items that are imbued with meaning and affective significance. Some regulatory requirements are not only counterproductive but may even be outdated. For example, regulations that discourage long-term care settings from using wood in preference to polyplastics err by specifying a substitute that actually burns more actively and creates a dense smoke by-product from combustion.

Budgetary Constraints

Frequently, the development of new ideas is met with conservative inertia, which can place narrow limits around the types of solutions the designer pursues. The lack of available information to test the costs and benefits of new ideas is often a problem that leads to the pursuit of a "safe" existing solution that has been tried and tested but that does not improve the state of the art.

Hesitancy of Manufacturers

Manufacturers have traditionally oriented their products toward a poorly defined aging market. Choices of building hardware and appliances that maximize safety and consider the sensory deficits of an aging population are only now beginning to be available in the marketplace. The aging of society has received enough recognition that corporations now carefully consider the impact of this market segment on their products. Much work has yet to be done, however, to represent those needs to manufacturers accurately.

A Lack of General Expertise in Design

Finally, the lack of expertise, or the lack of a general understanding about this user group, still creates problems. Many firms designing housing for the elderly find themselves confused by the literature and frequently make mistakes attempting to respond to what they perceive are the needs of senior citizens. A more careful segmentation of the particular social and physical characteristics of the older person is a necessary prerequisite in understanding perceived needs and desires. Designed environments that are overly supportive may be as much of a problem as those that err on the side of undersupport.

CONCLUSIONS

In summary, a few of the major problems that characterize the field of designing environments for the aging include the following:

- There is a lack of clear-cut traditions to integrate the behavioral aspects of design into a balanced process of design decision making that considers aesthetics, site constraints, and the needs of users/residents.
- The lack of effective communication strategies that sensitize designers and design decision makers to the philosophical, programmatic, and physiological needs of older people remains a problem. More effective avenues of communication and interactive design decision making must be pursued if the level of design sophistication and design response is to improve.
- Research must be structured and designed in such a way as to address the specific needs of design decision makers. Environmental design research that explores problems and ideas but does not deal with the application of those ideas to the physical environment may go unused.

There is much to be learned about the development of more effective research and the pursuit of better means of making that research useful and understandable to designers. Until these problems are addressed, designers will continue to be hampered and designed environments will continue to be fraught with insensitive mistakes and problems.

REFERENCES

American National Standards Institute (ANSI). 1980. *Specification for Making Building and Facilities Accessible To and Usable by Physically Handicapped People.* A 117.1. New York: The Institute.

Byerts, T., S. Howell, and L. Pastalan. 1979. *The Environmental Context of Aging: Lifestyles, Environmental Quality and Living Arrangements.* New York: Garland.

Carp, F. 1966. *A Future for the Aged: The Residents of Victoria Plaza.* Austin: University of Texas Press.

Hiatt, L. 1980. "Is Poor Light Dimming the Sight of Nursing Home Patients? Implications for Vision Screening and Care." *Nursing Homes* 29(5).

Howell, S. 1980. *Designing for Aging: Patterns of Use.* Cambridge, Mass.: MIT Press.

Kahana, E. 1982. "A Congruence Model of Person–Environmental Interaction." In *Aging and the Environment: Theoretical Approaches,* M. P. Lawton, P. Windley, and T. Byerts, eds. New York: Springer Publishing.
Koncelik, J. 1976. *Designing the Open Nursing Home.* Stroudsburg, Pa.: Dowden, Hutchinson, and Ross.
Koncelik, J. 1979. "Human Factors and Environmental Design for the Aging: Physiological Change and Sensory Loss as Design Criteria." In *Environmental Context of Aging,* T. Byerts, S. Howell, and L. Pastalan, eds. New York: Garland.
Lawton, M. P. 1975. *Planning and Managing Housing for the Elderly.* New York: John Wiley & Sons.
Lawton, M. P. 1977. "The Impact of the Environment on Aging and Behavior." In *Handbook of the Psychology of Aging,* J. E. Birren and K. Schaie, eds. New York: Van Nostrand.
Lawton, M. P. 1979. "Therapeutic Environments for the Aged." In *Designing for Therapeutic Environments,* D. Canter and S. Canter, eds. New York: John Wiley.
Lawton, M. P. 1980. *Environment and Aging.* Monterey, Calif: Brooks/Cole Publishing.
Lawton, M. P., P. Windley, and T. Byerts. 1982. *Aging and the Environment: Theoretical Approaches.* New York: Springer Publishing.
Lewin, K. 1951. *Field Theory in Social Science.* New York: Harper & Row.
Moore, G., P. Tuttle, and S. Howell. 1985. *Environmental Design Research Directions.* New York: Praeger.
Moos, R. 1976. *The Human Context: Environmental Determinants of Behavior.* New York: Wiley Interscience.
Moos, R., and S. Lemke. 1979. *Multiphasic Environmental Assessment Procedures: Preliminary Manual.* Palo Alto, Calif: Stanford University School of Medicine, Social Ecology Laboratory.
Morton, D. 1981. "Congregate Living." *Progressive Architecture* 62(8).
Murray, H. 1939. *Explorations in Personality.* New York: Harper & Row.
Pastalan, L. 1979. "Sensory Changes and Environmental Behavior." In *Environmental Context of Aging,* T. Byerts, S. Howell, and L. Pastalan, eds. New York: Garland.
Regnier, V. 1982. "The Neighborhood as a Support System for the Urban Elderly." In *Enriching Lifestyles for the Elderly,* J. McRae, ed. Gainesville, Fla.: University of Florida, College of Architecture.
Regnier, V. 1984. *Beverly Hills Congregate Housing: Participatory Design and Planning Feasibility Analysis.* Los Angeles: University of Southern California, Andrus Gerontology Center.
Regnier, V. 1985a. *Behavioral and Environmental Aspects of Outdoor Space Use in Housing for the Elderly.* Los Angeles, Calif: University of Southern California, School of Architecture, Andrus Gerontology Center.
Regnier, V. 1985b. "Congregate Housing for the Elderly: An Integrated and Participatory Planning Model." In *Proceedings of the Research and Design '85 Conference,* T. Vonier, ed. Washington, D.C.: American Institute of Architects.
Regnier, V., and T. Byerts. 1983. "Applying Research Findings to the Planning and Design of Housing for the Elderly." In *Housing for a Maturing Population,* F. Spink, ed. Washington, D.C.: Urban Land Institute.
Sommer, R., and B. Sommer. 1981. *A Practical Guide to Behavioral Research.* New York: Oxford University Press.
Steinfeld, E. 1979. *Adaptable Dwellings.* Washington, D.C.: U.S. Department of Housing and Urban Development.
Struyk, R. J. 1977a. "The Housing Expense Burden of Households Headed by the Elderly." *The Gerontologist* 17.

Struyk, R. J. 1977b. "The Housing Situation of Elderly Americans." *The Gerontologist* 17.

Struyk, R., and B. Soldo. 1980. *Improving the Elderly's Housing: A Key to Preserving the Nation's Housing Stock and Neighborhood.* Cambridge, Mass.: Ballinger Publishing.

U.S. Public Health Service. 1947. *Planning the Neighborhood.* Washington, D.C.: Government Printing Office.

Weisman, G. 1981. "Evaluating Architectural Eligibility: Way-finding in the Built Environment." *Environment and Behavior* 13.

Zeisel, J. 1981. *Inquiry by Design.* Monterey, Calif.: Brooks/Cole Publishing.

The Relation of Housing and Living Arrangements to the Productivity of Older People

James N. Morgan

The relevant literature on the relation of housing and living arrangements to the productivity of the elderly is diverse and often only marginally on target. A few items will be discussed, but a more extensive bibliography is provided at the end of this paper in which the titles are usually adequate for sorting. There is a large economics literature on the decision to retire from paid market work. In that area, the facts are gradually defeating the stereotypes, showing that retirement is both desired by most people and good for them. Most people retire as soon as they can afford to or when poor health or job obsolescence forces them to (Barfield and Morgan, 1969; Morgan, 1981a; Palmore, 1985, Parnes, 1981; Streib and Schneider, 1971). If there is to be an increase in productive activity by older people, it seems likely that it will not occur through a later retirement from regular jobs.

A second, much thinner stream deals with unpaid work—volunteer work or helping others—in which the evidence is that although people expect to do more of it when they retire, they do not report, after they retire, that they are doing more of it (Barfield and Morgan, 1969).

James N. Morgan is program director and professor of economics, Institute for Social Research, University of Michigan.

The stereotype that it is bad for older people to be "segregated" in communities of older people, like the stereotype that retirement is bad for people, has persisted in the face of contradictory evidence. One might discount the expressed attitudes or argue that the same stereotype affects the attitudes of older people when they opt for heterogeneous communities. Yet the data on activity and satisfaction levels of older people in various types of communities are also in favor of the age-homogeneous areas and are more convincing. They might, of course, exaggerate the difference because of selection biases—that is, if those who move to such communities do so because they expect to like them and be active in them. At a minimum, as Lawton has suggested, there is a substantial fraction of older people who would like to be in age-uniform communities (Lawton et al., 1984; Lawton et al., 1980; Rosow, 1967). Research and designs for environments for the frail elderly or for communities of the elderly have been extensively covered and summarized by M. Powell Lawton (Canter and Canter, 1979; Kasl, 1977; Koncelik, 1976; Lawton, various).

A burgeoning attention to care-giving, both institutional and by family or friends, reflects the nursing home crisis and the explosion of actual and threatened medical costs. It tends to focus on assessing the strain on people who provide care and on the relation of that strain to the decision to send the frail into nursing homes or other institutional care (Morycz, 1985; Silverstone, 1985). The finding that women care-givers report more strain than men may be another example of selection bias if women are more likely than men to be forced into such roles by the expectations and rules of society and the demographic facts of life. Interestingly enough, it is difficult to find in the studies of strain any attention to what apparently is the fact that many elderly with mental problems provide more difficulties for their spouses than for anyone else.

Finally, there is research on the design of the physical environment, which focuses almost entirely on increasing the efficiency and capacity for self-care or for professional care and not on the encouragement of care-giving by other older people (Koncelik, 1976; National Policy Center, no date).

If one asks about environments that might encourage productive activity on the part of older people, much of the literature does not appear relevant because it focuses productivity discussions on paid market work; the rest of the literature focuses attention on the delivery of services to the elderly or at most on facilitating more self-care. Surprisingly, this lack of breadth occurs at a time when we have a growing group of elderly, many of whom are reasonably fit, and yet the care of those who are not is provided either by one long-suffering, underrewarded spouse or by expensive professionals in expensive surroundings who provide many unnecessary services.

PRODUCTIVITY BROADLY CONSIDERED

We must expand our concept of productivity to include anything that produces goods or services. They need not be marketable, so long as they reduce the demand on goods or services produced by others. Even self-care is productive if the person might otherwise have required someone to provide that care. The potential for productive activities outside the usual paid employment by older people is both relatively and absolutely important.

The productivity of older people is a large and growing issue because the sheer number of relatively healthy older people is growing, and there is no evidence that they really want to stay longer in the paid labor force or that the younger workers want them there. Indeed, retirement from regular jobs is widely desired and enjoyed. Economists have recently discovered that it is not Social Security that induces early retirement but company pension schemes and the giving out of people's health or their jobs. Yet other kinds of productive activity, more flexibly scheduled and more discretionary, are a real possibility. The inequality among people in each generation increases as they age, leaving some hale and hearty and others in poor health. It is the potential demand of some older people for labor-intensive services, including nursing, that raises the question of whether or not others of them could provide many of those services. (Currently, unduly burdensome demands are often placed on spouses.)

Economists state that all issues of economic policy contain considerations of efficiency (resource allocation) and equity (fairness or redistributional effects). We must be careful in talking about increasing the productivity of older people to ask whether we are also increasing transfers to them by subsidizing activities or whether we are reducing their relative well-being by expecting them to do things without adequate compensation. Some older people do volunteer work, but coerced unpaid work is a form of taxation. Hence, we seek neutral policies that neither tax nor subsidize but that open up new options or opportunities and remove barriers.

There are three kinds of barriers that inhibit the productive activity of older people: (1) economic and legal, (2) social and organizational, and (3) environmental. I intend to discuss the third, namely, the effect of the built environment, housing and neighborhood, on the productivity of older people. But I must preface that discussion with a few words about the other two areas because we are talking about potentially substantial changes in people's behavior. It is well known that changing behavior requires multiple and powerful motivations, particularly among older people who have had a lifetime to become "set in their ways." We senior types have difficulty making up our minds, much less changing our way of life. On the other hand, we have fewer liquidity constraints. I know some people in Sun City West who are building a church with loans of $10,000 from each of the prospective new members. Indeed, there is some urgency in developing better designs for living arrangements for older people because many of them right now are committing themselves to investments in communities that, at least from the point of view of encouraging productive activities, are very badly designed.

What little research has been done has tended to follow the usual scientific paradigms of varying one thing at a time or at the least varying a few things in some kind of experimental design that is orthogonal so that the manipulated variables are uncorrelated. Yet if one sees real results only when all of the multiple motivations are in place and all of the major barriers are reduced, then such experimentation is a formula for failure, or at least for "proving" that each component does no good. The suggestions provided later in this paper may seem grandiose, but this may well be an area in which one must "think big" or fail.

Furthermore, we live in a changing and complicated world, and people are complex organisms. Hence, the success of any new physical or social or economic arrangements depends on their flexibility and on their capacity to adapt and solve the many unexpected problems that will arise. Our tradition of scientific experimentation must give way to trials not of rigidly predefined inputs but of problem-solving mechanisms. There are additional persuasive reasons for this approach. It is an insult to any group of people to experiment on them, but it is a compliment to provide new options and encourage them to get together and work out optimum new arrangements. There is very convincing research to show that offering older people more control over their environment and more opportunities will increase their activity level and even their indicators of health. We shall end by proposing a meta-experiment, trying out whole new flexible, self-regulated communities so that if some succeed we shall know what kind of living, problem-solving mechanisms show promise and not just what particular set of solutions worked in one situation.

It is our conviction that, to attract people to new opportunities, it may be necessary to change their social or organizational environment, their economic arrangements, and their physical or built environment. Each of the three depends on the others for its success. Consequently, let me postpone a discussion of the physical environment for just a little longer and briefly describe the economic and social structures or arrangements that I believe would have to accompany the better built environment if it were to work. I shall also indicate what those optimal arrangements imply about the required physical environment.

THE ECONOMIC ENVIRONMENT

We need economic arrangements that provide incentives and rewards for productive activities but that do not produce further inequities among a group that is experiencing widely diverging economic paths in any case. Inequality increases with age—inequality in income, wealth, and health. Hence, substantial economic incentives for those who are able to take advantage of them can seem like punishment to those who cannot. Most people in paid employment are relatively overpaid in their later years, and employers want to replace them with younger people with more energy and flexibility and lower salaries. Indeed, another of the stereotypes that is only slowly being dispelled by the facts is that Social Security encourages early retirement. In fact, it is the private pension plans that are twisted to reward those who retire early and punish those who stay on; Social

Security, particularly after the 1984 amendments, is actuarially unfair to those who retire early and provides undue rewards to those who keep working. This situation occurs despite the fact that many who retire early do so unavoidably because their health gives out or their job skills become obsolete, whereas many who continue to work are in pleasant, well-paid jobs they enjoy (Maxfield, 1985; Packard, 1985; Sherman, 1985).

I should propose for communities of older people a new alternate currency to be used for facilitating exchanges of services and helping each other. It is well known among economists that money (currency) facilitates exchange as well as providing a store of value that can be saved. It frees us from the constraints of barter, which would require us to stay in bilateral balance with each other individual. It facilitates the development and publication of market-clearing prices that can themselves reduce haggling and exploitation. It reveals real needs while discouraging undue demands. Many baby-sitting cooperatives use paper money to avoid the need to pay a secretary to make calls and keep the books. All one needs in such a group is a list of the members and rules against accumulating too much of the currency. Such cooperatives easily develop special prices in their currency for extra children in the house or for sitting after 11 p.m. in the evening. Because the currency is good for hours and not dollars, it does not depreciate. ("Prices" would, of course, be adjusted according to the amount of skill the help required.) Finally, by giving everyone an initial stock of the alternative currency, a certain initial equality is introduced even among people with wide differences in wealth and money income.

There is then an easy set of subsequent improvements: first, to have a small community tax in such currency so people can be paid for doing things for the community; then an insurance arrangement by which for an annual payment one can have emergency needs covered without running out of the currency; and finally, an annuity arrangement by which larger, early annual payments build a reserve to pay for the greater needs when one is very old.

Why not use ordinary money? Because it is taxable, because the "wages" in the new currency will be different, because a measure of altruism is involved, and because everyone starts out with the same initial stock of the new currency, reducing inequalities. As the currency is in units of hours of work adjusted for skill levels, it does not depreciate—indeed, its value goes up as real wages go up. Why any currency? Because it allows multilateral exchange—one need not stay in a balance of services given and received with each other individual. Others have discussed coordinating arrangements, and barter, and even a helper bank or "skills bank" (Goodman, 1984; Noberini and Berman, 1983; Pynoos, 1984). There has even been discussion of insurance arrangements, although not of an actual currency (Goodman, 1984). There is some research on attribution, which argues that rewards for good deeds erode the sense of altruism one attributes to oneself, but partial recognition in a new form should serve as an added incentive, and the increased sense of equity and balance are surely desirable. Indeed, there is now some research indicating that the opportunity to reciprocate encourages help-seeking behavior (Nadler et al., 1985).

If a community is to rely on its own internal markets to set prices for various productive activities, then there would have to be some system for keeping track of the prices being paid. Thus, at the beginning, it would be useful to start with some initial levels of those prices from which departures could be made. Services performed for others or for the community might initially be considered worth one "&" (if that is what we decide to call the new shadow currency) per quarter hour of unskilled time, plus a fourth of an "&" per mile driven transporting someone or running errands.

Another aspect of such economic arrangements would be a flexible choice as to how much money each individual invests in the community. Those with available assets and a desire to keep the tax advantages designed for home owners could make condominium-like arrangements with a large investment, taking tax deductions for their share of interest and taxes and achieving tax-free rent savings and a low monthly rental fee. Others might have almost nothing to invest and pay a high rental. And it should be possible to allow those with investments to consume them gradually by paying a lower rental, essentially by converting the investment into an annuity. There would, however, have to be a substantial flexible umbrella mortgage because most people could not invest much in the new community until they had sold their homes and moved. The amount of the mortgage would be large, at least temporarily, but the risk would be small because such a development would be attractive solely as a condominium project, even without the organization and other features designed to encourage productive activity.

In all of this, of course, an essential ingredient is flexibility, the capacity to change and adapt, and the involvement of the members in problem solving and managing. Indeed, a major productive activity for some members would be their contribution of time, energy, and expertise to solving the unpredictable problems that are bound to arise. Some of these problems would be legal as well as economic—such as securing the right to receive government payments for home nursing care, for example, and assuring favorable tax treatment of investments and of "earnings" from helping one another or the community.

Finally, if the shadow currency were to be used to tax members and pay for community services, and also to set up insurance and annuity arrangements allowing scheduled payments to cover unavoidable needs and heavier needs at older ages, then expert actuarial help would be needed, as well as clearance with the insurance regulations of the state. Note that an annuity-type arrangement would require a lump sum payment from new members who were joining at older ages because they would not have made the usual surplus payments in their earlier years that allow a flat set of payments to cover the higher risks later. Such a system would dramatize and quantify the need to maintain an age balance by starting with a wide age spread and then recruiting mostly young replacements.

It should be noted that these economic arrangements would only work well in cases in which there was excellent communication and an organizational structure to develop the rules, post the going prices, set up the pseudo insurance-annuity company, arrange the financing, and so forth. In addition, the economic exchanges of services surely require easy access—access to any other member of the group in a few minutes and without going outside in the cold or rain.

THE SOCIAL–ORGANIZATIONAL ENVIRONMENT

We need social–organizational arrangements because many of the productive activities that are most likely to result are services to the community or to other individuals, both of which require information, communication, and social support mechanisms. People need to know one another, to make new friends as the old ones die off, to be able to provide the kind of wise help only a friend can provide. And in starting any new activity—indeed, even in joining a new community—people need direct, personal encouragement and help. Transitions are difficult, particularly if they involve moving from the old family home and neighborhood, however inappropriate they were and however few friends remained there.

The socialization of new members into such a community would involve more than simply helping them make the traumatic move and adjust to a new set of norms and relationships. Such new members would also need training in providing social support for others and in certain skills such as nursing care, which are sure to be in demand in such a community. Indeed a major advantage of this type of community would be the potential for spreading the burden of care among many people rather than concentrating it on a single spouse or close relative. The gerontological literature is full of studies of the strain of caregiving and the resulting demand for nursing home care merely to relieve the strain and not because highly skilled nursing is needed (Morycz, 1985; Silverstone, 1985). Providing social support also requires skills most of us must acquire. Social support means more than just affective support and friendship; it also means an affirmation of the worth of the other person and aid tailored to the person's needs. Developing new friendships is increasingly difficult as one gets older, and one cannot expect to like everyone in any community. But the focus on doing things for others, and being rewarded with both thanks and payments so that no one feels in debt, would help. In addition, the variety of jobs organizing and keeping track of such activities and arranging deals would itself facilitate getting to know and like people.

Many of the services members would do for each other are currently provided either by professionals (although most of what is done even in a nursing home is not highly skilled) or by spouses. The economic advantage of reducing the use of highly paid (insurance-bloated) professionals on the one hand and the psychic advantage of reducing the excess burden on spouses on the other should be clear.

Again, it is necessary to stress the need for flexibility and problem solving as such a community develops. The history of most successful institutions and communities is a history of the smart solving of a variety of unpredictable problems and emergencies. It would probably be ideal to start with a number of two-generation pairs of member families, one in their sixties and one or more of their parents in their eighties or nineties, with separate dwellings but able to share burdens. (It is often easier to deal with helping a nonrelative, particularly in more extreme situations such as memory loss.) Should the same economic arrangements and "prices" apply to the two-generational helping relationships? The answer is probably yes.

How much recordkeeping and monitoring of prices is needed to ensure convergence on market clearing norms? I feel sure the community would be able to work such things out. It is likely, however, that there would have to be at least 200 people involved in order to have a variety of skills, needs, time schedules, and enough transactions to establish norms ("prices"). There are many issues to be decided: for example, what about visitors, who will range from friends to relatives to noisy grandchildren to nosy observers of this new experiment? The community itself will have to decide how to protect itself from excessive costs in disruption and perhaps excessive self-consciousness that might come from becoming a news item. Although the community would want to keep some intimate connections with the larger surrounding community, it would also want protection and privacy, particularly from the more noxious aspects of society. Surely it would appear useful to have barriers to keep burglars out and keep some forgetful members from wandering off. Indeed, the best protection against unwanted intruders may well be the development of a community in which everyone knows everyone else well and even recognizes their neighbors' family, friends, and visitors.

As with the social–organizational environment, these economic arrangements might be possible among a set of dispersed families, but they would surely be more likely to succeed if people were in easy contact, had regular, casual interactions with others, shared some space and equipment, and could easily keep up with everything that was going on. Thus, the built environment may be a crucial element in facilitating the productive activity of older people.

THE BUILT ENVIRONMENT

Finally, then, we come to the built environment. If the economic and social arrangements of the aging are to be improved, what is there about the physical environment that matters? It seems obvious that a major barrier to most of the productive activities I have been talking about, except perhaps some gardening and home maintenance, is remaining in an isolated single-family home. It reduces communication and contact and makes giving or receiving help difficult because it requires transportation and communication. It is also wasteful of resources to have very large homes occupied by one or two people, even if they only heat part of them in the winter. Yet the familiar is difficult to give up, even if the economic arrangements in a new environment could mimic those to be had with single-family homes.

In a design workshop with students given an assignment to design such a physical environment, it took a quantum change in their orientation (away from a focus on auto traffic and parking and the aesthetic aspects of design) before they could achieve success. They were not used to asking what would facilitate each person's access to others or reduce barriers to potentially productive activities. There was some uncertainty about whether people would respond favorably to such notions as clothes washers and dryers shared by a few nearby units—to facilitate friendly, casual meetings and the making of friends—as well as doing a neighbor's wash when he or she was ill because we are all so used to total access and no sharing of such equipment. Similar issues will arise with any shared equipment or shared space. In terms of shared space, economists believe that putting prices on things helps allocate them fairly and efficiently. Thus, as an example, groups could get together and rent space for their meetings. Only experience would tell whether such tests of need were necessary to avoid conflict.

A major issue is the relative amount of space devoted to common or group use. Clearly, in a community of several hundred units, every square foot of private space given up by each family frees up several hundred square feet of common space. Decisions would have to be made about how to divide the common space among subgroups defined physically (one wing) or by interests (garden space, swimming pool).

Another issue is the paradox of privacy versus encouraging and facilitating interaction with and easy access to one another. Television monitors and other electronic gadgets are always a possibility, but there are advantages to easy visibility in some areas (so that any one of a number of others can be sure that a person is all right) that can be closed off when privacy is wanted. Some hospitals have begun putting windows in rooms that look into halls or common spaces—the windows have curtains that can be drawn. Some community members will want easy access to their cars; others will use public transport, taxis, or rides provided by other members and will need sheltered pick-up space. Casual contacts during the day would surely facilitate arranging for helping activities. What should be available is access to the rest of the community through a private door or garage for those who want it but, more importantly, access to everyone in the group through inside corridors or space, without stairs or other barriers.

There are many small mechanical "fixes," ranging from emergency signaling systems (usually with cords reaching to the floor) to elaborate monitoring from central stations. There are stoves that turn themselves off and ways of converting beds to the needs of the handicapped. What I see little of is designs that make it easy for a not-very-strong older person to do things to help others. (My grandfather cared for my grandmother, who was paralyzed on one entire side, in an isolated farmhouse in southern Indiana for many years, using some ingenious aids like a pulley-hoist to get her up onto a wheelchair or toilet and a party-line telephone so she could be the communication link for the whole community.) Sequential changes along these lines may be required, although initial pretesting pays off. Experience in designing the new University of Michigan hospital revealed that only going through actual procedures in mocked-up rooms uncovered many of the problems. Substantial changes could thus be made before construction took place in things like door widths and room dimensions that would have been difficult to change later.

There has been a great deal of work on design to facilitate caring for older people, and some has even been devoted to making it easier for them to care for themselves. What we have not had the imagination to discuss yet is design that will help older people care for each other and do things for their community.

Instead of more studies of the strain of care-giving when it is concentrated on one spouse, we need designs that allow the burden to be spread. And we also need to make these new environments so attractive that people will want to move to them before any of them are desperate or frail, committing themselves to provide some support for whoever becomes frail in return for a promise that others will support them if they need help—with some compensation, of course. Such a community would be ideal for two-generation families, with separate housing units for the very old and for their old children but easy monitoring, contact, and care when needed.

What characteristics would we seek in an optimal housing and community layout, optimal including the facilitating of productive activities, including the organizing and problem solving that is in itself a productive activity? The following seven seem desirable:

1. *Autonomy and self-determination.* This characteristic is another reason for insisting that such new communities be self-supporting without either subsidies or taxes or the expectation of unpaid work for the larger community, which is itself a kind of extra tax. However, because not all of its members will want to invest in the community (not unlike the situation in a condominium) and because many of them will not have the funds until they sell their present homes, some interim financing will be essential. A flexible mortgage that can be rapidly reduced as members move their investment from some minimum to a full share or more would be required. Perhaps temporary mortgages on present homes could be used, mortgages that would be transferable to an investment in the community when people can actually sell their homes and move.
2. *Privacy and individual freedom, combined somehow with easy access to others to give and receive social support and various kinds of help.* Students in a design seminar at the University of Michigan worked on such a project, and they found it quite challenging. It was necessary, however, to keep reminding them of the criteria; otherwise, they tended to revert to lovely designs that restricted access to others or focused on cars and parking. It seems likely that the best design might be one that allowed a great deal of change and adjustment by the members of the community as experience and preferences dictated. Ideally, a

founders group could give advice on basic issues of layout before the project started building.

It is quite unlikely that telephones and computers can overcome distance and the lack of regular, casual contact in stimulating mutual help patterns or community help activities. At best, it seems probable that various bulletin boards, secretaries, central offices, or other devices would facilitate and encourage cooperative exchanges. Economic arrangements can ensure equity and incentives, and social–organizational arrangements can provide the norm and the emotional support that should go along with the productive activities. Yet seeing others regularly, and being able to get to their living quarters without going out in the rain (or up and down stairs) would seem to be extremely important. Of all the discussion and writing on better physical environments for the aged, almost none focuses on the activities of the aged, except perhaps in terms of their improved capacity to care for themselves—requiring alarm systems, hand-rails, stoves that shut off, chairs it is easier to get out of, and the like. The ideal way to arrange helping is during regular or even casual meetings at meals, the laundry, or in shared spaces rather than formally, through an exchange center (however much computers may facilitate such "markets").

Access to the wider community is also important, ideally with the new community within the service area of public transportation. Perhaps some members of the community might provide child care for children of the area while their parents are at work, all day or just after school.

3. *Reasonable homogeneity of status to facilitate everything but embedded in a larger community to allow interactions with other age groups and other economic levels.* There is much discussion about "age ghettos," but many old people prefer to be able to get away from the noise and confusion of modern life. Most like occasional contact with their own grandchildren. (Some might want to run a day-care nursery, but again, the emphasis must be on self-determination, not predetermination.) The basic design tends to determine some general level of cost, however, and hence of the affluence of the average member. I would personally opt for a level that is sufficiently modest so that middle-income children with dependent parents would be willing to pay to house them there.

4. *A maintained age spread,* which means starting with an

even distribution from age 55 up but then encouraging mostly the younger old to join so that there are always younger people providing more of the services and building up their community credit for when they may need more help than they can give. Two-generation families would also be welcome, however. A major reason for insisting that all features must be attractive is that otherwise people will not move to the community until they become desperate, and it could become one more dismal nursing home, assembling all those who need help.

5. *A size sufficient to allow a real community to develop, diverse talents to be shared, and "markets" to set the "wages" for services to others and to the community in the new currency.* The perils of the too-small community were dramatically described by Nathaniel Hawthorne after his brief experience at Brook Farm: "an unfriendly state of feeling could not occur between any two members, without the whole society being more or less commoted and made uncomfortable thereby . . ." (*The Blithdale Romance,* 1852).

There need to be at least several hundred people in such a community, but there is also an upper limit beyond which it is difficult to develop warm friendship groups, even subgroups, or for the community to govern itself.

6. *Homelike living quarters, but with the capacity to introduce special equipment to facilitate remaining there even when disabled or ill.* A combination of equipment for self-care and easy communication and accessibility for calling for help is obviously needed. Home health care is generally a myth for those living alone, even in apartments, because although they need care only occasionally, it is economically and physically inefficient to provide it. Often, simple emergency help for a few minutes is all that is needed, and such help can be easily provided by someone close at hand, often requiring little skill. Having people nearby without the developed networks and support arrangements, helps little. Having emergency call systems (as in retirement homes) without the social and economic arrangements leads to expensive professional services and/or inhibitions against asking for help. A recent study of the impact of the ending of a home help service indicated little effect, prompting the conclusion that the service had not provided the personal care that is the most burdensome and most time-specific (Hooyman, 1985).

7. *The crucial qualities of flexibility and adaptability,* particu-

larly to minimize the need to move again. Each living unit should have wide doors and be capable of having hoists added to facilitate getting into and out of a bed or a wheelchair, ways of allowing the visual monitoring of activities when necessary through windows or by TV, and the delivery of meals. It should be possible to advertise that people would never have to move again (studies in England have shown that is what happens even when different levels of care are provided for in different projects).

There are some requirements that make it unlikely that the easy conversion of older structures would suffice. Overall, it would be difficult to provide hierarchies of shared space—for example, some shared locally by 4 to 12 families, some by larger groups or the whole community, and some by smaller groups from the whole community. It would be difficult to provide both privacy and access to the outside and one's car and also easy access (without going out in the wind and rain and cold) to most of the other members of the community. In addition, common space that is protected from outsiders but easily visible by insiders (so that those who need it could be kept under observation without that burden falling on one person) is impossible in older areas of either low or high density.

At the level of design of individual spaces, ceilings strong enough to allow the installation of pulleys (so that people can be moved between bed and wheelchair and toilet without much main strength) and doorways and spaces that allow such maneuvering could be designed inexpensively in new areas, but they would be very difficult to install in older ones. In particular, to avoid the need for moving to other quarters, one would want the capability of space adaptation without the investment of fitting out every space for every contingency. There is ample evidence that moving is difficult for the elderly and will be resisted and that providing several stages of residence does not work—people tend to stay wherever they first move. Furthermore, it seems likely that friendship groups will develop, and people may want to live near their friends (sharing the small-group spaces with them), rather then near others with the same level of handicaps. There may, of course, be some who require a kind of segregation to avoid disturbing others, and the community would have to solve such problems as they arose.

There can also be shared equipment, including not just wheelchairs and hospital beds and pulleys but such items as tools, videotapes, and sports equipment. Here, again, many problems may arise (as anyone knows who has tried to share woodworking tools with people who never sharpen anything); but again, one of the productive activities such communities would induce is the solving of this kind of problem. There are, after all, real economies in sharing things that are used only occasionally and advantages in specialization—"paying" skilled perfectionists who will keep the planes sharp in the woodworking shop.

Is there no way we can make do with arrangements that allow people to stay where they are? Or could we start with existing retirement communities and attempt to work just on the economic and organizational arrangements? I do not believe there is much promise in the first of these alternatives, however appealing it may seem. The problems of communication and transportation are just too great to overcome. We might consider, in a few of the more appropriate places in which older people are concentrated, trying the other environmental changes, particularly the economic ones. Indeed, newspapers have reported some attempts at recognizing community services with credits that can be used to purchase other needed services. Finally, in line with my general insistence that the people involved should make as many of their own decisions as possible, we need designs that are flexible and that allow each unique group with its backgrounds, preferences, and experiences to adapt the physical environment to its own needs.

Do we need more studies of existing situations to seek out approaches that work or to know what modes of reciprocity and patterns of time use prevail in existing communities? I suspect that what we would learn would be that existing communities have various barriers that prevent any but the most limited patterns of mutual help or other productive activities. Perhaps cataloging all of the possible barriers in their diversity would help prove our contention that we need built environments that solve all the problems at once, rather than more experiments that would continue to show that partial solutions are not much use.

It is important to keep certain distinctions in mind. Efficiency must be gained without destroying equity, which means providing for reciprocity among members and self-sufficiency for the whole community. Facilitating productive activity and opening up new possibilities is different from applying incentives or rules or penalties. All of the latter are likely to benefit many unnecessarily and punish others unfairly. We are talking about new communities—not communes—with freedom, individuality preserved, and the right to be as much or as little involved in activities as one likes. We are proposing trials by people of new possibilities, not experiments on people. And finally, we suggest the dramatic change to whole new environments but with great concern for minimizing the trauma that any change brings, particularly for older people.

CONCLUSION

New environments, particularly if they are to attract people before they are desperate and ready for a nursing home, must be appealing in multiple ways and have no important drawbacks. It will be a real challenge to design them. Our only avenue is to focus on the crucial elements and hope that the first applicants will solve the problems and adapt the design to make it still better. The only help required would be loan guarantees, some original organizing advice, and perhaps some research to report systematically and quantitatively on which problem-solving mechanisms work and not just on the particular solutions that were found. Measures of change in satisfaction would be more compelling by the addition of quantitative measures of changes in the amount of time devoted to productive activities and in the sizes of helping networks.

REFERENCES

Abrams, P. 1978. "Neighbourhood Care and Social Policy: A Research Perspective." Berkhamsted, Herts, England: The Volunteer Centre.

Abrams, P. 1980. "Social Change, Social Networks and Neighbourhood Care." *Social Work Service* 22:12–23.

Abrams, P. 1985. "Policies to Promote Informal Social Care: Some Reflections on Voluntary Action, Neighborhood Involvement and Neighborhood Care." *Aging and Society* 5(March):1–18.

Abrams, P., S. Abrams, R. Humphrey, and R. Snaith. 1981. "Action for Care: A Review of Good Neighbour Schemes in England." Berkhamsted, Herts, England: The Volunteer Centre.

Abrams, P., S. Abrams, R. Humphrey, and R. Snaith. 1982. *A Handbook of Good*

Neighbour Schemes in England. Berkhamsted, Herts, England: The Volunteer Centre.

Altman, I., J. Wohlwill, and M. P. Lawton, eds. 1984. *Human Behavior and the Environment: Current Theory and Research,* vol. 7. New York: Plenum.

Antonucci, T. C., and C. E. Depner. 1983. "Social Support and Informal Helping Relationship." Pp. 233–253 in *Basic Processes in Helping Relationships,* T. A. Wills, ed. New York: Academic Press.

Babchuck, N., and A. Booth. 1969. "Voluntary Association Membership: A Longitudinal Analysis." *American Sociological Review* 34:31–45.

Barfield, R., and J. Morgan. 1969. *Early Retirement, The Decision and the Experience.* Ann Arbor, Mich.: Institute for Social Research.

Barnes, J., and N. Conelly, eds. 1978. *Social Care Research.* London: Policy Studies Institute and Bedford Square Press.

Barnes, W. D. 1979. "The Economics of Retirement Communities." *Aging Leisure Living* 2(8):5–7.

Bar-Tal, D., Y. B. Zohar, M. S. Greenberg, and M. Hermon. 1977. "Reciprocity in the Relationship Between Donor and Recipient and Between Harm Doer and Victim." *Sociometry* 40:293–298.

Bednar, M. J. 1977. *Barrier-free Environments.* Stroudsburg, Pa.: Hutchinson and Ross.

Bivens, G. E., and C. B. Volker. 1982. "Value Added in Household Food Preparation: A Preliminary Report of a Changed Approach to Valuing Household Production." In *Confronting Change: Dimensions Diversity Decisions,* V. Dickenson and G. Olson, eds. Proceedings of the 22nd Western Region Home Management-Family Economics Educators' Conference, Portland, Oregon, November.

Bladeck, B. C. 1980. *Unloving Care.* New York: Basic Books.

Breuer, J. M. 1982. "A Handbook of Assistive Devices for the Handicapped Elderly: New Help for Independent Living." *Physical and Occupational Therapy in Geriatrics* 1(2):1–77.

Brickman, P., L. H. Kidder, D. Coates, V. Rabinowitz, E. Cohn, and J. Karuza. "The Dilemmas of Helping: Making Aid Fair and Effective." Pp. 19–45 in *New Directions in Helping,* J. D. Fisher, A. Nadler, and B. M. DePaulo, eds. Vol. 1, *Recipient Reactions to Aid.* New York: Academic Press.

Brody, E. M. 1981. "Women in the Middle and Family Help to Older People." *The Gerontologist* 21:471–480.

Brody, E. M., P. T. Johnsen, and M. C. Fulcomer. 1984. "What Should Adult Children Do for Elderly Parents—Opinions and Preferences of Three Generations of Women." *Journal of Gerontology* 39(November):736–746.

Brody, E. M. 1985. "Parent Care as a Normative Family Stress." *The Gerontologist* 25(February):19–29.

Brody, E., P. Johnson, M. Fulcomer, and A. Lang. 1983. "Women's Changing Roles and Help to Elderly Parents: Attitudes of Three Generations of Women." *Journal of Gerontology* 38:597–607.

Bronson, E. P. 1972. "An Experiment in Intermediate Housing Facilities for the Elderly." *Gerontologist* 12(Spring):22–26.

Brubaker, T. H., ed. 1983. *Family Relations in Later Life.* Beverly Hills, Calif.: Sage Publications.

Bultena, G. G. 1974. "Structural Effects on the Morale of the Aged—A Comparison of Age-Segregated and Age-Integrated Communities." Pp. 18–31 in *Late Life: Communities and Environmental Policy,* J. F. Gubrium, ed. Springfield, Ill.: Charles C. Thomas.

Butler, A., C. Oldman, and J. Greve. 1983. *Sheltered Housing for the Elderly: Policy,*

Practice, and the Consumer. National Institute Social Sources Library no. 44. London: George Allen and Unwin.

Byerts, T. O. 1982. "The Congregate-Housing Model: Integrating Facilities and Services." In *Congregate Housing for Older People: A Solution for the 1980's,* R. D. Chellis, J. F. Seagel, and B. M. Seagle, eds. Lexington, Mass.: Lexington Books.

Byerts, T. O., S. C. Howell, and L. A. Pastalen, eds. 1979. *The Environmental Context of Aging.* New York: Garland STPM Press.

Canter, D., and S. Canter, eds. 1979. *Designing for Therapeutic Environments.* London: John Wiley.

Cantor, M. H. 1979. "Neighbors and Friends: An Overlooked Resource in the Informal Support System." *Research on Aging* 1:434–463.

Cantor, M. H. 1980. "The Informal Support System: Its Relevance in the Lives of the Elderly." In *Aging and Society,* E. Gorgatta and N. McCluskey, eds. Beverly Hills, Calif.: Sage Publications.

Cantor, M. H. 1983. "Strain Among Caregivers: A Study of Experience in the United States." *The Gerontologist* 23(6):597–604.

Caplan, G., and M. Killilea. 1976. *Support Systems and Mutual Help.* New York: Greene and Stratton.

Carlin, V. F., and R. Fox. 1981. "An Alternative for Elderly Housing: Housing Conversion." In *Community Housing Choices for Older Americans,* M. P. Lawton and S. L. Hoover, eds. New York: Springer Publishing.

Carp, F. M. 1966. *A Future for the Aged.* Austin: University of Texas Press.

Castro, M. A. "Reactions to Receiving Aid as a Function of Cost to the Donor and Opportunity to Aid." *Journal of Applied Social Psychology* 4:194–209.

Chapman, N. J., and D. L. Pancoast. 1985. "Working with the Informal Helping Networks of the Elderly: The Experiences of Three Programs." *Journal of Social Issues* 41:47–64.

Chatters, L. M., R. J. Taylor, and J. S. Jackson. 1985. "Size and Composition of the Informal Helper Networks of Elderly Blacks." *Journal of Gerontology* 40(September):605–614.

Cicirelli, V. G. 1981. *Helping Elderly Parents: The Role of Adult Children.* Boston: Auburn House.

Clark, M., and B. Anderson. 1967. *Culture and Aging.* Springfield, Ill.: Charles C Thomas.

Clark, M. S. 1983. "Reactions to Aid in Communal and Exchange Relationships." Pp. 281–304 in *New Directions in Helping,* J. D. Fisher, A. Nadler, and B. M. DePaulo, eds. Vol. 1, *Recipient Reactions to Aid.* New York: Academic Press.

Clark, M. S. 1983. "Some Implications of Close Social Bonds for Help Seeking." Pp. 205–233 in *New Directions in Helping,* J. D. Fisher, A. Nadler, and B. M. DePaulo, eds. New York: Academic Press.

Clark, M. S., and J. Mills. 1979. "Interpersonal Attention in Communal and Exchange Relationships." *Journal of Personality and Social Psychology* 37:12–24.

Cumming, E., and W. E. Henry. 1971. *Growing Old: The Process of Disengagement.* New York: Basic Books.

Currie, L. J. 1977. *Designing Environments for the Aging.*

Cutler, S. J. 1975. "Age Differences in Voluntary Association Memberships." *Social Forces* 55(September):43–58.

Cutler, S. J. 1977. "Aging and Voluntary Association Participation." *Journal of Gerontology* 32:470–479.

DePaulo, B. M. 1982. "Social Psychological Processes in Informal Help Seeking." In *Basic Processes in Helping Relations,* T. A. Wills, ed. New York: Academic Press.

DePaulo, B. M, and J. D. Fisher. 1980. "The Costs of Asking for Help." *Basic and Applied Social Psychology* 1:23–35.

DePaulo, B. M., A. Nadler, and J. D. Fisher, eds. 1983. *New Directions in Helping.* Vol. 2, *Help Seeking.* New York: Academic Press.

Doherty, W. J. 1985. "Family Interventions in Health Care." *Family Relations* 34(January):129–137.

Doherty, W. J., and H. I. McCubbin. 1985. "Families and Health Care: An Emerging Arena of Theory, Research, and Clinical Intervention." *Family Relations* 34(January):5–12.

Dubrof, R., and E. Litwak. 1977. *Maintenance of Family Ties of Long-Term Care Patients: Theory and Guide to Practice.* Washington, D.C.: U.S. Department of Health, Education, and Welfare.

Eckert, J. K., and M. Haug. 1984. "The Impact of Forced Residential Relocation on the Health of the Elderly Hotel Dweller." *Journal of Gerontology* 39(November):753–755.

Editorial Research Reports. 1982. "Housing Options for the Elderly." II(5): Washington, D.C.: Congressional Quarterly, Inc. August 6.

Ehrlich, P., I. Ehrlich, and P. Woehlke. 1982. "Congregate Housing Thirteen Years Later." *The Gerontologist* 22:399–403.

Epp, G. 1981. "Furnishing the Unit from the Viewpoint of the Elderly, the Designer, and HUD." Pp. 312–317 in *Design Research Interactions,* A. Osterberg, C. Tierman, and R. Findlay, eds. Proceedings of the Twelfth International Conference of the Environmental Design Research Association. Washington, D.C.: Environmental Design Research Association.

Feller, B. A. 1983. "Americans Needing Help to Function at Home." In *Advance Data from Vital and Health Statistics,* No. 92. National Center for Health Statistics, Division of Health Interview Statistics. September 14.

Fillenbaum, G. G., L. K. George, and E. B. Palmore. 1985. "Determinants and Consequences of Retirement Among Men of Different Races and Economic Levels." *Journal of Gerontology* 40(January):85–94.

Finch, J., and D. Groves, eds. 1983. *A Labour of Love: Women, Work and Caring.* London: Routledge & Kegan Paul.

Findlay, R. A., and E. W. Morris. 1976. "Social Determinants of the Design of Housing for the Elderly." In *The Behavioral Basis of Design,* vol. 2, P. Suedfeld et al., eds. Stroudsburg, Pa.: Dowden, Hutchinson, and Ross.

Fisher, J. D., B. M. DePaulo, and A. Nadler. "Extending Altruism Beyond the Altruistic Act: The Mixed Effects of Aid on the Help-Recipient." Pp. 205–37 in *Altruism and Helping Behavior: Social Personality, and Developmental Perspectives,* J. P. Rushton and R. M. Sorrentino, eds. Hillsdale, N.J.: Erlbaum.

Flagler, A. P., and N. Goodrich. 1979. "Wives of Elderly Disabled Men: The Hidden Patients." *The Gerontologist* 19(April):175–183.

Fleishman, R., and A. Schmueli. 1984. "Patterns of Informal Social Support of the Elderly: An International Comparison." *The Gerontologist* 24(June):303–312.

Fozard, J. L. 1981. "Person–Environment Relationships in Adulthood: Implications for Human Factors Engineering." *Human Factors* 23:7–27.

Froland, C., D. Pancoast, N. Chapman, and P. Kimboko. 1981. *Helping Networks and Human Services.* Beverly Hills, Calif.: Sage Publications.

Gelwicks, L. E., and R. J. Newcomer. 1974. *Planning Housing Environments for the Aging.*

Gilhooly, M. 1984. "The Impact of Caregiving on Caregivers: Factors Associated with the Psychological Wellbeing of People Caring for a Dementia Relative in the Community." *British Journal of Medical Psychology* 57:35–44.

Golant, S. M. 1976. "Intraurban Transportation Needs and Problems of the Elderly."

In *Community Planning for an Aged Society,* M. P. Lawton, R. J. Newcomer, and T. O. Byorts, eds. Stroudsburg, Pa.: Dowden, Hutchinson, and Ross.

Gold, M. 1984. *The Older American's Guide to Housing and Living Arrangements.* Mount Vernon, N.Y.: Institute for Consumer Policy Research, Consumers Union.

Goldschmidt-Clermont, L. 1982. "Product Related Evaluations of Unpaid Household Work: A Challenge for Time Use Studies." Unpublished paper.

Goodman, C. C. 1984. "Natural Helping Among Older Adults." *The Gerontologist* 24(2, April):138–140.

Goodman, C. C. 1984. "Helper Bank: A Reciprocal Services Program for Older Adults." *Social Work* July–August:397–398.

Green, I., B. E. Fedewa, C. A. Johnston, W. M. Jackson, and H. L. Deerdorff. 1975. *Housing for the Elderly: The Development and Design Process.* New York: Van Nostrand.

Greenberg, M. S. 1980. "A Theory of Indebtedness." Pp. 87–102 in *Social Exchange: Advances in Theory and Research,* K. J. Gergen, M. S. Greenberg, and R. H. Willis, eds. New York: Wiley.

Greenberg, M. S., and D. R. Westcott. 1983. "Indebtedness as a Mediator of Reactions to Aid," In *New Directions in Helping: Recipient Reactions to Aid,* J. D. Fisher, A. Nadler, and B. M. DePaulo, eds. New York: Academic Press.

Haber, D. 1983. "Promoting Mutual Help Groups Among Older Persons." *The Gerontologist* 23(June):251–253.

Hall, F. T., and M. P. Schroeder. 1970. "Effects of Family Housing Characteristics on Time Spent on Household Tasks." *Journal of Home Economics* 62:23–29.

Hare, P. H., S. Connor, and D. Merriam. 1981. *Accessory Apartments: Using Surplus Space in Single Family Houses.* Report No. 365. Chicago: American Planning Association.

Hatfield, E., and S. Sprecher. 1983. "Equity Theory and Recipient Reactions to Aid." In *New Directions in Helping,* vol. 1, *Recipient Reactions to Aid,* J. D. Fisher, A. Nadler, and B. M. DePaulo, eds. New York: Academic Press.

Hershbergger, R. G. 1972. "Toward a Set of Semantic Scales to Measure the Meaning of Architectural Environments." In *Environmental Design: Research and Practice,* W. J. Mitchell, ed. Los Angeles: University of California, Los Angeles.

Hinrichsen, G. A. 1985. "The Impact of Age-Concentrated, Policy Assisted Housing on Older People's Social and Emotional Wellbeing." *Journal of Gerontology* 40(November):758–760.

Hoenig, J., and G. Honach. 1985. "Partial Retirement as a Separate Mode of Retirement Behavior." *Journal of Human Resources* 20(Winter):21–46.

Hoenig, J., and M. Hamilton. 1966. "Elderly Psychiatric Patients and the Burden on the Household." *Psychiatria et Neurologia,* 152–281.

Hooyman, N., J. Gonyea, and R. Montgomery. 1985. "Impacts of In-Home Services Termination on Family Caregivers." *The Gerontologist* 25(April):141–145.

Horowitz, A., and L. Shindelman. 1983. "Reciprocity and Affection: Past Influences on Current Caregiving." *Gerontological Social Work* 5:5–20.

Israel, B. A. 1982. "Social Networks and Health Status: Linking Theory Research and Practice." *Patient Counseling and Health Education* 4(2):65–79.

Jacobs, J. 1975. *Older Persons and Retirement Communities.* Springfield, Ill.: Charles C Thomas.

Jarrett, W. H. 1985. "Caregiving Within Kinship Systems: Is Affection Really Necessary?" *The Gerontologist* 25(February):5–10.

Johnson, C. L., and D. J. Catalano. 1983. "A Longitudinal Study of Family Supports to Impaired Elderly." *The Gerontologist* 23(6, December).

Juster, T. J., and F. P. Stafford, eds. 1985. *Time, Goods, and Well-Being.* Ann Arbor, Mich.: Institute for Social Research, University of Michigan.

Kahn, R. L. 1981. *Work and Health.* New York: John Wiley & Sons.

Kanter, R. M. 1972. *Commitment and Community: Communes and Utopias in Sociological Perspective.* Cambridge, Mass.: Harvard University Press.

Kasl, S. W. 1977. "The Effects of the Residential Environment on Health and Behavior: A Review." In *The Effect of the Man-Made Environment on Health and Behavior,* O. E. Hinkle and W. C. Loring, eds. Washington, D.C.: Government Printing Office.

Kerckhoff, A. 1965. "Nuclear and Extended Family Relationships: Normative and Behavioral Analysis." In *Social Structure and the Family: Generational Relations,* E. Shanas and G. F. Streib, eds. Englewood Cliffs, N.J.: Prentice-Hall.

Kira, A. 1976. *The Bathroom,* rev. ed. New York: The Viking Press.

Knight, E., and M. Menchik. 1974. *Residential Environmental Attitudes and Preferences: Report of a Questionnaire Survey.* Report No. 27. Madison: University of Wisconsin-Madison, Institute for Environmental Studies.

Kodner, D. C., C. Snyder, and T. Taphael. 1985. "Older People as Co-Producers of Their Own Long-Term Care: The Potential of 'Service Credits' to Stimulate Informal Caregiving Among Elders Enrolled in Prepaid Health Plans." Paper presented at the 1985 annual meetings of the Gerontological Society of America (abstract in *Gerontologist* 25 [October]).

Koncelik, J. A. 1976. *Designing the Open Nursing Home.* Stroudsburg, Pa.: Dowden, Hutchinson, and Ross.

Kulys, R., and S. S. Tobin. 1980. "Older People and their 'Responsible Others.'" *Social Work* 25:25.

Lan, A., and E. Brody. 1983. "Characteristics of Middle-Age Daughters and Help to their Elderly Mothers." *Journal of Marriage and Family* 45(February):193–202.

Lawton, M. P. 1970. "Ecology and Aging." In *Spatial Behavior of Older People,* L. A. Pastalan and D. H. Carson, eds. Ann Arbor, Mich.: University of Michigan, Institute of Gerontology.

Lawton, M. P. 1970. "Planners Notebook: Planning Environments for Older People." *Journal of the American Institute of Planners* 36:124–129.

Lawton, M. P. 1972. "The Dimensions of Morale." In *Research, Planning and Action for the Elderly,* D. P. Kent et al., eds. New York: Behavioral Publications.

Lawton, M. P. 1973. "Interior Design as an Aid to Effective Living by Institutional Residents." In *Nonprofit Homes for the Aging,* R. H. Davis, ed. Los Angeles: University of Southern California, Andrus Gerontology Center.

Lawton, M. P. 1974. "Coping Behavior and the Environment of Older People." In *Professional Obligations and Approaches to the Aged,* I. Mensh and A. Schwartz, eds. Springfield, Ill.: Charles C Thomas.

Lawton, M. P. 1975. *Planning and Managing Housing for the Elderly.* New York: Wiley-Interscience.

Lawton, M. P. 1976. "Homogeneity and Heterogeneity in Housing for the Elderly." In *Community Planning for an Aging Society,* M. P. Lawton, R. J. Newcomer, and T. O. Byerts, eds. Stroudsburg, Pa.: Dowden, Hutchinson, and Ross.

Lawton, M. P. 1976. "The Relative Impact of Congregate and Traditional Housing on Elderly Tenants." *Gerontologist* 237–242.

Lawton, M. P. 1977. "Applying Research Knowledge to Congregate Housing." In *Congregate Housing for Older People,* W. T. Donahue, M. M. Thompson, and D. J. Curren, eds. Washington, D.C.: Government Printing Office, 1977.

Lawton, M. P. 1978. "Environments for the Aged." In *Therapeutic Environments,* D. Canter and S. Canter, eds. London: Architectural Press.
Lawton, M. P. 1979. "How the Elderly Live." In *The Environmental Context of Aging,* T. O. Byerts, L. A. Pastalan, and S. C. Howell, eds. New York: Garland Publishers.
Lawton, M. P. 1980. *Environment and Aging.* Monterey, Calif.: Brooks/Cole.
Lawton, M. P. 1980. *Environment and Aging.* Belmont, Calif.: Wadsworth.
Lawton, M. P. 1980. "Environmental Change: The Older Person as Initiator and Responder." In *Transitions of Aging,* N. Datan and N. Lohmann, eds. New York: Academic Press.
Lawton, M. P. 1980. "Residential Quality and Residential Satisfaction Among the Elderly." *Research on Aging* 2:309–328.
Lawton, M. P. 1980. *Social and Medical Services in Housing for the Aged.* Rockville, Md.: National Institute of Mental Health.
Lawton, M. P. 1981. "Alternative Housing." *Journal of Gerontological Social Work* 3:61–80.
Lawton, M. P. 1981. "An Ecological View of Living Arrangements." *The Gerontologist* 21:59–66.
Lawton, M. P. 1982. "Community Supports for the Aged." *Journal of Social Issues* 37:102–115.
Lawton, M. P. 1982. "Competence, Environmental Press, and the Adaptation of Older People." In *Aging and the Environment: Theoretical Approaches,* M. P. Lawton, P. G. Windley, and T. O. Byerts, eds. New York: Springer.
Lawton, M. P. 1982. "Environments and Living Arrangements." In *International Perspectives on Aging: Patterns, Policies, and Challenges,* R. H. Binstock and J. Schulz, eds. New York: United Nations.
Lawton, M. P. 1982. "Time, Space, and Activity Patterns." In *Aging and Milieu,* G. Rowles and R. Ohta, eds. New York: Academic Press.
Lawton, M. P. Forthcoming. "Activities and Leisure." In *Annual Review of Gerontology and Geriatrics,* vol. 5, M. P. Lawton and G. Maddox, eds. New York: Springer Publishing Co.
Lawton, M. P. Forthcoming. "Designing the Environment for the Senile Dementia Patient." In *Treating the Older Dementia Patient,* G. Cohen and T. Crook, eds. Rockville, Md.: National Institute of Mental Health.
Lawton, M. P. Forthcoming. "Housing and Living Environments of Older People." In *Handbook of Aging and the Social Sciences,* 2d ed., R. H. Binstock and E. Shanas, eds. New York: Van Nostrand, Reinhold.
Lawton, M. P. Forthcoming. "Housing Preferences and Choices." In *Housing an Aging Society,* R. J. Newcomer, M. P. Lawton, and T. O. Byerts, eds. Stroudsburg, Pa.: Dowden, Hutchinson, and Ross.
Lawton, M. P. Forthcoming. "The Impact of the Environment on Aging and Behavior." In *Aging and Technology,* J. E. Birren and F. W. Schaie, eds. New York: Plenum.
Lawton, M. P. Forthcoming. "The Older Person in the Residential Environment." In *Aging and Technology,* J. E. Birren and J. Livingstone, eds. New York: Plenum.
Lawton, M. P., and J. Bader. 1970. "Wish for Privacy by Young and Old." *Journal of Gerontology* 25:48–54.
Lawton, M. P., and E. Brody. 1969. "Assessment of Older People, Self-Maintaining and Instrumental Activities of Daily Living." *Gerontologist* 9:179–188.
Lawton, M. P., and J. Cohen. 1974. "Environment and the Wellbeing of Elderly Inner City Residents." *Environment and Behavior* 6:194–211.

Lawton, M. P., and J. Cohen. 1974. "The Generality of Housing Impact on the Wellbeing of Older People." *Journal of Gerontology* 29:194–204.

Lawton, M. P., and S. L. Hoover, eds. 1981. *Community Housing Choices for Older Americans.* New York: Springer.

Lawton, M. P., and L. Nahemow. 1973. "Ecology and the Aging Process." In *The Psychology of Adult Development and Aging,* C. Eisdorfer and M. P. Lawton, eds. Washington, D.C.: American Psychological Association.

Lawton, M. P., and L. Nahemow. 1979. "Social Areas and the Wellbeing of Tenants in Planned Housing for the Elderly." *Multivariate Behavioral Research* 14:463–484.

Lawton, M. P., and B. Simon. 1968. "The Ecology of Social Relationships in Housing for the Elderly." *Gerontologist* 8:108–115.

Lawton, M. P., P. Altman, and J. F. Wohlwill. 1984. "Dimensions of Environment-Behavior Research." In *Elderly People and the Environment,* I. Altman, M. P. Lawton, and J. F. Wohlwill, eds. New York: Plenum.

Lawton, M. P., T. O. Byerts, and P. Windley, eds. 1982. *Environment Theory and Aging.* New York: Springer.

Lawton, M. P., M. Greenbaum, and B. Liebowitz. 1980."The Lifespan of Housing Environments for the Aging." *The Gerontologist* 20(1):56–64.

Lawton, M. P., M. Moss, and M. Grimes. 1985. "The Changing Service Needs of Older Tenants in Planned Housing." *The Gerontologist* 25(June):258–264.

Lawton, M. P., M. Moss, and M. H. Kleban. Forthcoming. "Marital Status, Living Arrangements, and the Wellbeing of Older People." *Research on Aging.*

Lawton, M. P., M. Moss, and E. Moles. 1984. "The Suprapersonal Neighborhood Context of Older People: Age Heterogeneity and Wellbeing." *Environment and Behavior* 16(January):89–109.

Lawton, M. P., L. Nahemow, and J. Teaff. 1975. "Housing Characteristics and the Wellbeing of Elderly Tenants in Federally Assisted Housing." *Journal of Gerontology* 30:601–607.

Lawton, M. P., L. Nahemow, and T. M. Yeh. 1980. "Neighborhood Environment and the Wellbeing of Elder Tenants in Planned Housing." *International Journal of Aging and Human Development* 11:211–277.

Lawton, M. P., R. J. Newcomer, and T. O. Byerts, eds. 1977. *Community Planning for an Aging Society.* Stroudsburg, Pa.: Dowden, Hutchinson, and Ross.

Lawton, M. P., L. Nahemow, S. Yaffe, and S. Feldman. 1976. "Psychological Impact of Crime and Fear of Crime: The Elderly and Public Housing." In *Crime and the Elderly: Challenge and Response,* J. Goldsmith and S. Goldsmith, eds. New York: Heath.

Lee, G. R. 1979. "Children and the Elderly: Interaction and Morale." *Research on Aging* 1:335–360.

Lee, G. R. 1985. "Kinship and Social Support of the Elderly: The Case of the United States." *Aging and Society* 5(March):19–38.

Lees, R., and G. Smith, eds. 1975. *Action–Research in Community Development.* London: Routledge and Kegan Paul.

Lemon, B. W., V. L. Bengston, and J. A. Peterson. 1972. "An Exploration of the 'Activity Theory' of Aging." *Journal of Gerontology* 27:511–523.

Lemon, B. W., et al. 1972. "An Exploration of the Activity Theory of Aging: Activity Types and Life Satisfaction Among In-Movers to a Retirement Community." *Journal of Gerontology* 27:511–523.

Levin, I. S. 1977. "Self-Care and Health Planning." *Social Policy* (November–December).

Levin, I. S., A. H. Katz, and E. Holst. 1976. *Self-Care—Lay Initiatives in Health.* New York: Prodest.

Litman, T. J. 1971. "Health Care and the Family: A Three Generational Analysis." *Medical Care* 9:67.

Litwak, E., and I. Szelenyi. 1969. "Primary Group Structure and Their Functions: Kin, Neighbors, and Friends." *American Sociological Review* 34:465–481.

Loney, M. 1983. *Community Against Government: The British Community Development Project 1968–1978.* London: Heinemann.

Maddox, G. L. 1975. "Families as Context and Resources in Chronic Illness." In *Long Term Care: A Handbook for Researchers, Planners and Providers,* S. Sherwood, ed. New York: Spectrum Publications.

Marans, R. W. 1976. "High Density–High Rise Living and the Elderly." Paper presented at the Singapore Professional Center Conference on High Rise–High Density Living, September 5–9.

Mastroieni, M., and M. P. Lawton, eds. Forthcoming. *Designing and Redesigning Mental Health Settings.* Stroudsburg, Pa.: Hutchinson and Ross.

Maxfield, L. D. 1985. "Income of Retired Workers by Age at First Benefit Receipt: Findings from the New Beneficiary Survey." *Social Security Bulletin* 48(July):7–26.

McAuley, W. J., and R. Blieszner. 1985. "Selection of Long-Term Care Arrangements by Older Community Residents." *The Gerontologist* 25(April):188–193.

Ministry of Community and Social Services, Applied Program Technology Unit, Province of Ontario, Canada. 1984. "Older People Use a Young Technology to Maintain Their Independence." *Window on Technology* 1(2, February).

Ministry of Social Affairs and Health Research Department. 1982. *Housework Study.* Helsinki: Official Statistics of Finland.

Montgomery, R. J. V., J. G. Gonyea, and N. R. Hooyman. 1985. "Caregiving and the Experience of Subjective and Objective Burden." *Family Relations* 34(January):19–26.

Moon, M. 1983. "The Role of the Family in the Economic Wellbeing of the Elderly." *The Gerontologist* 23:45–50.

Morgan, J. 1984. "The Role of Time in the Measurement of Transfers and Wellbeing." In *Economic Transfers in the United States,* M. Moon, ed. Chicago: University of Chicago Press.

Morgan, J. 1985. "Mobilitaet des Arbeitsmarktes in Groessern Zusammenhang." In *Mobilitaetsprozesse auf dem Arbeitsmarkt,* H. Knepel and R. Hujer, eds. Frankfurt/Main: Campus Verlag.

Morgan, J. N. 1981. "Antecedents and Consequences of Retirement." In *Five Thousand American Families,* vol. 9, M. Hill, D. Hill, and J. Morgan, eds. Ann Arbor, Mich.: Institute for Social Research.

Morgan, J. N. 1981. "Behavioral and Social Science Research and the Future Elderly." In *Aging: Social Change,* S. B. Kiesler, J. N. Morgan, and V. K. Oppenheimer, eds. New York: Academic Press.

Morycz, R. M. 1985. "Caregiving Strain and the Desire to Institutionalize Family Members with Alzheimer's Disease." *Research on Aging* 7(September):329–361.

Moss, F., and M. P. Lawton. 1982. "The Time Budgets of Older People." *Journal of Gerontology* 37:115–123.

Nadler, A., D. Bar-Tal, and O. Drukman. 1982. "Density Does Not Help: Help-Giving, Seeking, and Reciprocating of Students Living in High Rise and Lower Dormitories." *Population and Environment: Behavioral and Social Issues* 5:6–42.

Nadler, A., J. D. Fisher, and S. Streufert. 1976. "When Helping Hurts: The Effects of Donor-Recipient Similarity and Recipient Self-Esteem on Recipient Reactions to Aid." *Journal of Personality* 44:392–409.

Nadler, A., J. D. Fisher, and S. Ben-Itzhak. 1983. "With a Little Help from My Friend: Effects of Single or Multiple Act Aid as a Function of Donor and Task Characteristics." *Journal of Personality and Social Psychology* 44:392–409.

Nadler, A., O. Mayseless, N. Peri, and A. Chemirinski. 1985. "Effect of Opportunity to Reciprocate and Self Esteem on Help-Seeking Behavior." *Journal of Personality* 53(March):23–35.

Nahemow, L., and M. P. Lawton. 1975. "Similarity and Propinquity in Friendship Formation." *Journal of Personality and Social Psychology* 32:205–213.

National Council on the Aging. 1975. *The Myth and Reality of Aging in America.* Washington, D.C.: National Council on the Aging.

National Policy Center on Housing and Living Arrangements for Older Americans. N.d. *Elderly Housing Guidelines.* Ann Arbor, Mich.: College of Architecture and Urban Planning, University of Michigan.

Neumann, L. 1981. "The Function of Different Sheltered Housing Categories for the Semi-Independent Elderly." *Social Policy and Administration* 15(Summer):164–180.

Newcomer, R. J. 1975. "Group Housing for the Elderly: Defining Neighborhood Service Convenience for Public Housing and Section 202 Residents." Unpublished Ph.D. Dissertation, University of Southern California.

Newcomer, R. 1976. "An Evaluation of Neighborhood Service Convenience for Elderly Housing Project Residents." In *The Behavioral Basis of Design,* P. Suedfeld and J. Russell, eds. Stroudsburg, Pa.: Dowden, Hutchinson, and Ross.

Newcomer, R. J., M. P. Lawton, and T. O. Byerts, eds. Forthcoming. *Housing an Aging Society.* Stroudsburg, Pa.: Hutchinson and Ross.

Newman, S. J. 1976. "Housing Adjustments of the Disabled Elderly." *Gerontologist* 16:312–317.

Newman, S., et al. 1976. *Housing Adjustments of Older People: A Report of Findings from the Second Phase.* Ann Arbor, Mich.: Institute for Social Research, University of Michigan.

Noberini, M. R., and R. U. Berman. 1983. "Barter to Beat Inflation: Developing a Neighborhood Network for Swapping Services on Behalf of the Aged." *The Gerontologist* 23(October):467–470.

O'Bryant, S. L. 1985. "Neighbors' Support of Older Widows Who Live Alone in Their Own Homes." *The Gerontologist* 25(June):305–310.

Osterberg, A. "Post-Occupancy Evaluation of a Retirement Home." Pp. 301–311 in *Design Research Interactions: Proceedings of the Twelfth International Conference of the Environmental Design Research Association,* A. Osterberg, C. Tiernan, and R. Findlay, eds. Washington, D.C.

Packard, M. 1985. "Health Status of New Retired-Worker Beneficiaries: Findings from the New Beneficiary Study." *Social Security Bulletin* 48(February):5–16.

Palmore, E., et al., 1985. *Retirement, Causes and Consequences.* New York: Springer.

Parker, R. 1981. "Tending and Social Policy." Pp. 17–34 in *A New Look at the Personal Social Services,* E. M. Goldberg and S. Hatch, eds. London: Policy Studies Institute.

Parker, S. 1980. *Older Workers and Retirement.* London: Office of Population Censuses and Surveys, Social Survey Division, Her Majesty's Stationery Office.

Parnes, H. 1981. *Work and Retirement.* Cambridge, Mass.: MIT Press.

Parsall, S., and E. M. Tagliareni. 1974. "Cancer Patients Help Each Other." *American Journal of Nursing* 74(April).

Parsons, H. M. 1981. "Residential Design for the Aging." *Human Factors* 23:39–58.

Pastalan, L. A. 1973. "How the Elderly Negotiate Their Environment." In *Housing and Environments for the Elderly,* T. O. Byerts, ed. Washington, D.C.: Gerontological Society.

Pastalan, L. A. 1977. "Designing Housing Environments for the Aging." *Journal of Architectural Education* 31(September):11–13.

Pastalan, L. A. Forthcoming. "Sensory Changes and Environmental Behavior." In *The Environmental Context of Aging,* T. O. Byerts, L. A. Pastalan, and S. C. Howell, eds. New York: Garland.

Pastalan, L. A., and D. H. Carson, eds. 1970. *The Spatial Behavior of Older People.* Ann Arbor: Institute of Gerontology, University of Michigan.

Peterson, G. L. 1967. "A Model of Preference: Qualitative Analysis of the Perception of the Visual Appearance of Residential Neighborhoods." *Journal of Regional Science* 8(1):19–32.

Poulshock, S. W., and G. T. Deimling. 1984. "Families Caring for Elders in Residence: Issues in the Measurement of Burden." *Journal of Gerontology* 39(2):230–239.

Poulshock, S. W., and L. S. Noelker. 1982. *The Effects on Families of Caring for Impaired Elderly in Residence.* Final Report on the Administration on Aging. Washington, D.C.: Administration on Aging. April.

Pratt, C., V. Schmall, S. Wright, and M. Cleland. 1985. "Burden and Coping Strategies of Caregivers to Alzheimer's Patients." *Family Relations* 34(January):27–34.

Pynoos, J., B. Hade-Kaplan, and D. Fleisher. "Intergenerational Neighborhood Networks: A Basis for Aiding the Frail Elderly." *The Gerontologist* 24(June):233–237.

Raschko, B. B. 1982. *Housing Interiors for the Disabled and Elderly.* New York: Van Nostrand Reinhold.

Redden, M. R., and V. W. Stern, eds. 1983. *Technology for Independent Living II.* Proceedings of the 1981 workshops, "Science and Technology for the Handicapped." Washington, D.C.: American Association for the Advancement of Science.

Reece, D., T. Walz, and H. Hageboeck. 1983. "Intergenerational Care Providers of Non-Institutionalized Frail Elderly: Characteristics and Consequences." *Journal of Gerontological Social Work* 5:21–34.

Regnier, V. 1976. "Neighborhoods as Service Systems." In *Community Planning for an Aging Society,* M. P. Lawton, R. J. Newcomer, and T. O. Byerts, eds. Stroudsburg, Pa.: Dowden, Hutchinson and Ross.

Regnier, V., ed. 1979. *Planning for the Elderly: Alternative Community Analysis Techniques.* Los Angeles: University of Southern California Press.

Regnier, V., and J. Bonar. 1981. "Recycled Buildings for Elderly Housing." In *Community Housing Choices for Older Americans,* M. P. Lawton and S. L. Hoover, eds. New York: Springer.

Roberts, P. R. 1974. "Human Warehouses: A Boarding Home Study." *American Journal of Public Health* 64(3, March).

Robinson, F., and P. Abrams. 1977. *What We Know About the Neighbours.* Rowntree Research Unit, Department of Sociology and Social Policy, University of Durham.

Robinson, F., and S. Robinson. 1981. *Neighbourhood Care: An Exploratory Bibliography.* Berkhamsted, Herts, England: The Volunteer Centre.

Rosenberg, G. G. 1970. *The Worker Grows Old.* San Francisco: Jossey-Bass.

Russell, L. B. 1981. "An Aging Population and the Use of Medical Care." *Medical Care* 19(June):633–643.

Sainsbury, P., and J. Grad de Alardon. 1970. "The Effects of Community Care on the Family and the Geriatric Patient." *Journal of Geriatric Psychiatry* 4:23.

Schooler, K. 1975. "Response of the Elderly to Environment: A Stress-Theoretical Perspective." Pp. 157–175 in *Theory Development in Environment and Aging,* T. O. Byerts and G. F. Ernst, eds. Washington, D.C.: The Gerontological Society. May.

Schooler, K. 1976. "Environmental Change and the Elderly." In *Human Behavior and Environment,* vol. 1, I. Altman and J. F. Wohwill, eds. New York: Plenum Press.

Schram, V. R., and J. L. Hafstrom. 1984. "Household Production: A Conceptual Model for Time-Use Study in the United States and Japan." *Journal of Consumer Studies and Home Economics* 8(December):283–292.

Schwartz, S., S. Danziger, and E. Smolensky. "The Choice of Living Arrangements by the Elderly." In *Retirement and Economic Behavior,* H. Aaron and G. Burtless, eds. Washington, D.C.: Brookings Institution.

Seelbach, W. C., and W. J. Sauer. 1977. "Filial Responsibility Expectations and Morale Among Aged Parents." *The Gerontologist* 17:492–499.

Seidl, R., R. Applebaum, C. Austin, and K. Mahoney. 1983. *Delivery of In-Home Services to the Aged and Disabled.* Lexington, Mass.: Lexington Books.

Shanas, E. 1979. "Social Myth as Hypothesis: The Case of the Family Relations of Old People." *The Gerontologist* 19:3–9.

Shanas, E. 1979. "The Family as a Social Support System in Old Age." *Gerontologies* 19:169–174.

Shanas, E. 1980. "Older People and Their Families: The New Pioneers." *Journal of Marriage and the Family* 42:9–15.

Shanas, E., et al. 1968. *Older People in Three Industrial Societies.* New York: Atherton Press.

Sherman, S. R. 1985. "Reported Reasons Retired Workers Left Their Last Job: Findings from the New Beneficiary Survey." *Social Security Bulletin* 48(March):22–30.

Sherwood, S., D. S. Grier, J. N. Morris, and C. C. Sherwood. 1972. *The Highland Heights Experiment.* Washington, D.C.: U.S. Department of Housing and Urban Development.

Silverman, P. C. 1975. "Mutual Help and the Elderly Widow." *Journal of Geriatric Psychiatry* 8:9.

Silverstone, B. 1985. "Informal Social Support Systems for the Frail Elderly." In *America's Aging: Health in an Older Society,* Committee on an Aging Society, Institute of Medicine and National Research Council. Washington, D.C.: National Academy Press.

Silverstone, B., and S. Miller 1980. "Isolation in the Aged: Individual Dynamics, Community and Family Involvement." *Journal of Geriatric Psychiatry* 13:27.

Smallegan, M. 1985. "There Was Nothing Else to Do: Needs for Care Before Nursing Home Admission." *The Gerontologist* 25(August):364–369.

Smith, D. H., R. D. Ready, and B. R. Baldwin, eds. 1973. *Voluntary Action Research.* Lexington, Mass.: Lexington Books, D.C. Heath.

Smithson, S., P. Amato, and P. Pearce. 1983. *Dimensions of Helping Behavior.* Oxford: Pergamon Press.

Soldo, B. J., and J. Myllyluoma. 1983. "Caregivers Who Live with Dependent Elderly." *The Gerontologist* 23(December):5–61.

Spilerman, S., and E. Litwak. "Reward Structures and Organizational Design: An Analysis of Institutions for the Elderly." *Research on Aging.*

Steinfield, E. 1975. *Barrier-Free Design for the Elderly and Disabled.* Syracuse, N.Y.: Syracuse University.

Steinmetz, S. K. 1983. "Dependency, Stress, and Violence Between Middle-Aged Caregivers and Their Elderly Parents." Pp. 134–149 in *Abuse and Maltreatment of the Elderly: Causes and Intervention,* J. I. Kosberg, ed. Boston: John Wright.

Stephens, M. A., and E. P. Willems. 1979. "Everyday Behavior of Older Persons in Institutional Housing: Some Implications for Design." Pp. 344–348 in *Environmental Design: Research, Theory and Application: Proceedings of the Tenth Annual Conference of the Environmental Design Research Association,* A. D. Seidel and S. Danford, eds. Washington, D.C.: Environmental Research Association.

Stoller, E. P. 1983. "Parental Caregiving by Adult Children." *Journal of Marriage and the Family* 45:851–858.

Stoller, E. P. 1985. "Elder-Caregiver Relationships in Shared Households." *Research on Aging* 7(June):175–194.

Stoller, E. P., and L. L. Earl. 1983. "Help with Activities of Everyday Living: Sources of Support for the Non-Institutionalized Elderly." *Gerontologies* 23(February):64–70.

Streib, G, and C. Schneider. 1971. *Retirement in American Society: Impact and Process.* Ithaca, N.Y.: Cornell University Press.

Struyk, R. J. 1982. *The Demand for Specially Adapted Housing by Elderly-Headed Households.* Washington, D.C.: The Urban Institute.

Suedfeld, P., and J. A. Russell, eds. 1976. *The Behavioral Basis of Design,* vol. 1. Stroudsburg, Pa.: Dowden, Hutchinson, and Ross.

Suedfeld, P., J. A. Russell, L. M. Ward, F. Szigeti, and G. Davis, eds. 1976. *The Behavioral Basis of Design,* vol. 2. Stroudsburg, Pa.: Dowden, Hutchinson, and Ross.

Suviranta, A., and A. Mynttinen. 1981. *Housework Study.* Official Statistics. Helsinki: Ministry of Social Affairs and Health Research Department of Finland, Special Social Studies.

Teaff, J. D., M. P. Lawton, L. Nahemow, and D. Carlson. 1978. "Impact of Age Integration on the Wellbeing of Elderly Tenants in Public Housing." *Journal of Gerontology* 33:126–133.

Teresi, J., M. Holmes, and D. Homes. 1982. *Sheltered Living Environments for the Elderly.* Community Research Applications. August.

Thompson, E., and W. Doll. 1982. "The Burden of Families Coping with the Mentally Ill: An Invisible Crisis." *Family Relations* 31:379–398.

Tucker, S. 1975. "Independent Housing for the Elderly: The Human Element in Design." *The Gerontologist* (February):73–76.

U.S. Congress, House of Representatives, Select Committee on Aging. 1982. *Shared Housing.* Hearing Before the Subcommittee on Housing and Consumer Interests, November 17, 1981. Washington, D.C.: Government Printing Office.

U.S. Congress, Office of Technology Assessment. 1985. *Technology and Aging in America.* Washington, D.C.: Government Printing Office. June.

U.S. Department of Housing and Urban Development. 1982. "Third Annual Report to Congress on the Congregate Housing Services Program, 1982." Washington, D.C.

U.S. General Accounting Office, Comptroller General of the United States. 1977. *The Wellbeing of Older People in Cleveland, Ohio.* Washington, D.C.

Weisman, J. 1981. "Evaluating Architectural Legibility: Way-Finding in the Built Environment." *Environment and Behavior* 13:189.

Weiss, R. S. 1973. "The Provisions of Social Relationships." Pp. 17–26 in *Doing unto Others: Joining, Molding, Conforming, Helping, Loving,* Z. Rubin, ed. Englewood Cliffs, N.J.: Prentice-Hall.

Whitaker, J., and J. Garbarino, eds. 1983. *Social Support Networks: Informal Helping in the Human Services.* New York: Aldine.

Winiecke, L. 1973. "The Appeal of Age-Segregated Housing to the Elderly Poor." *International Journal of Aging and Human Development* 4:293–306.

The Wolfenden Report. 1978. *The Future of Voluntary Organizations.* London: Croom Helm.

Wright, C. R., and H. H. Hyman. 1958. "Voluntary Association Memberships of American Adults: Evidence from National Sample Survey." *American Sociological Review* 23:284–294.

Zais, J. P., R. J. Struyk, and T. Thibodeau. 1982. *Housing Assistance for Older Americans: The Reagan Prescription.* Washington, D.C.: The Urban Institute Press.

Zarit, S., K. Reever, and J. Bach-Peterson. 1980. "Relatives of the Impaired Elderly: Correlates of Feelings of Burden." *The Gerontologist* 20:649–655.

Index

M

N

O

P

Q

R

W